THE SEVEN DEADLY SINS

nakaba suzuki presents

19

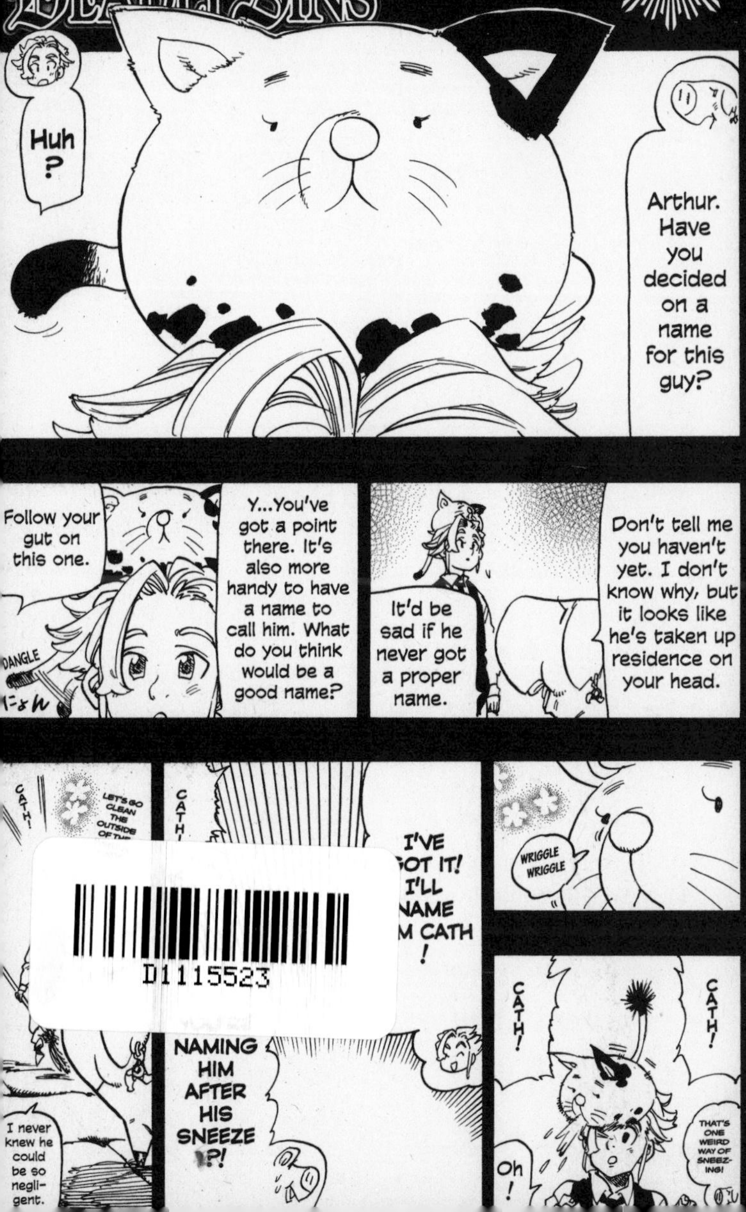
Arthur. Have you decided on a name for this guy?
Huh?
Don't tell me you haven't yet. I don't know why, but it looks like he's taken up residence on your head.
It'd be sad if he never got a proper name.
Y...You've got a point there. It's also more handy to have a name to call him. What do you think would be a good name?
Follow your gut on this one.
DANGLE
WRIGGLE WRIGGLE
CATH!
CATH!
Oh!
THAT'S ONE WEIRD WAY OF SNEEZING!
CATH!
I'VE
OT IT! I'LL
NAME
M CATH!
NAMING HIM AFTER HIS SNEEZE?!
CATH!
LET'S GO CLEAN THE OUTSIDE OF THE
I never knew he could be so negli-gent.

CONTENTS

BOAR HAT

The Seven Deadly Sins

Chapter 145 - Beautiful Soul

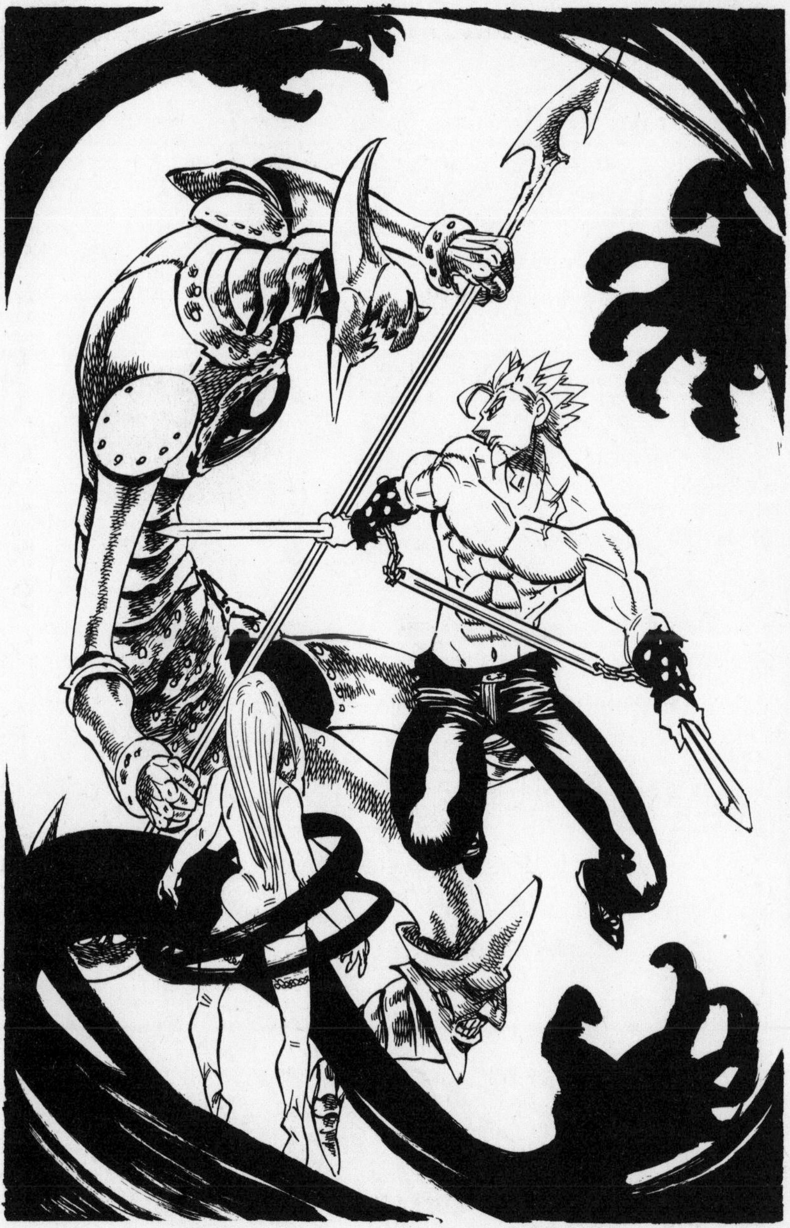

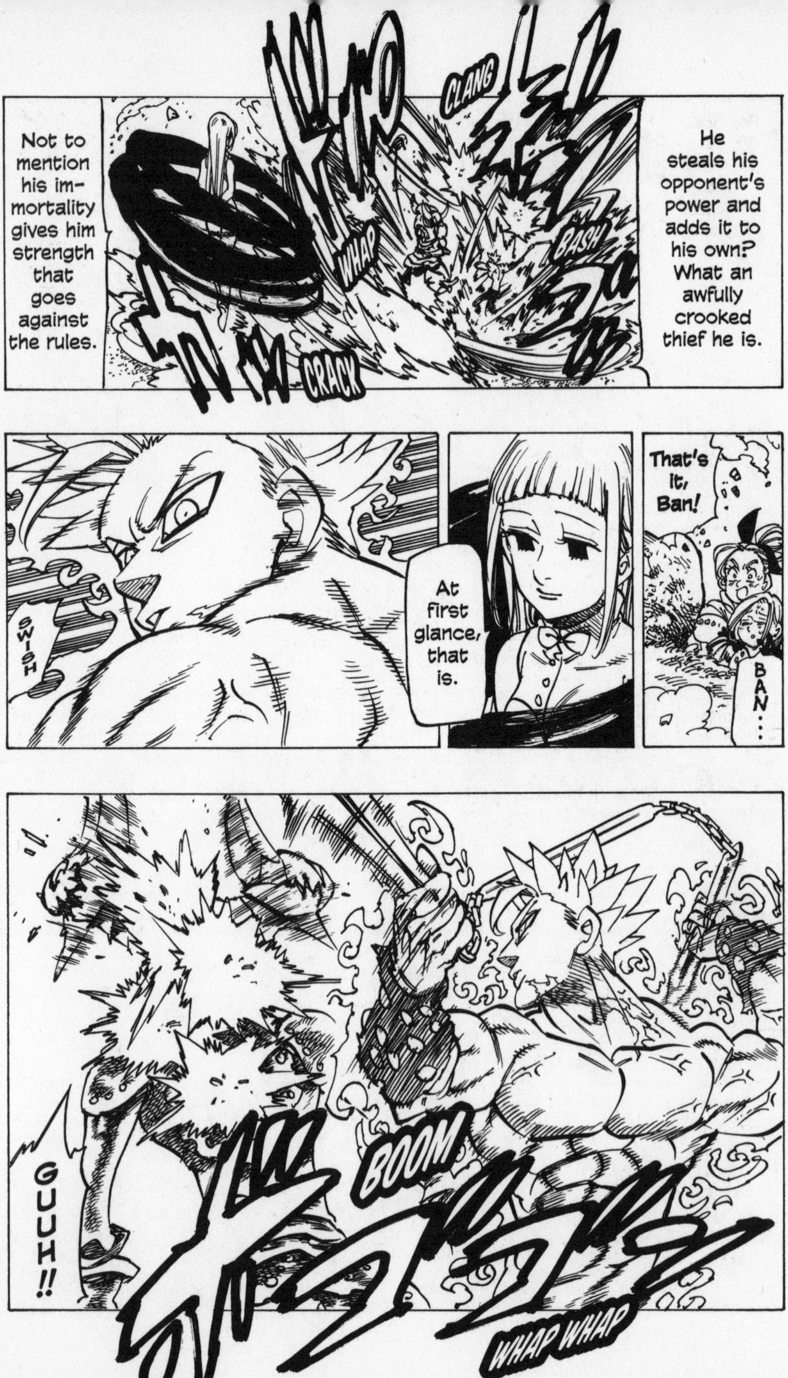
CLANG
He steals his opponent's power and adds it to his own? What an awfully crooked thief he is.
BASH
WHAP
Not to mention his immortality gives him strength that goes against the rules.
CRACK
That's it, Ban!
BAN...
At first glance, that is.
SWISH
BOOM
GUUH!!
WHAP WHAP

REEL
YOU CHEEKY LITTLE HUMAN!
Sheesh, what kind of power do you have, Cap'n? ♪
SCHING
For now, I'm just thinking about how I'll split that dumb-looking helmet of yours in half. ♪
Then you ought to steal more of his power.
!
Mela-scula, have you lost your mind?!
JAB
Steal every last drop of his strength until he can't even move. Then deliver the final blow.
That's how I'd do it.
And yet, what keeps you from doing it?
...
A warrior's pride? No, you don't seem the type.
The answer is "you can't."
It's prob-ably a problem with your body's tolerance level.

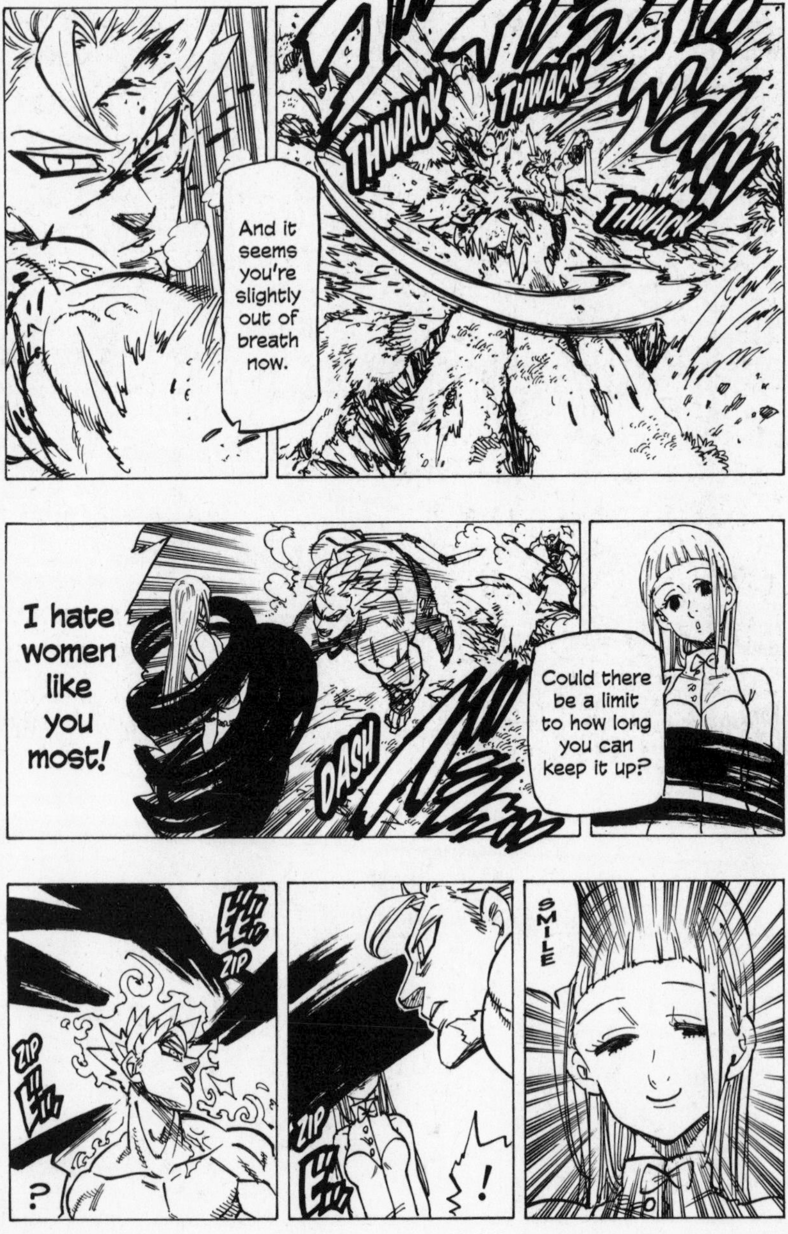
THWACK
THWACK
THWACK
THWACK
And it seems you're slightly out of breath now.
Could there be a limit to how long you can keep it up?
I hate women like you most!
DASH
SMILE
ZIP
!
ZIP
ZIP
?

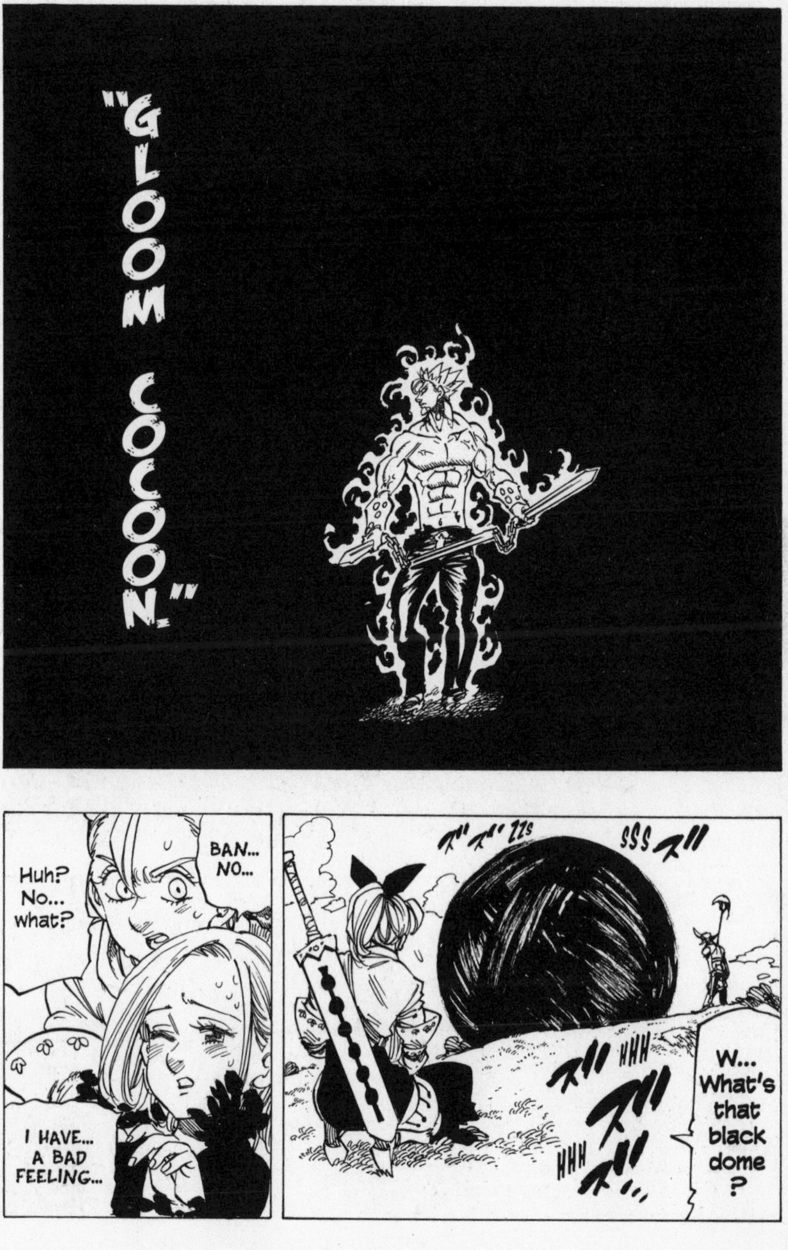
"GLOOM COCOON."
SSS ズ
ズズ ZZS
W... What's that black dome?
ズ HHH
ズズ HHH
ズ...
BAN... NO...
Huh? No... what?
I HAVE... A BAD FEELING...

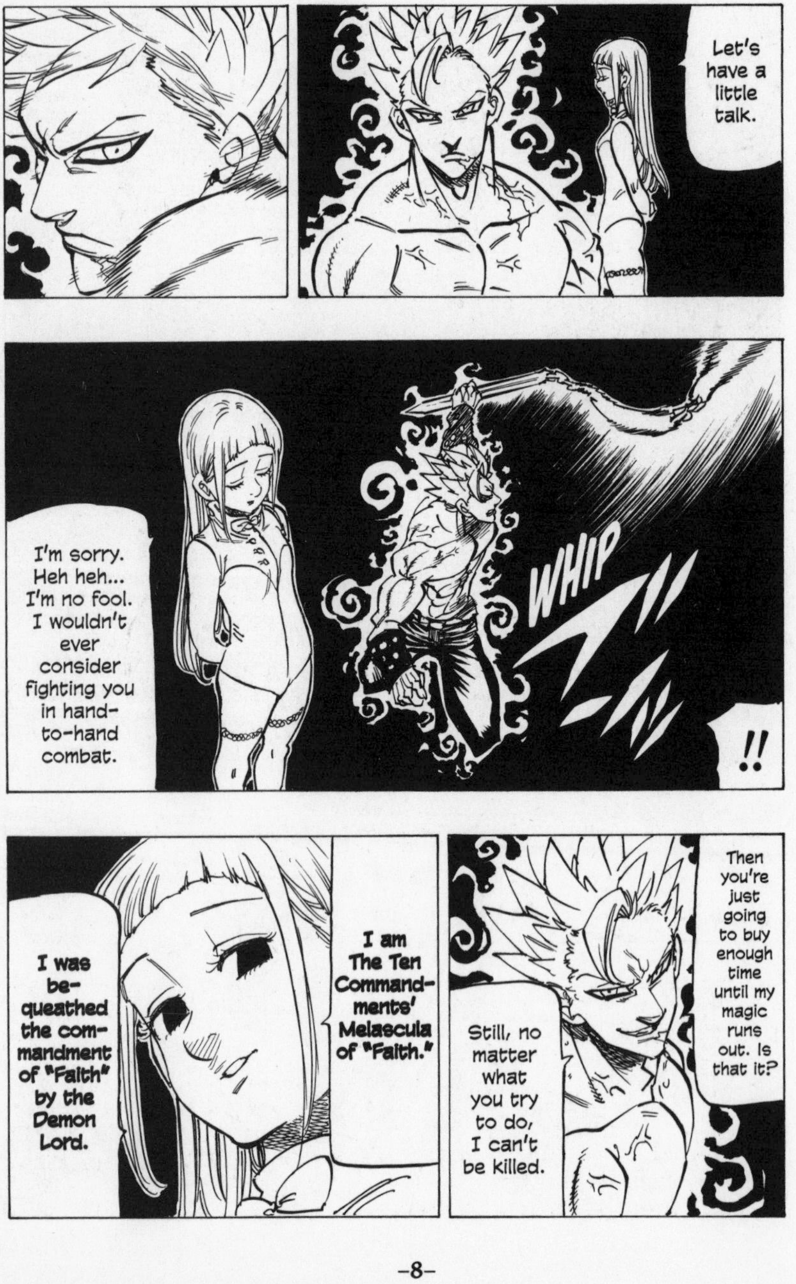
Let's have a little talk.
WHIP
!!
I'm sorry. Heh heh... I'm no fool. I wouldn't ever consider fighting you in hand-to-hand combat.
Then you're just going to buy enough time until my magic runs out. Is that it?
Still, no matter what you try to do, I can't be killed.
I am The Ten Commandments' Melascula of "Faith."
I was bequeathed the commandment of "Faith" by the Demon Lord.

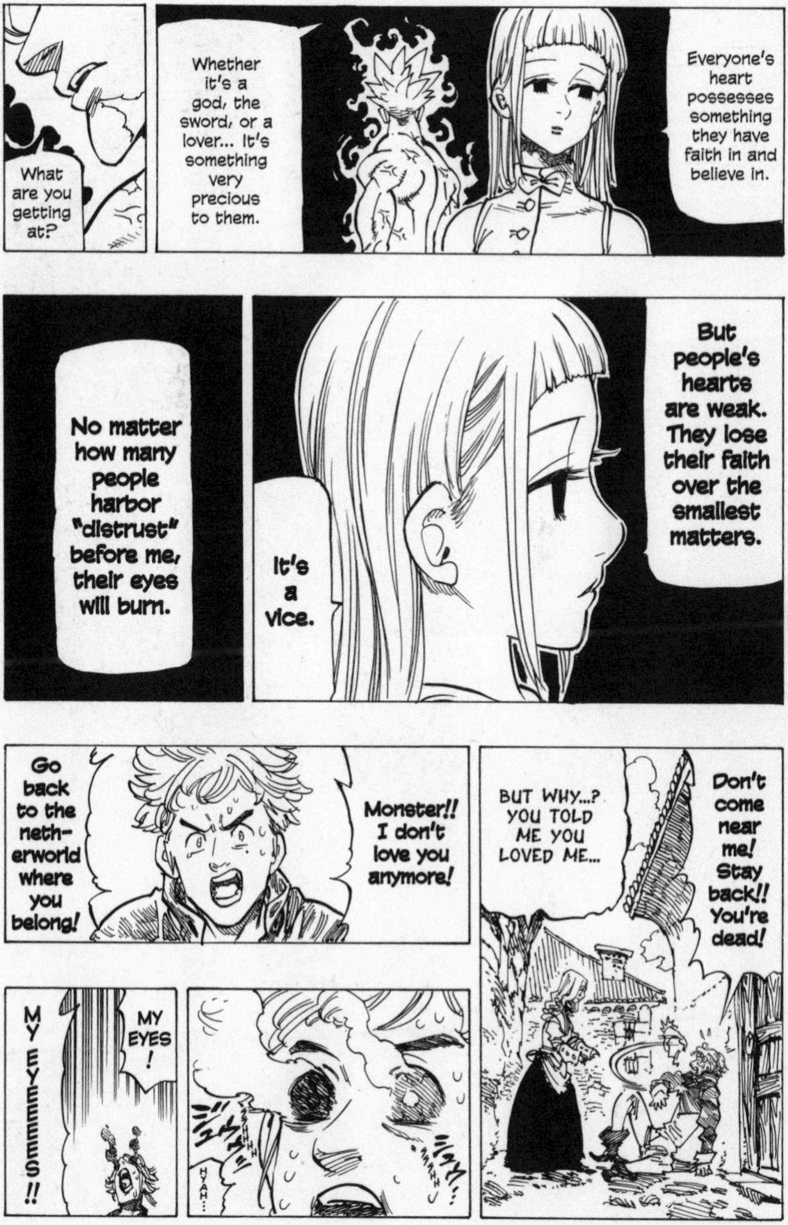
Everyone's heart possesses something they have faith in and believe in.
Whether it's a god, the sword, or a lover... It's something very precious to them.
What are you getting at?
But people's hearts are weak. They lose their faith over the smallest matters.
It's a vice.
No matter how many people harbor "distrust" before me, their eyes will burn.
Don't come near me! Stay back!! You're dead!
BUT WHY...? YOU TOLD ME YOU LOVED ME...
Monster!! I don't love you anymore!
Go back to the netherworld where you belong!
HYAH...
MY EYES!
MY EYEEEES!!

Even after your lover's irrational anger bore its fangs at you, you didn't doubt or hate her for a moment.

You pass.

Such an innocent and beautiful soul.

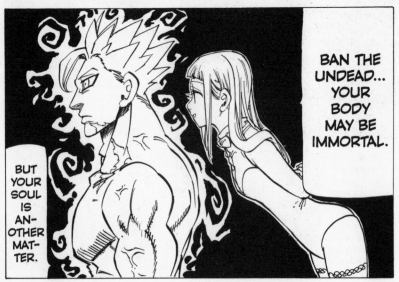

BAN THE UNDEAD... YOUR BODY MAY BE IMMORTAL.

BUT YOUR SOUL IS ANOTHER MATTER.

Kuh!

WHIP

CHILL

When your body dies, your soul travels to the afterlife. But when a soul dies, the body becomes a living, hollow shell.

What do you think will happen to you when your soul dies?

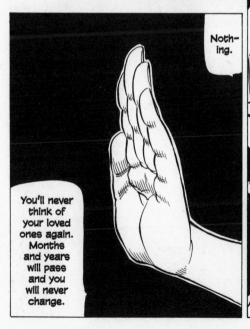

Noth-ing.

You'll never think of your loved ones again. Months and years will pass and you will never change.

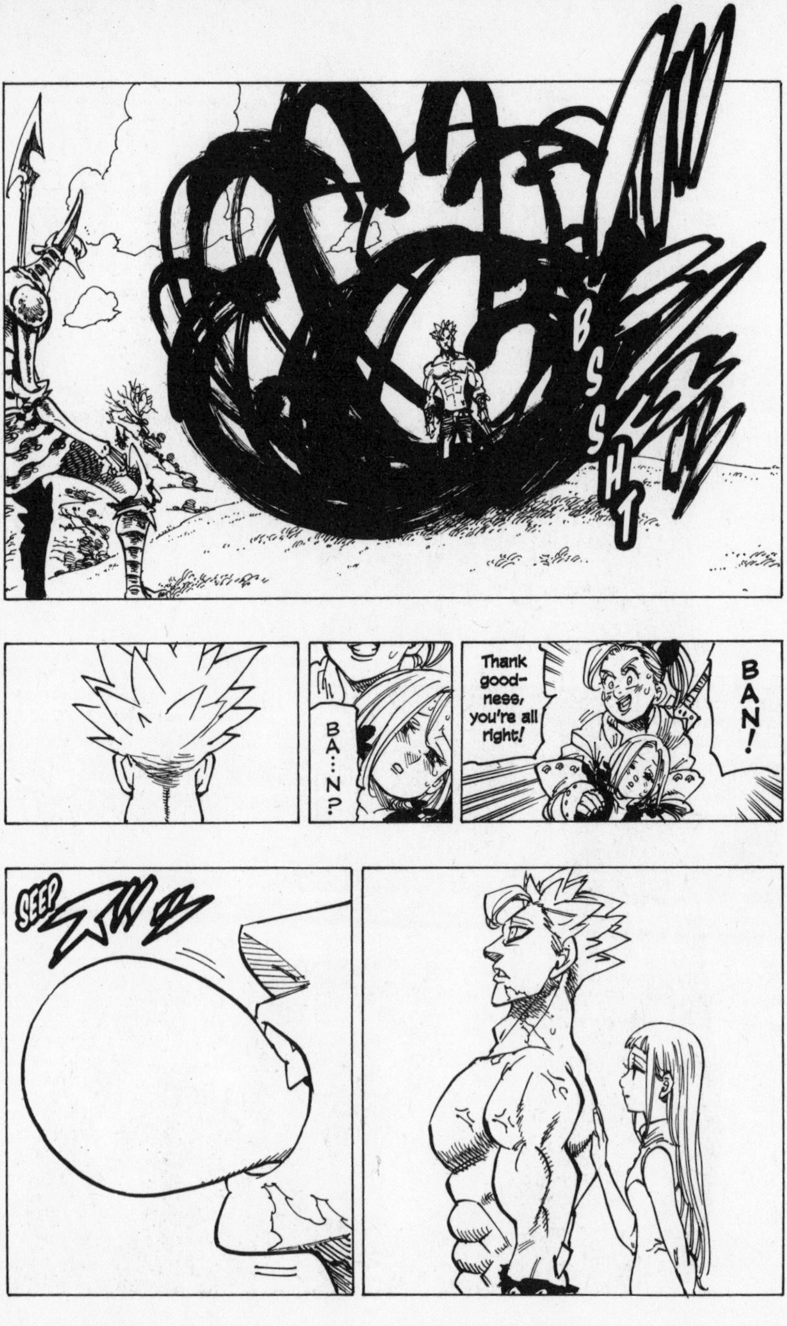
BSSHT
BAN!
Thank goodness, you're all right!
BA...N?
SEEP

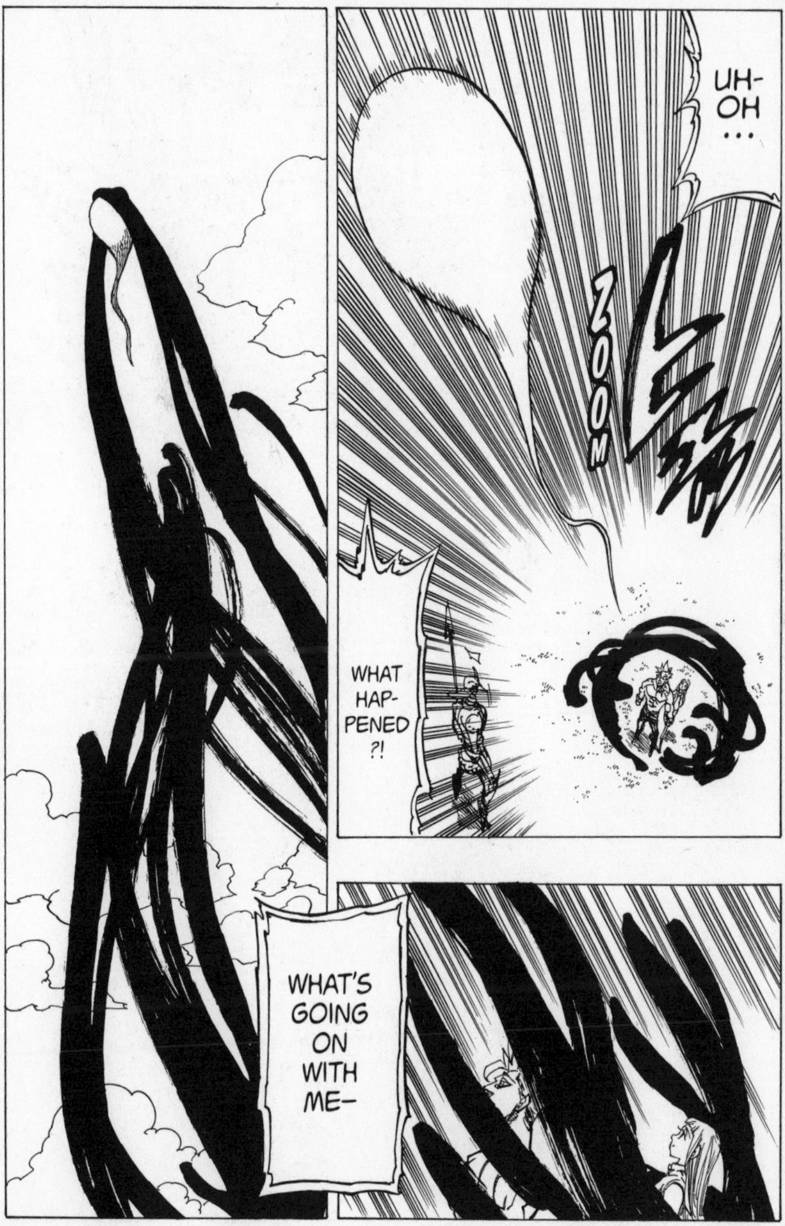
UH-OH ...
ZOOM
WHAT HAP-PENED ?!
WHAT'S GOING ON WITH ME–

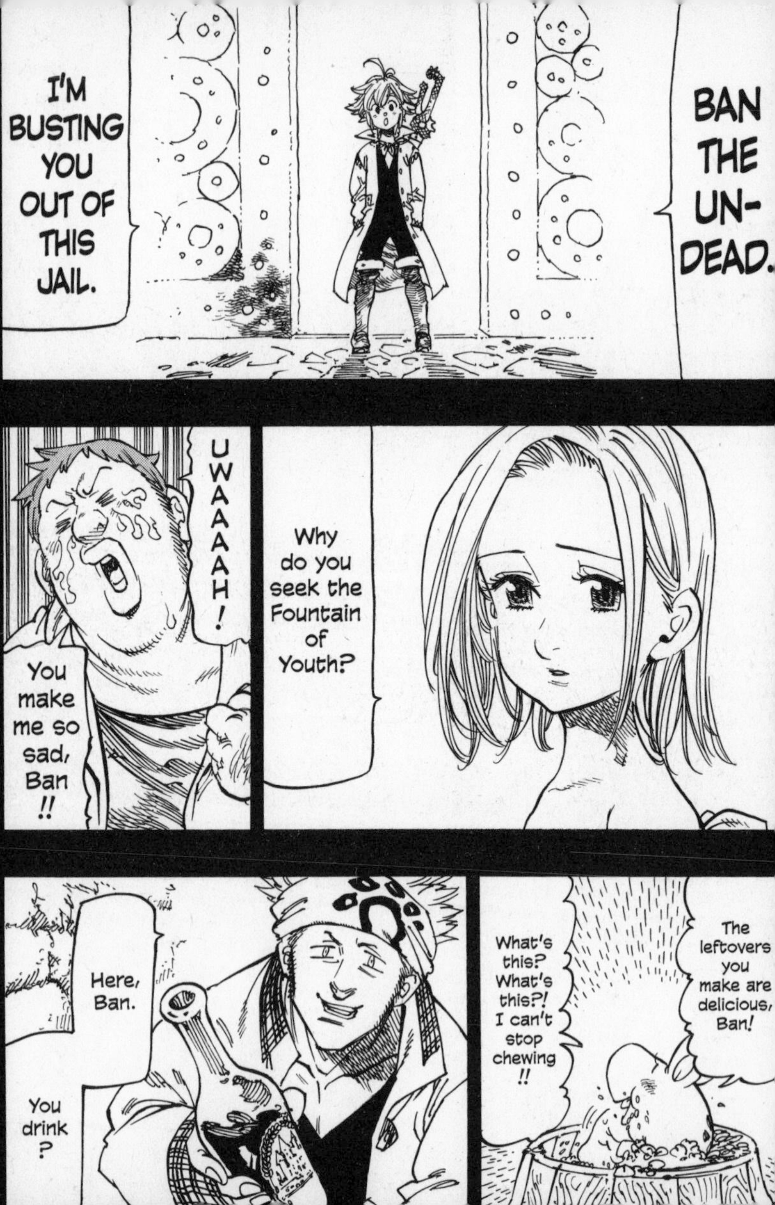
BAN THE UN-DEAD.
I'M BUSTING YOU OUT OF THIS JAIL.
Why do you seek the Fountain of Youth?
UWAAAAAH!
You make me so sad, Ban!!
The leftovers you make are delicious, Ban!
What's this? What's this?! I can't stop chewing!!
Here, Ban.
You drink?

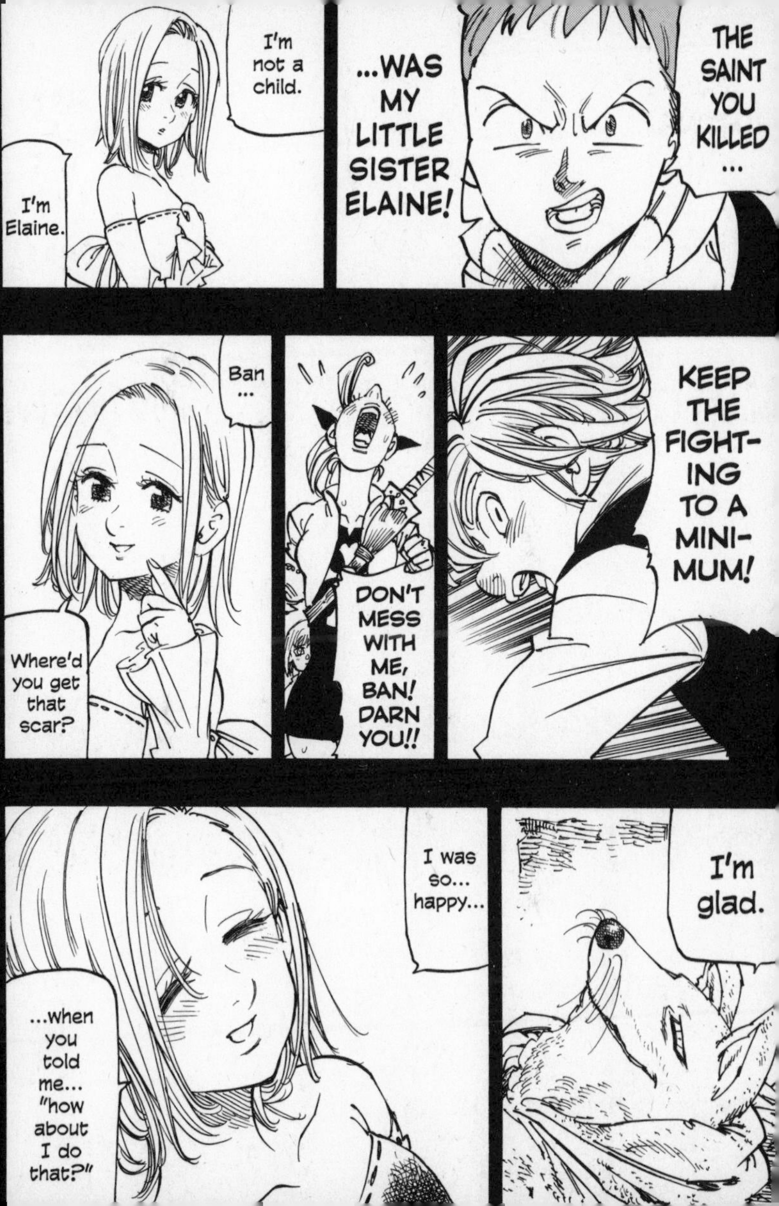
THE SAINT YOU KILLED ...
...WAS MY LITTLE SISTER ELAINE!
I'm not a child.
I'm Elaine.
KEEP THE FIGHTING TO A MINIMUM!
DON'T MESS WITH ME, BAN! DARN YOU!!
Ban ...
Where'd you get that scar?
I'm glad.
I was so... happy...
...when you told me... "how about I do that?"

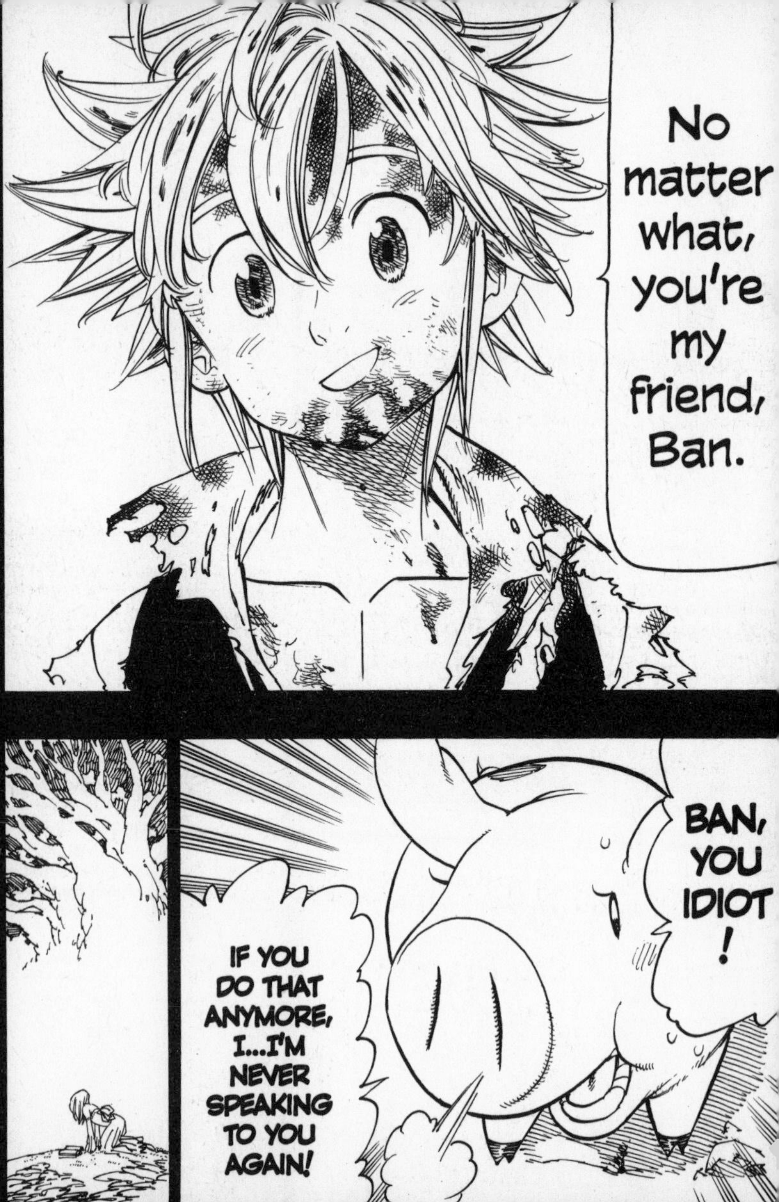
No matter what, you're my friend, Ban.
BAN, YOU IDIOT!
IF YOU DO THAT ANYMORE, I...I'M NEVER SPEAKING TO YOU AGAIN!

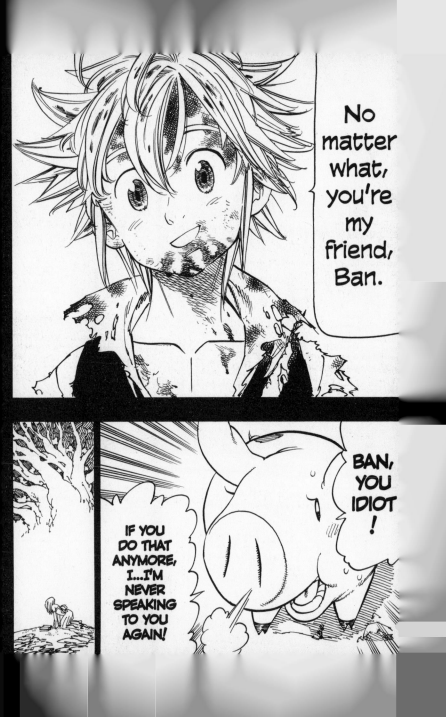

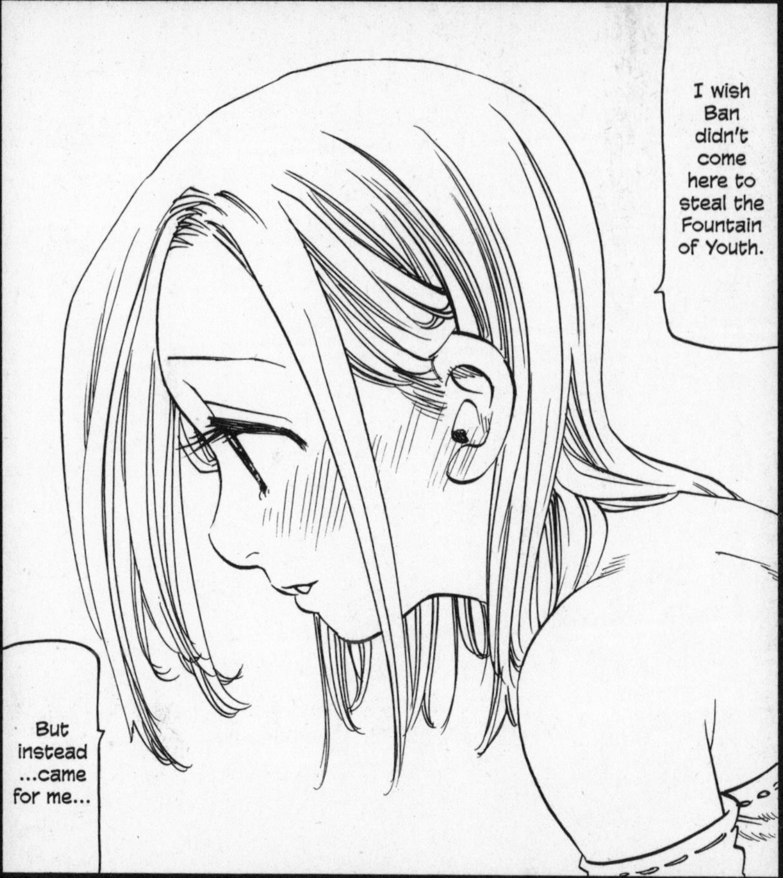
I wish Ban didn't come here to steal the Fountain of Youth.
But instead ...came for me...
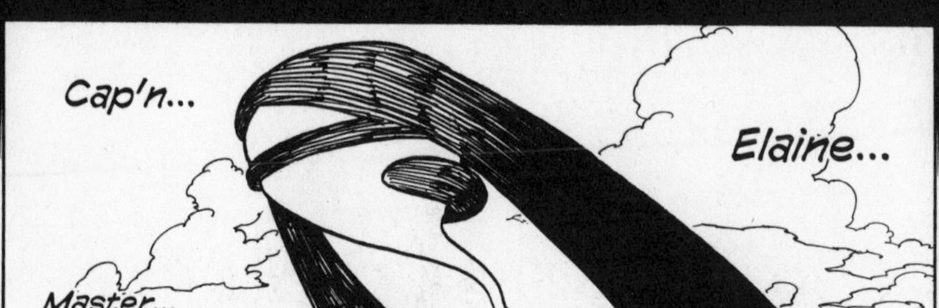
Elaine...
Cap'n...
Master...

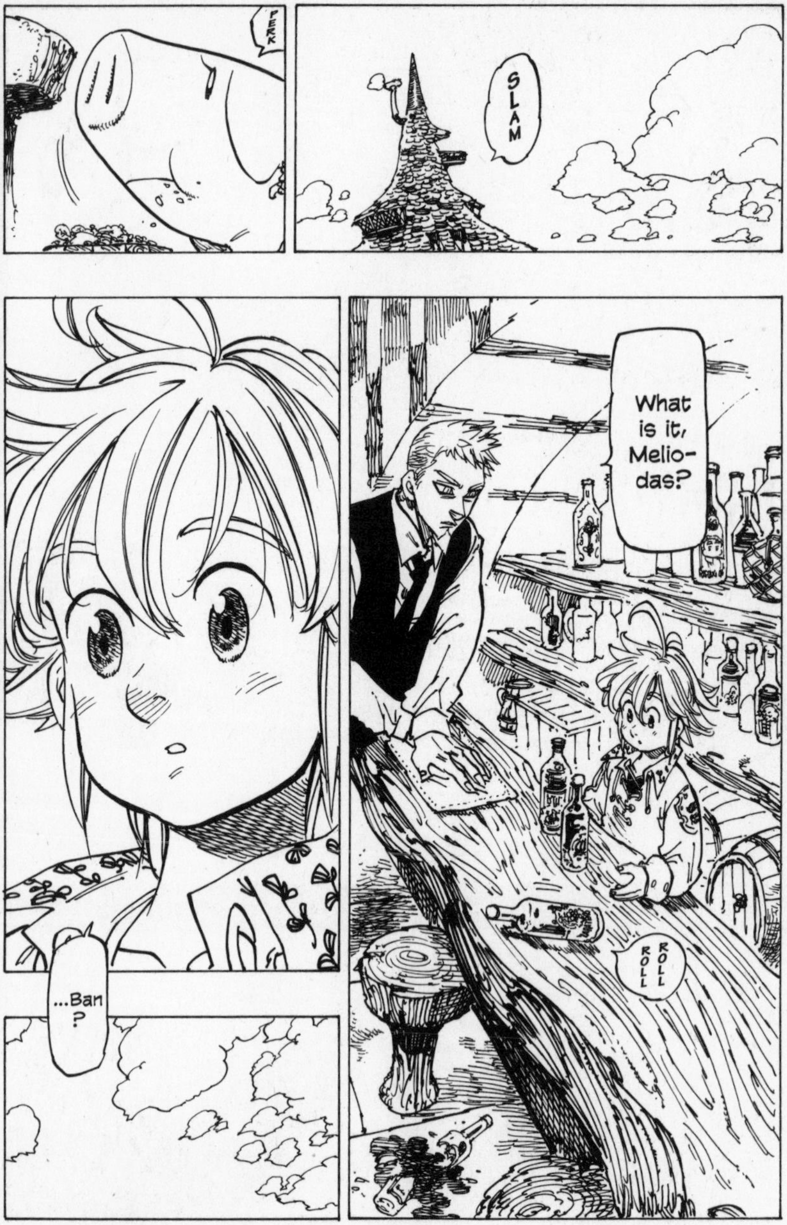
SLAM
PERK
What is it, Melio-das?
ROLL ROLL
...Ban?

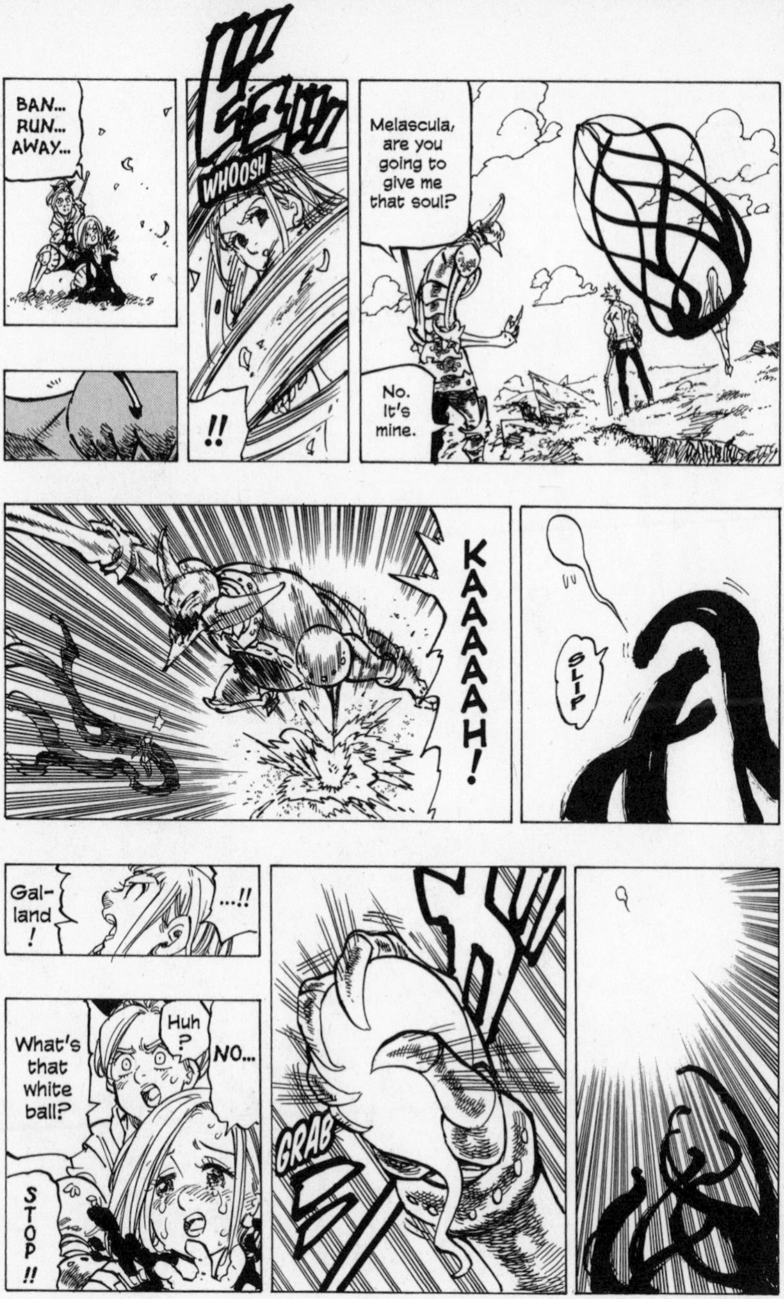

Melascula, are you going to give me that soul?
No. It's mine.
WHOOSH
!!
BAN... RUN... AWAY...
SLIP
KAAAAAAH!
GRAB
...!!
Galland!
Huh?
NO...
What's that white ball?
STOP!!

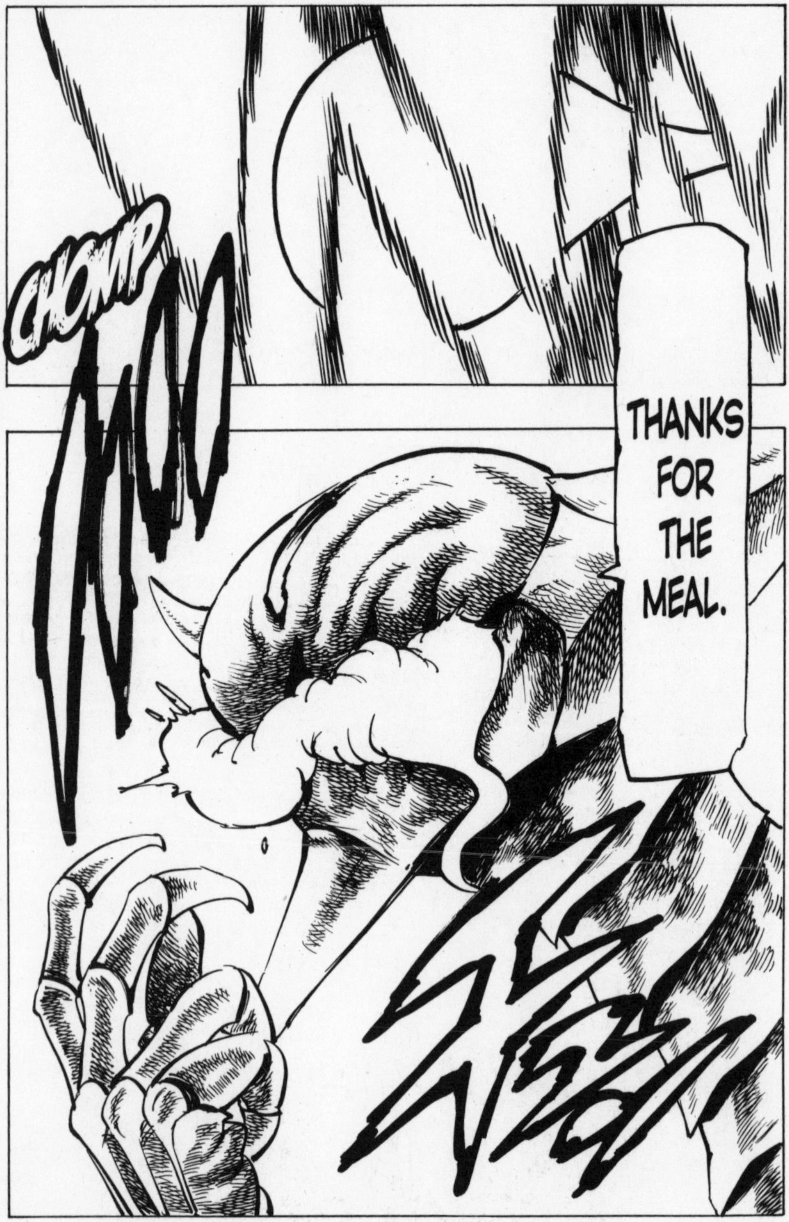
CHOMP
THANKS FOR THE MEAL.

Chapter 146 - Farewell, Beloved Thief

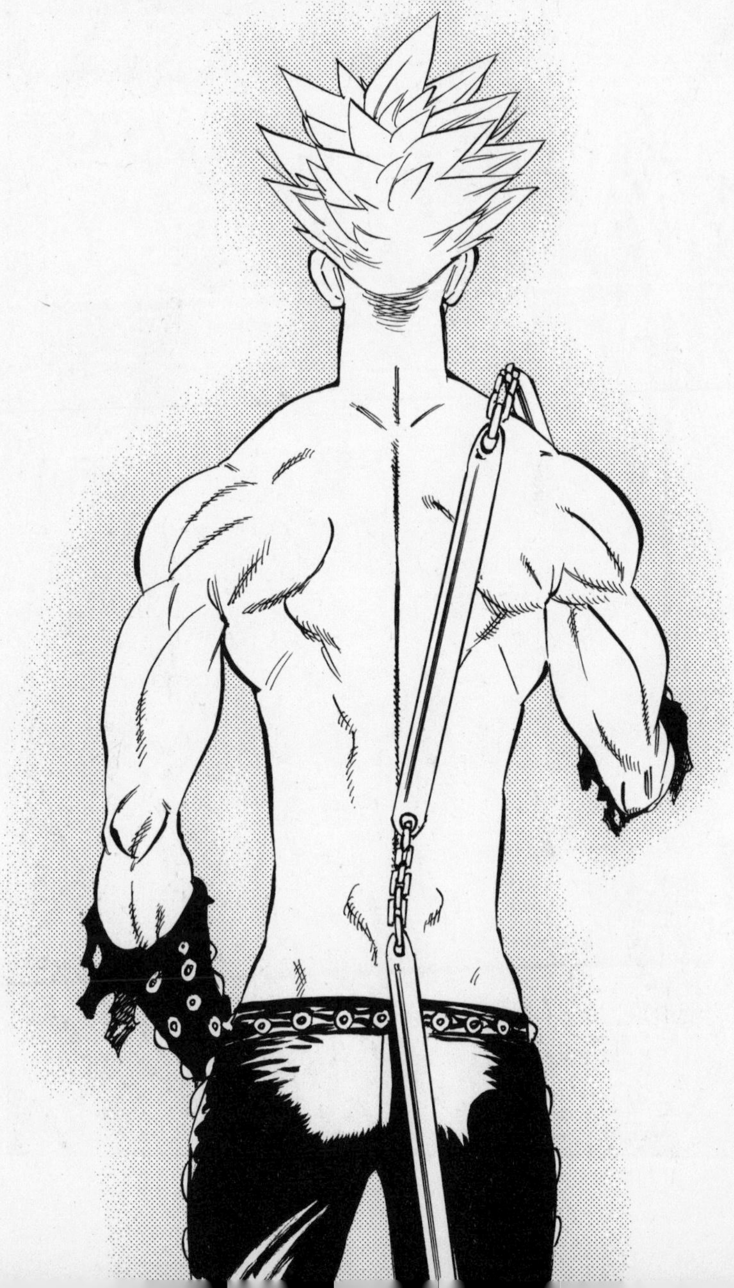

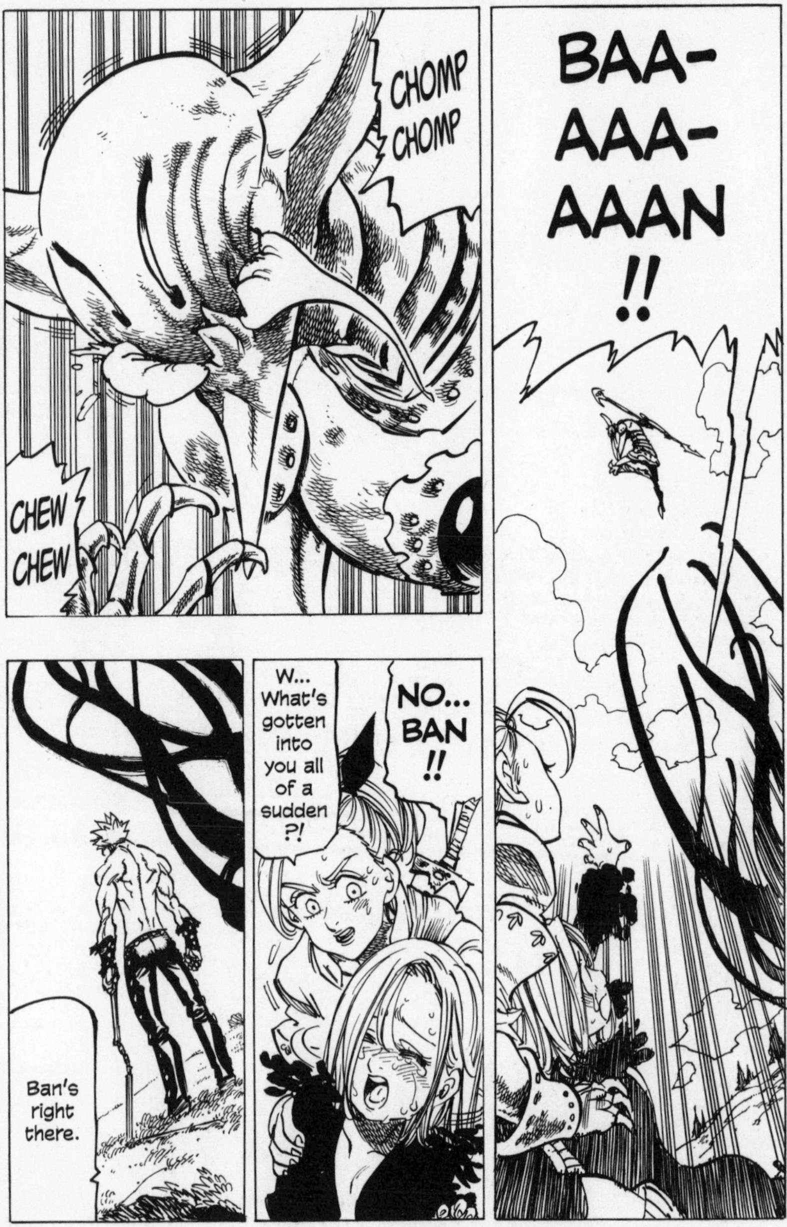
BAA-AAA-AAAN!!
CHOMP CHOMP
CHEW CHEW
NO... BAN!!
W... What's gotten into you all of a sudden?!
Ban's right there.

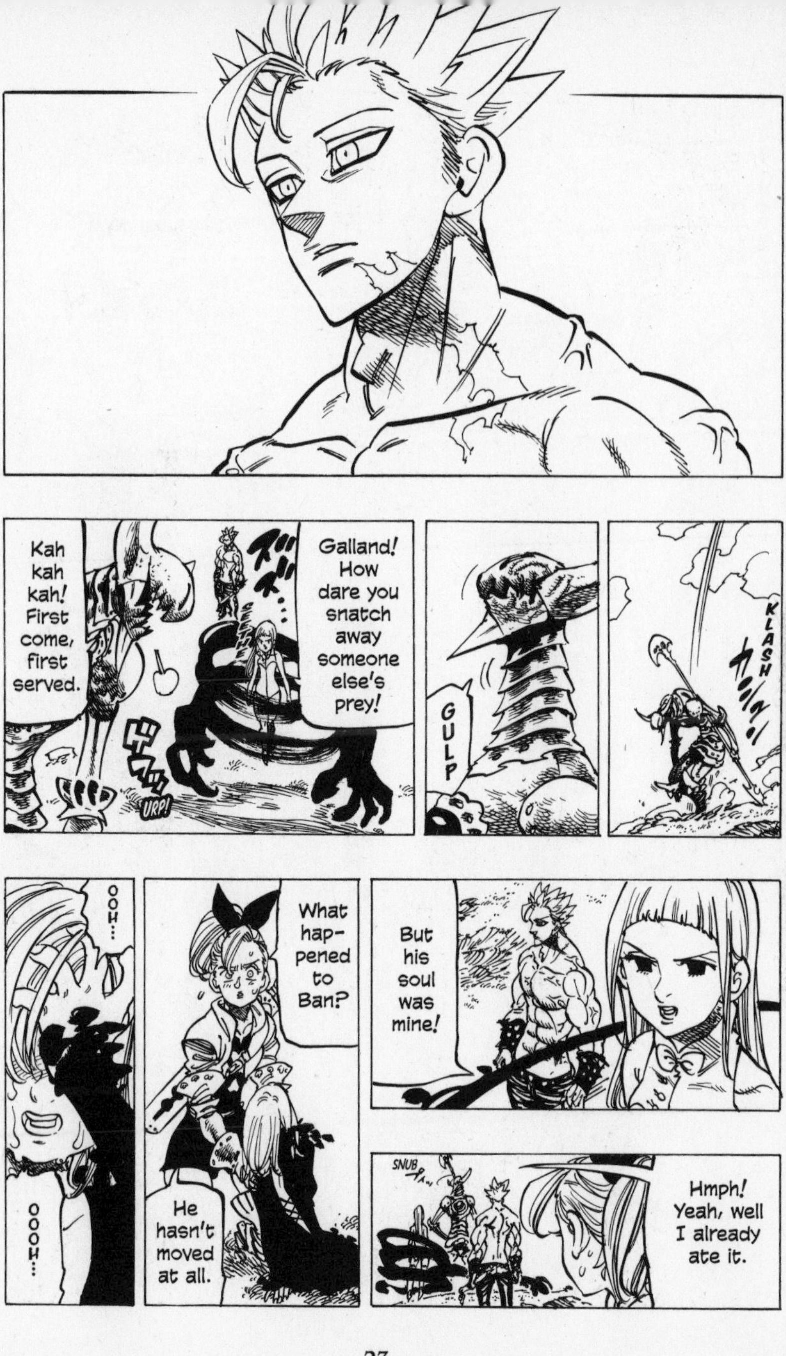
KLASH
GULP
Galland! How dare you snatch away someone else's prey!
Kah kah kah! First come, first served.
URP!
But his soul was mine!
Hmph! Yeah, well I already ate it.
SNUB
What hap-pened to Ban?
He hasn't moved at all.
OOH...
OOOH...

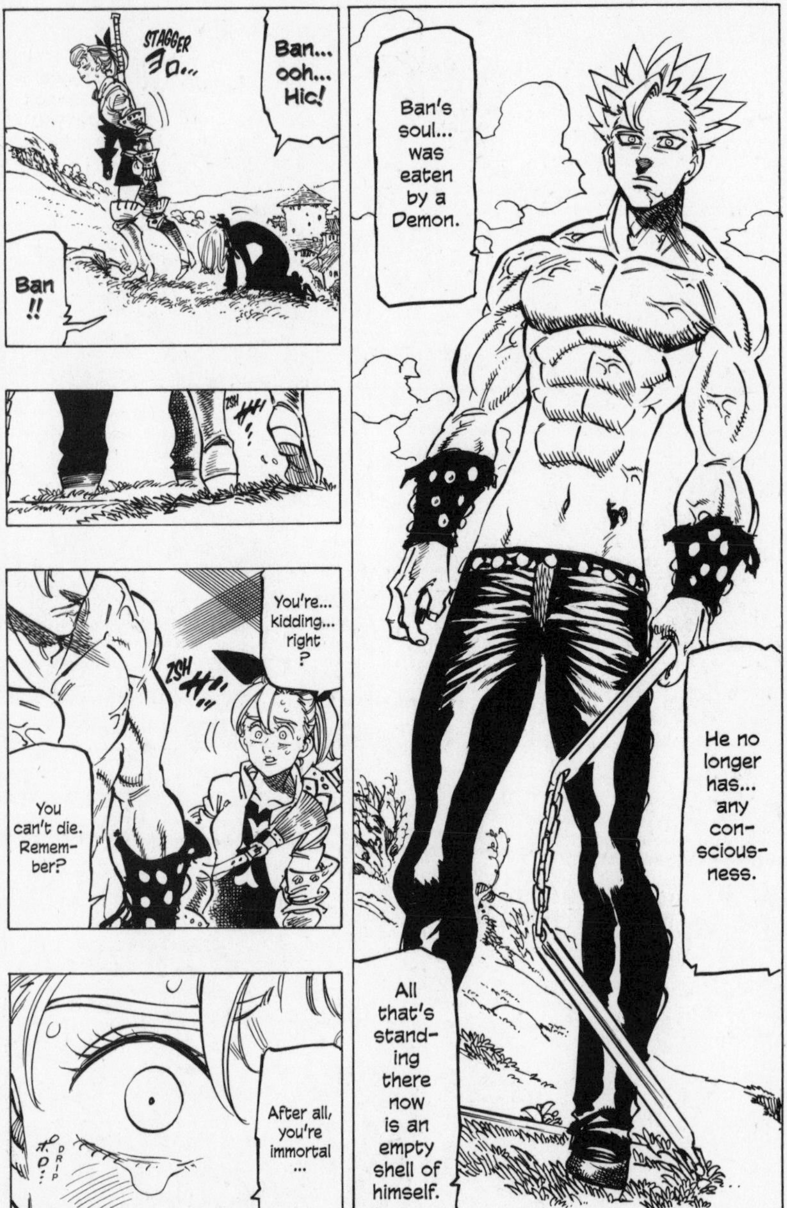
Ban's soul... was eaten by a Demon.
He no longer has... any consciousness.
All that's standing there now is an empty shell of himself.
Ban... ooh... Hic!
STAGGER
Ban!!
ZSH
You're... kidding... right?
ZSH
You can't die. Remember?
After all, you're immortal...
DRIP

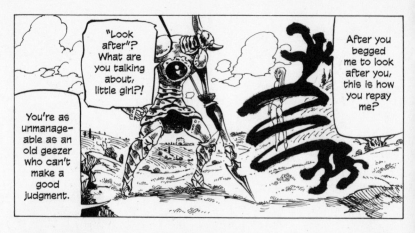

After you begged me to look after you, this is how you repay me?
"Look after"? What are you talking about, little girl?!
You're as unmanage-able as an old geezer who can't make a good judgment.
ZSH ZSH
SLIDE
Ban... I'm going to avenge you!
GRAB
Huh?

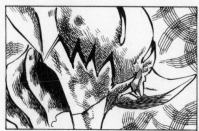

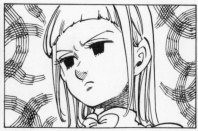

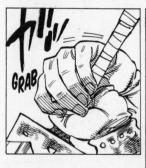

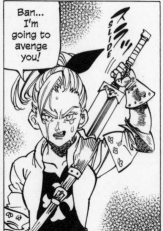

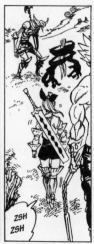

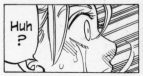

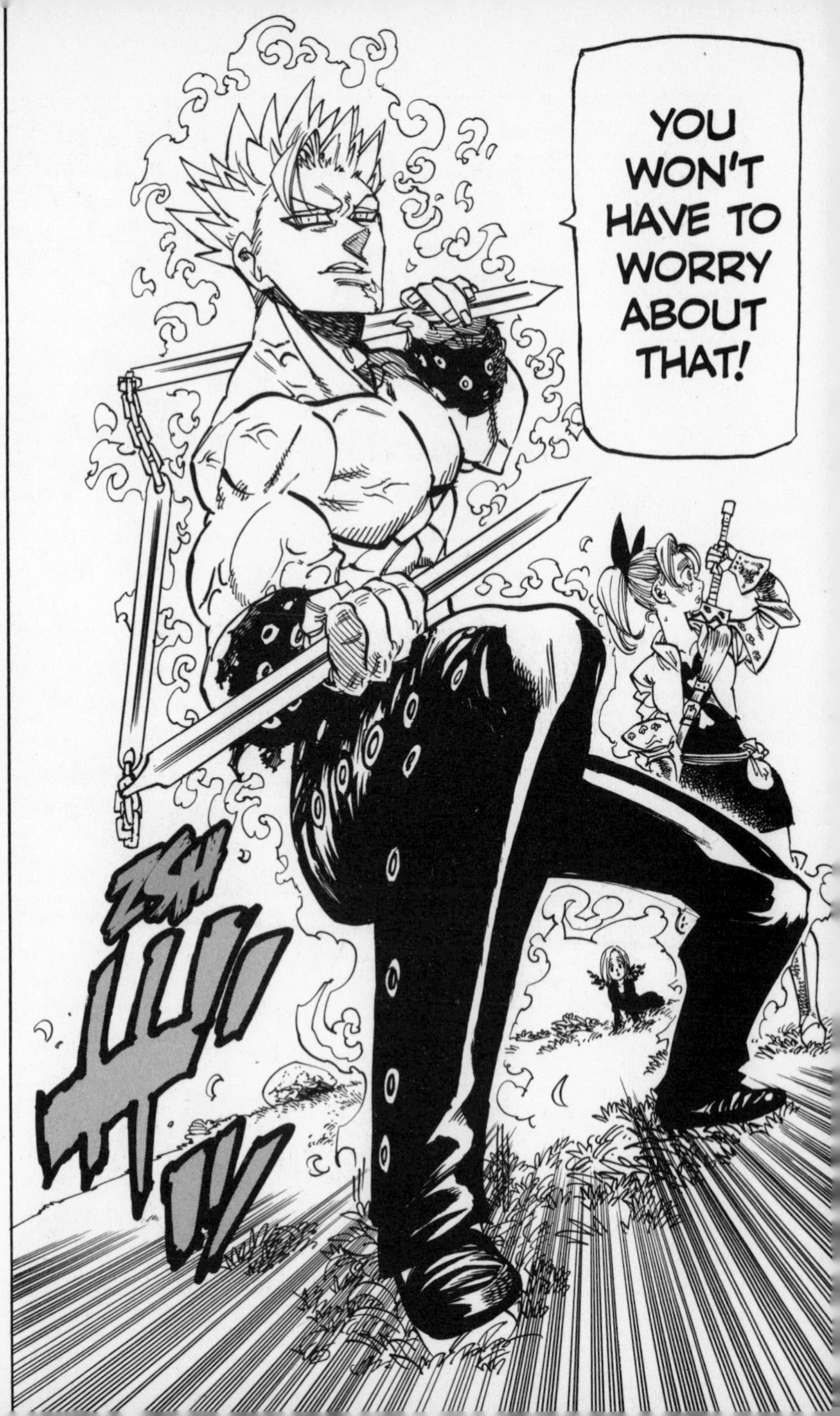
YOU WON'T HAVE TO WORRY ABOUT THAT!
ZSH

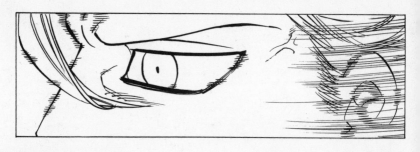

"FOX HUNT."

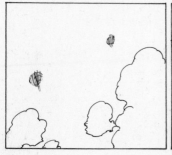

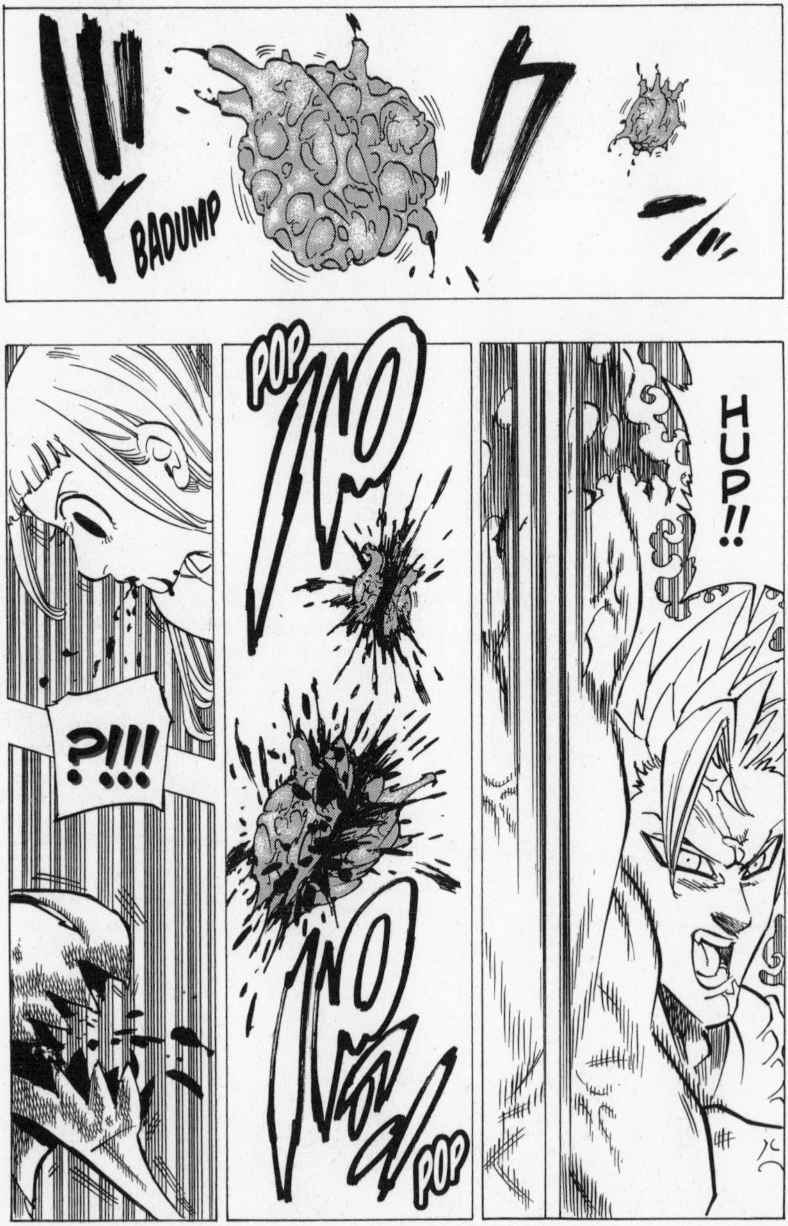
BADUMP
HUP!!
POP
POP
?!!!

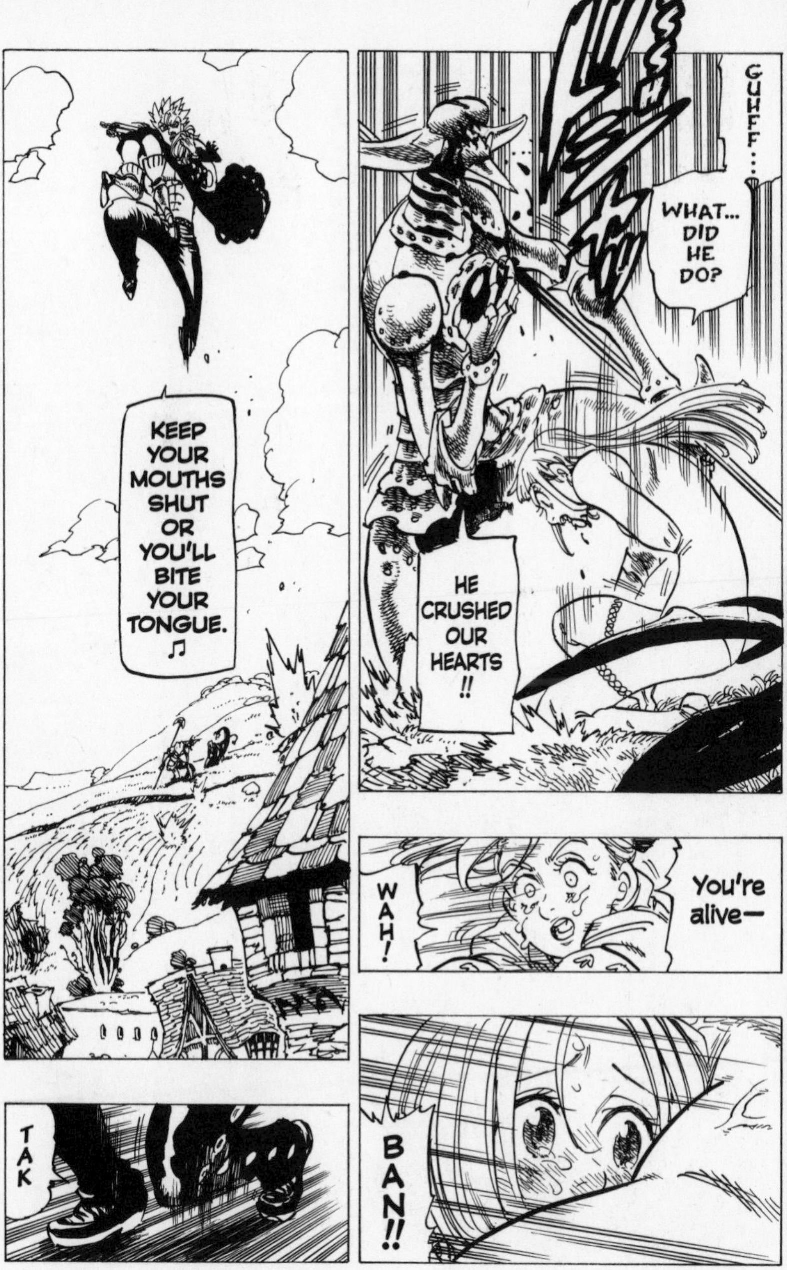
DSSHH
GUHFF...
WHAT... DID HE DO?
HE CRUSHED OUR HEARTS!!
WAH!
You're alive—
BAN!!
KEEP YOUR MOUTHS SHUT OR YOU'LL BITE YOUR TONGUE. ♫
TAK

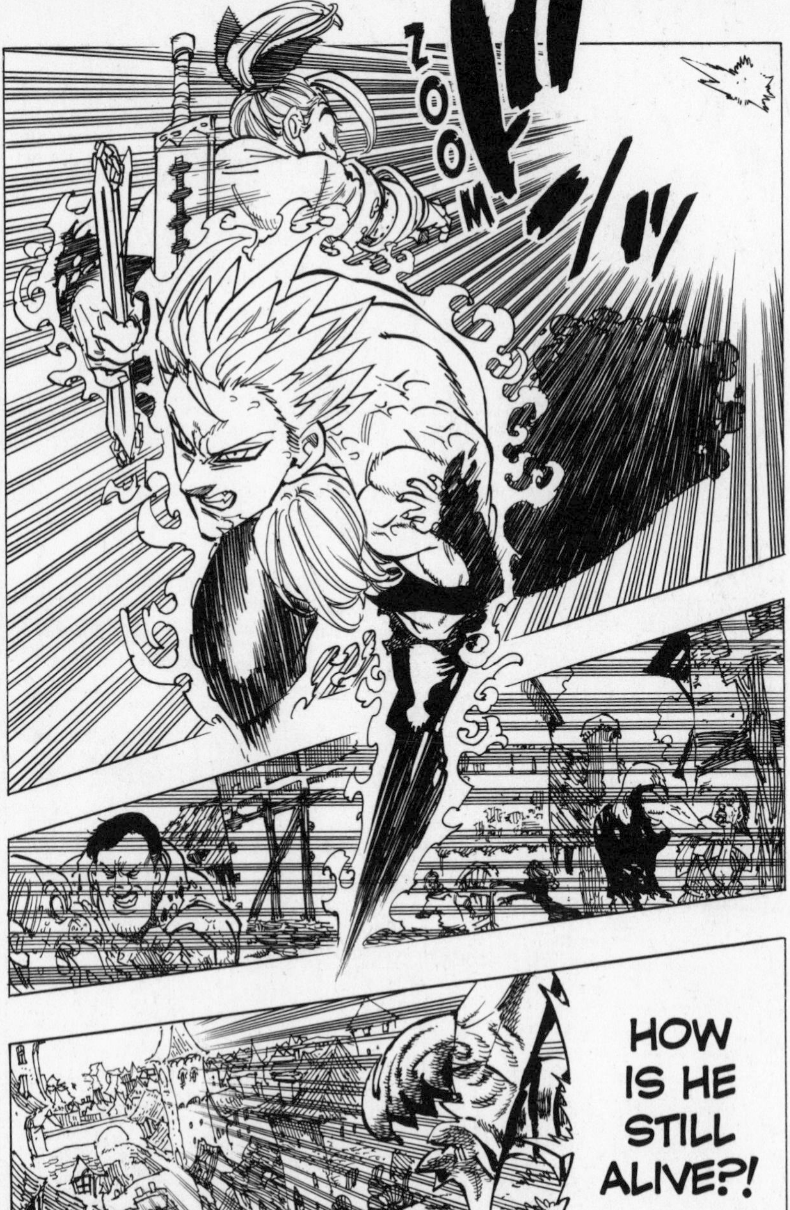
ZOOOM
HOW IS HE STILL ALIVE?!

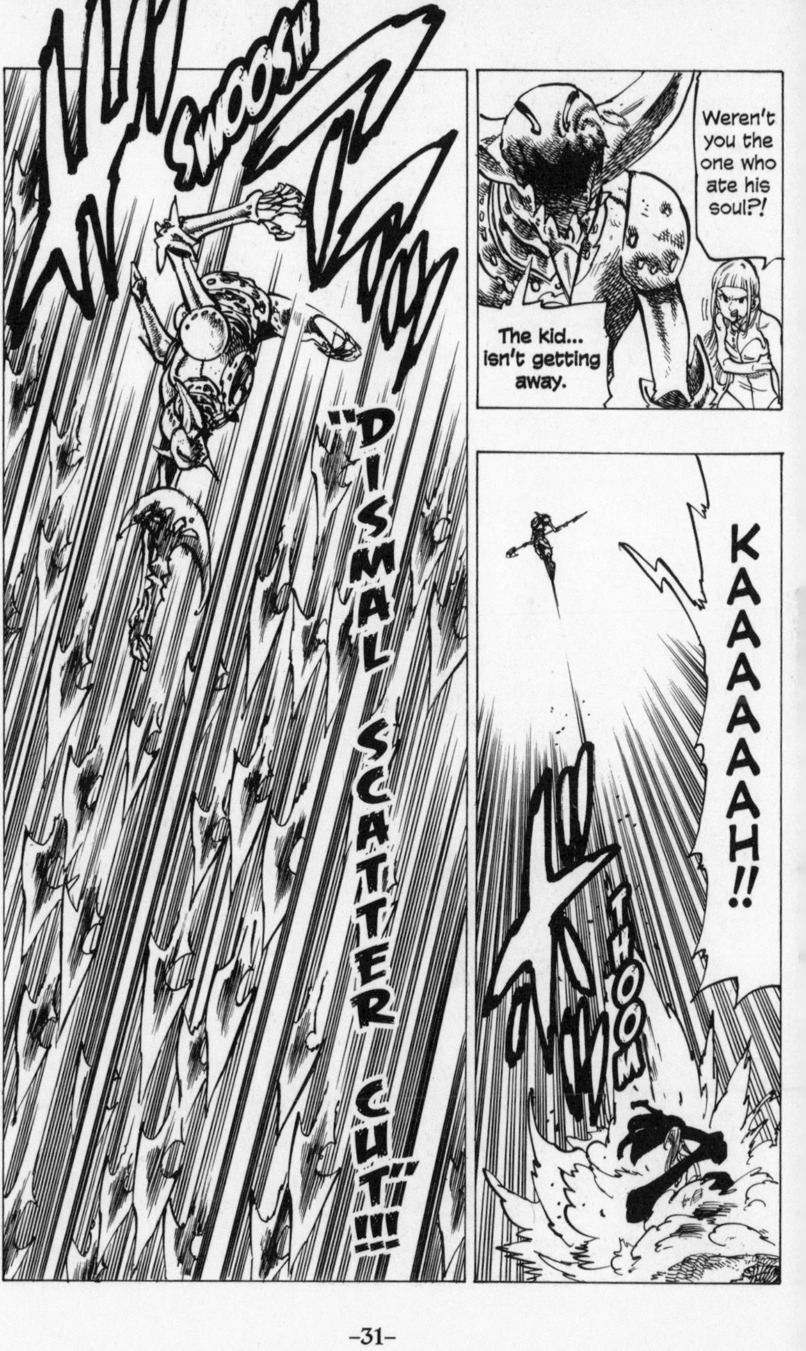
Weren't you the one who ate his soul?!
The kid... isn't getting away.
KAAAAAAAH!!
THOOM
SWOOSH
"DISMAL SCATTER CUT"!!!

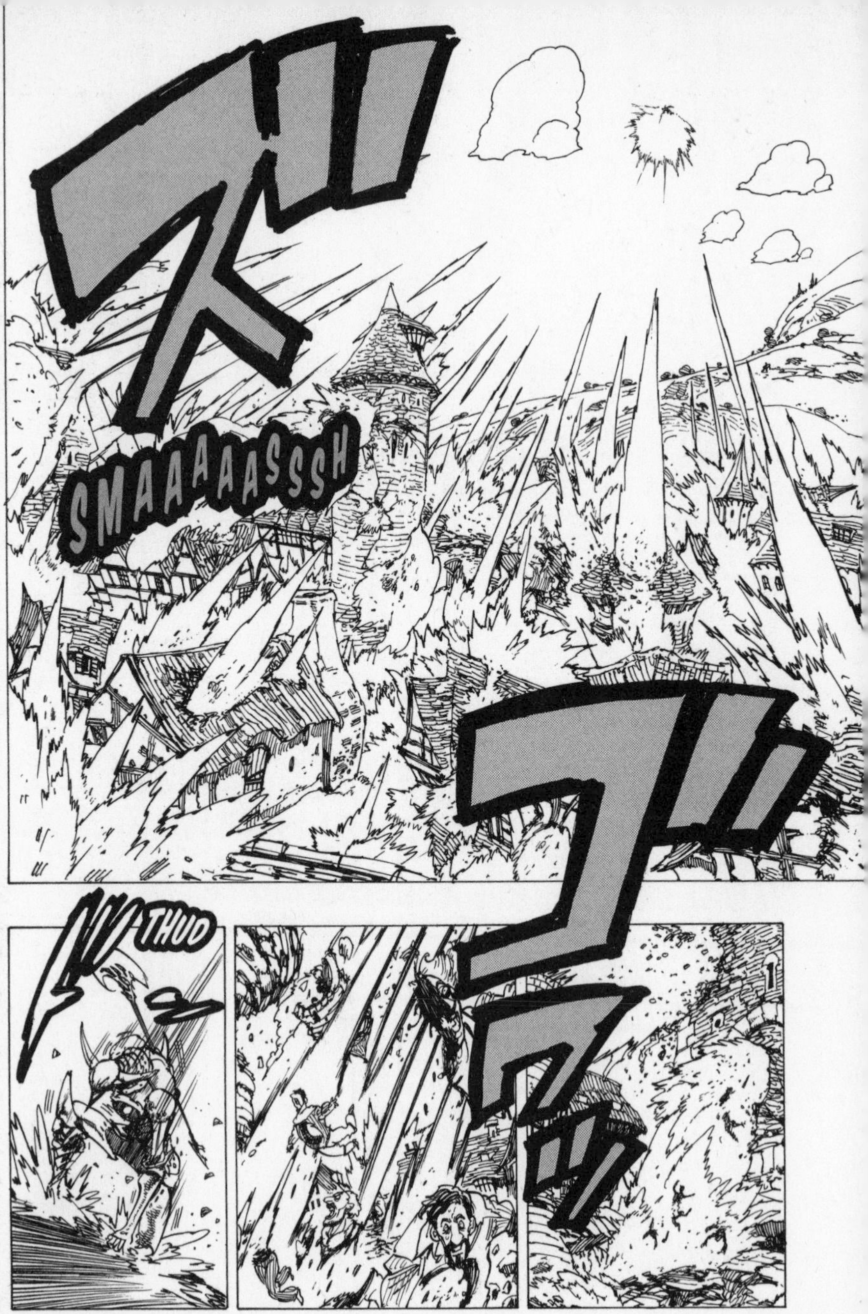
SMAAAAASSSH
THUD

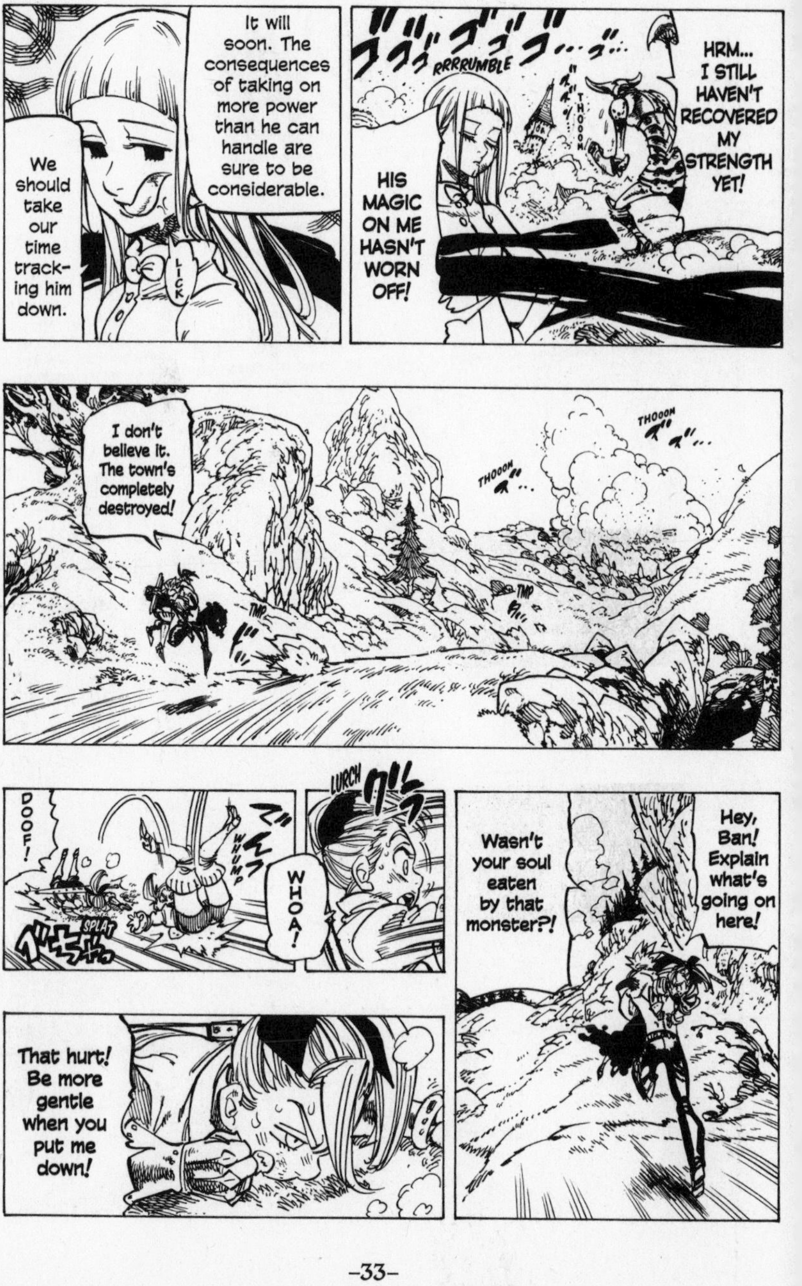
RRRRUMBLE
THOOOM
HRM... I STILL HAVEN'T RECOVERED MY STRENGTH YET!
HIS MAGIC ON ME HASN'T WORN OFF!
It will soon. The consequences of taking on more power than he can handle are sure to be considerable.
LICK
We should take our time tracking him down.
THOOOM
THOOOM
I don't believe it. The town's completely destroyed!
TMP
TMP
Hey, Ban! Explain what's going on here!
Wasn't your soul eaten by that monster?!
LURCH
WHOA!
WHUMP
DOOF!
SPLAT
That hurt! Be more gentle when you put me down!

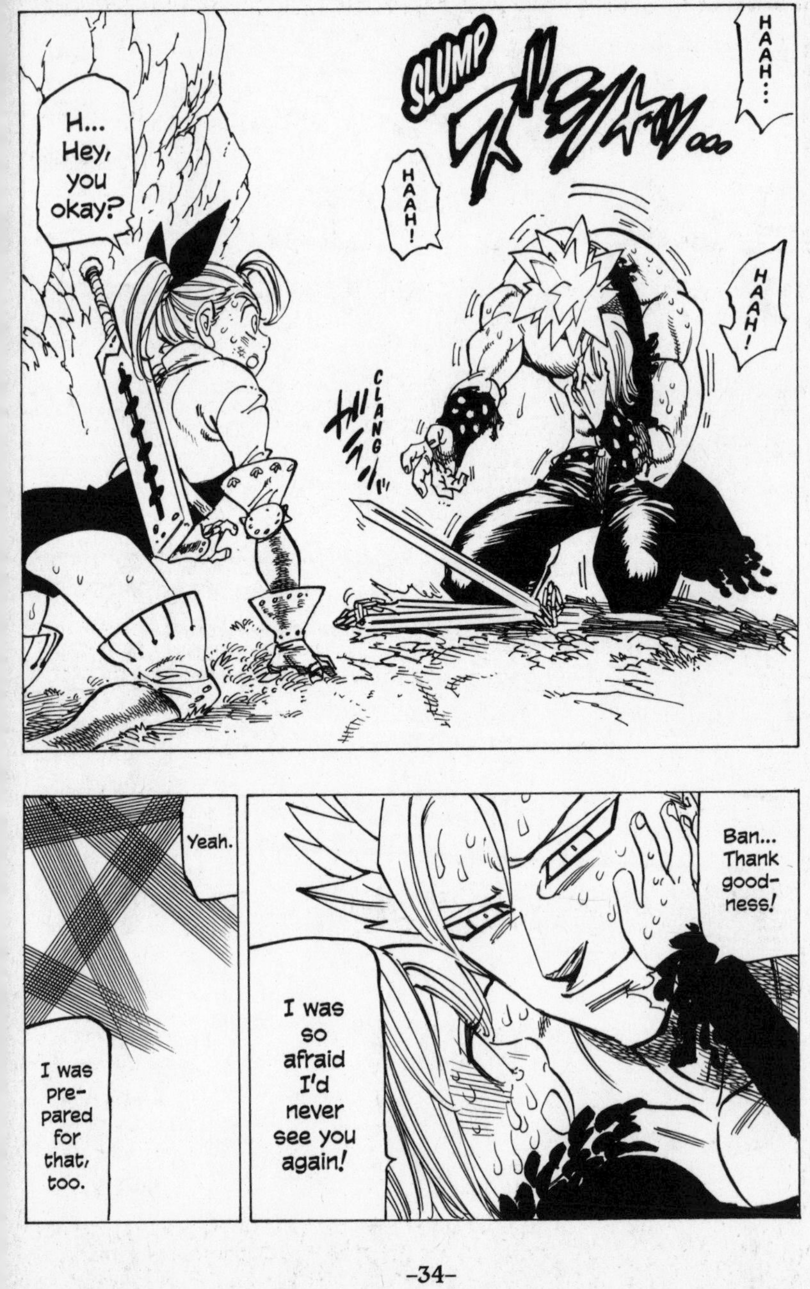
HAAAH...
SLUMP
HAAH!
HAAAH!
CLANG
H... Hey, you okay?
Ban... Thank goodness!
I was so afraid I'd never see you again!
Yeah.
I was prepared for that, too.

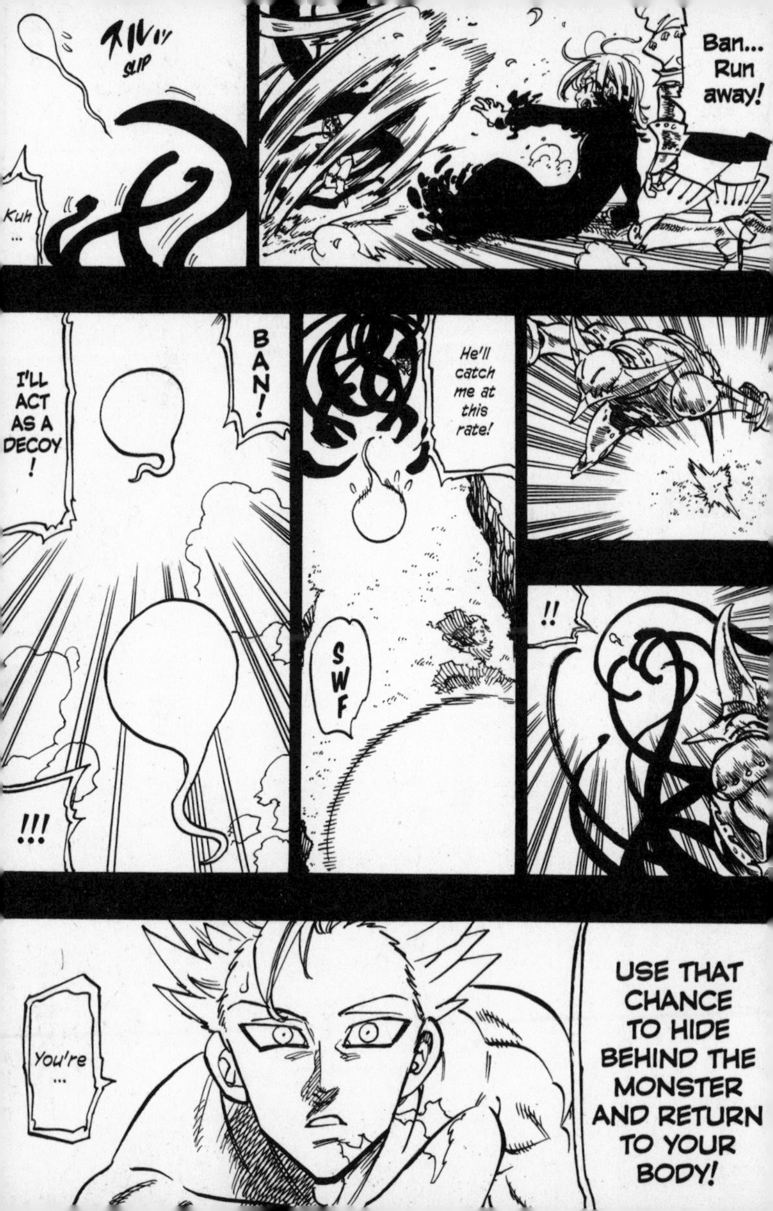
Ban... Run away!
スルッ
SLIP
Kuh ...
!!
He'll catch me at this rate!
SWF
BAN!
I'LL ACT AS A DECOY!
!!!
USE THAT CHANCE TO HIDE BEHIND THE MONSTER AND RETURN TO YOUR BODY!
You're ...

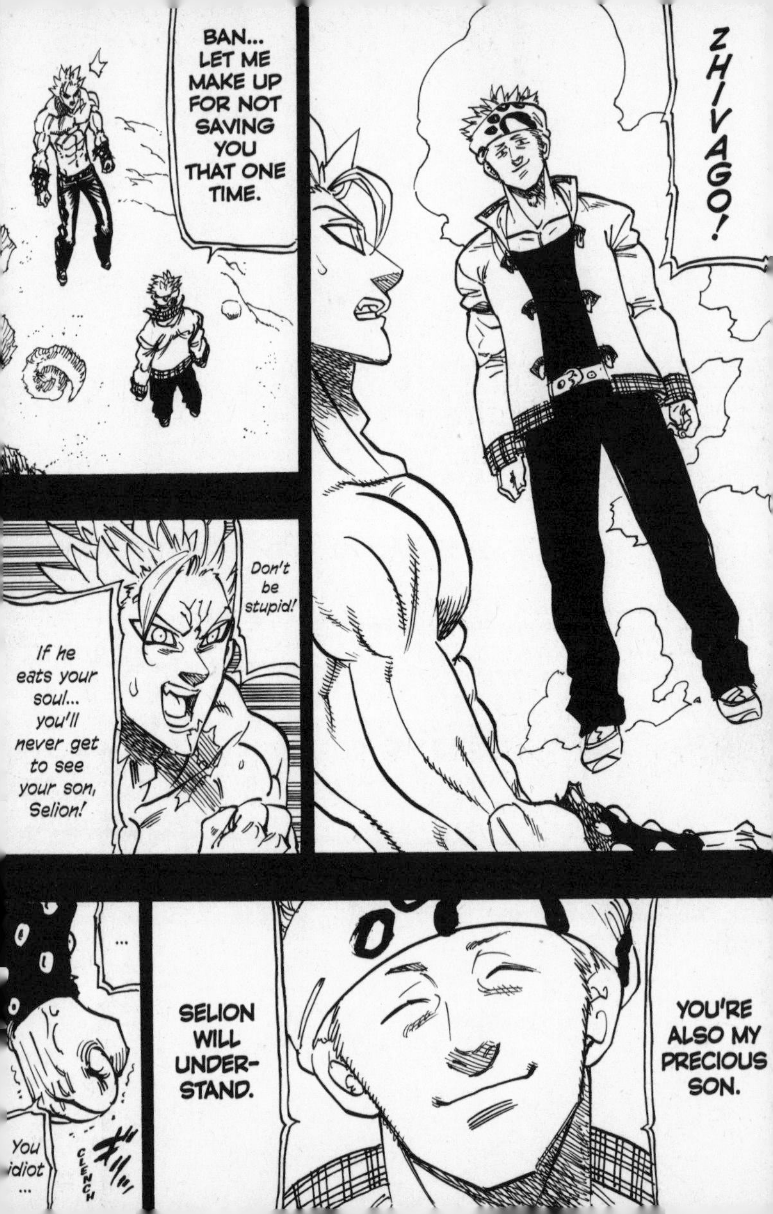
ZHIVAGO!
BAN... LET ME MAKE UP FOR NOT SAVING YOU THAT ONE TIME.
...
Don't be stupid!
If he eats your soul... you'll never get to see your son, Selion!
YOU'RE ALSO MY PRECIOUS SON.
SELION WILL UNDERSTAND.
...
You idiot...
CLENCH

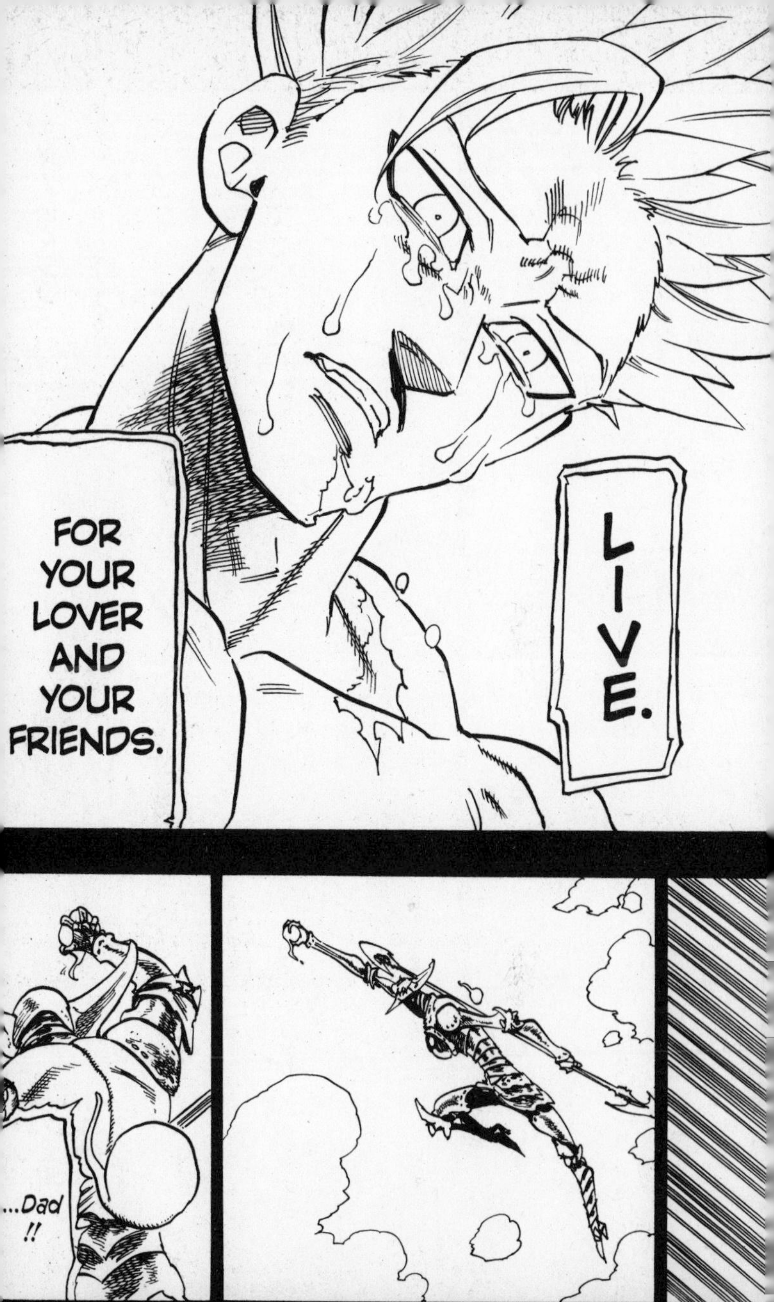
LIVE.
FOR YOUR LOVER AND YOUR FRIENDS.
...Dad !!

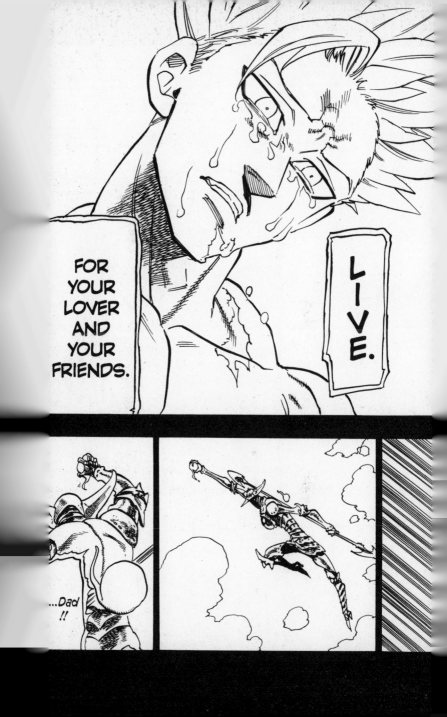

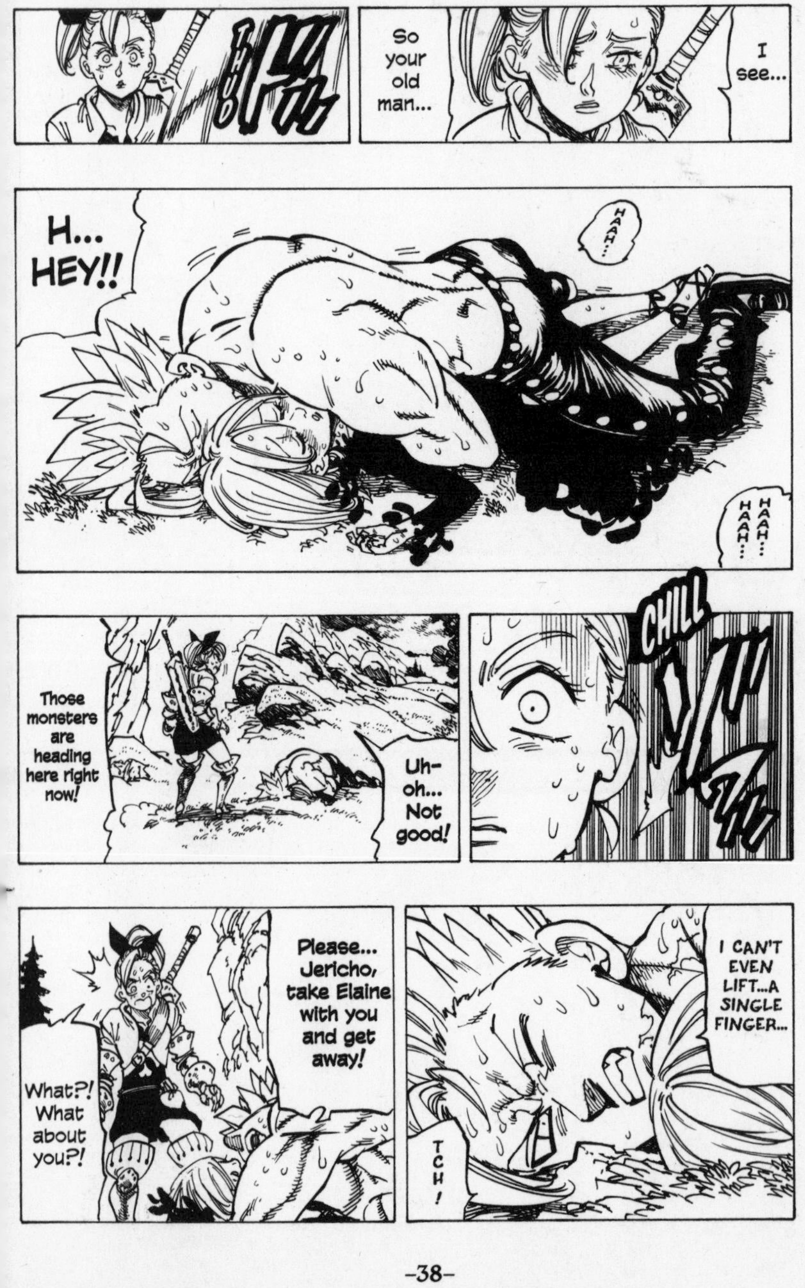
I see...
So your old man...
THUD
H... HEY!!
HAAH...
HAAH... HAAH...
CHILL
Uh-oh... Not good!
Those monsters are heading here right now!
I CAN'T EVEN LIFT...A SINGLE FINGER...
TCH!
Please... Jericho, take Elaine with you and get away!
What?! What about you?!

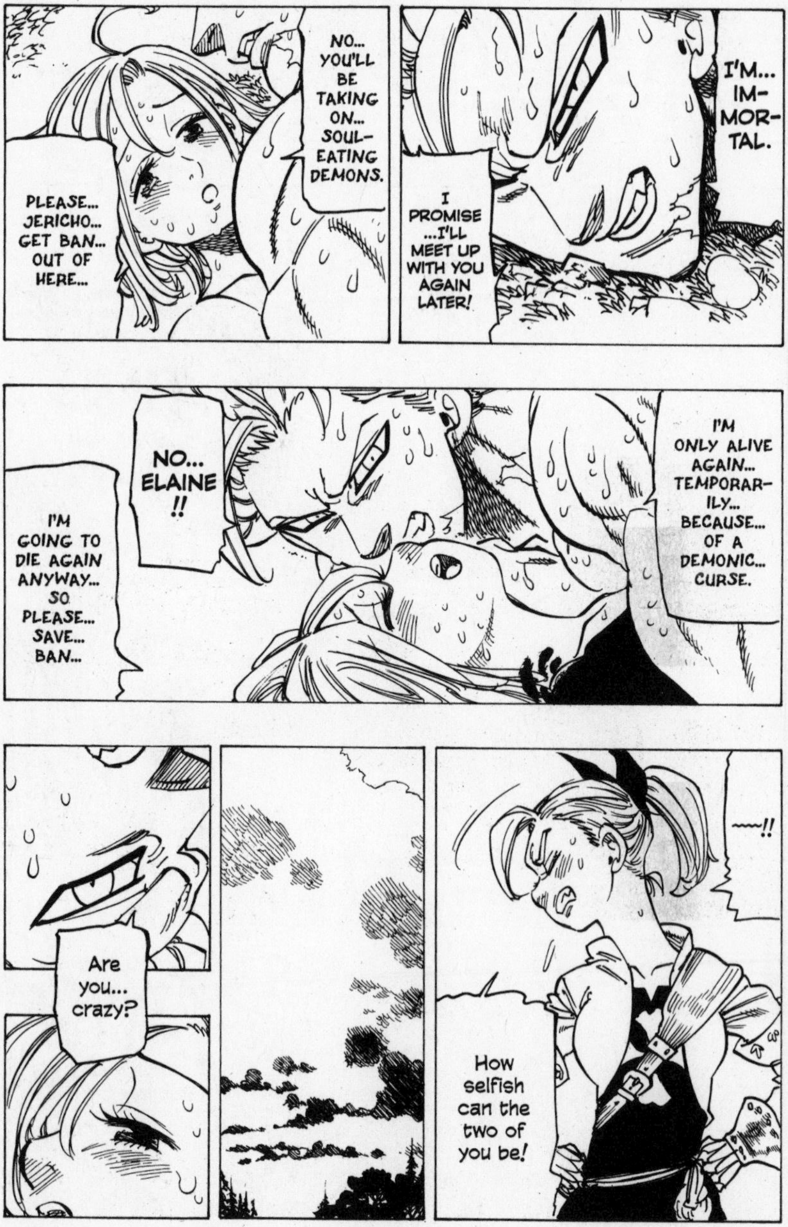
I'M... IMMORTAL.
I PROMISE ...I'LL MEET UP WITH YOU AGAIN LATER!
NO... YOU'LL BE TAKING ON... SOUL-EATING DEMONS.
PLEASE... JERICHO... GET BAN... OUT OF HERE...
I'M ONLY ALIVE AGAIN... TEMPORARILY... BECAUSE... OF A DEMONIC... CURSE.
NO... ELAINE!!
I'M GOING TO DIE AGAIN ANYWAY... SO PLEASE... SAVE... BAN...
~~!!
How selfish can the two of you be!
Are you... crazy?

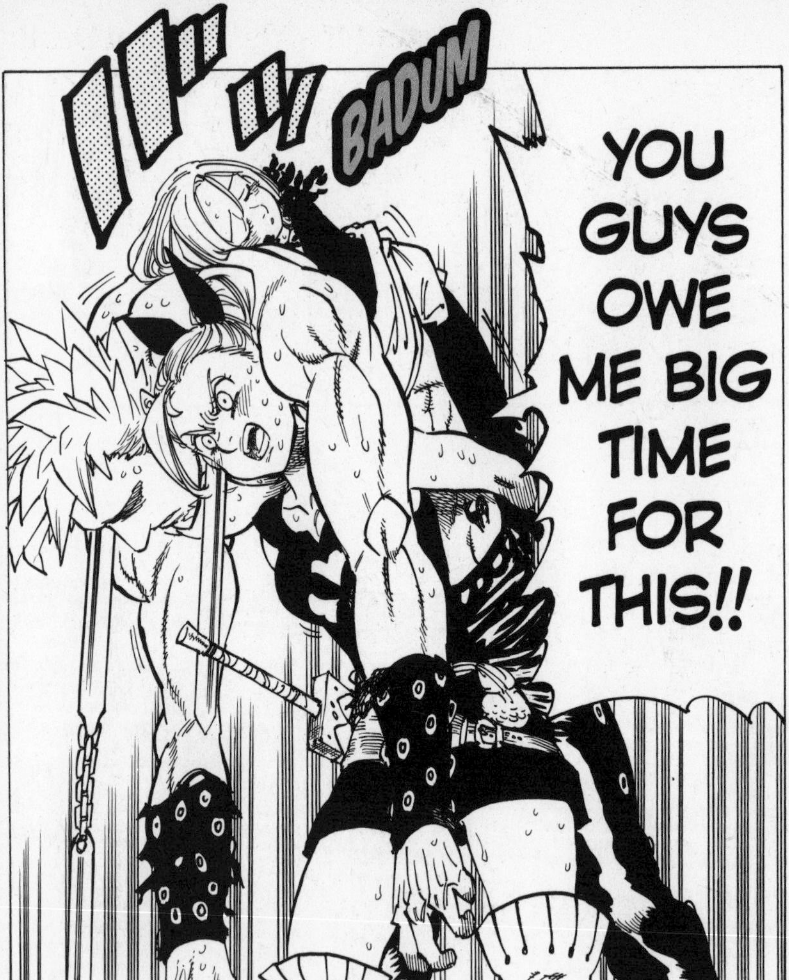
BADUM
YOU GUYS OWE ME BIG TIME FOR THIS!!
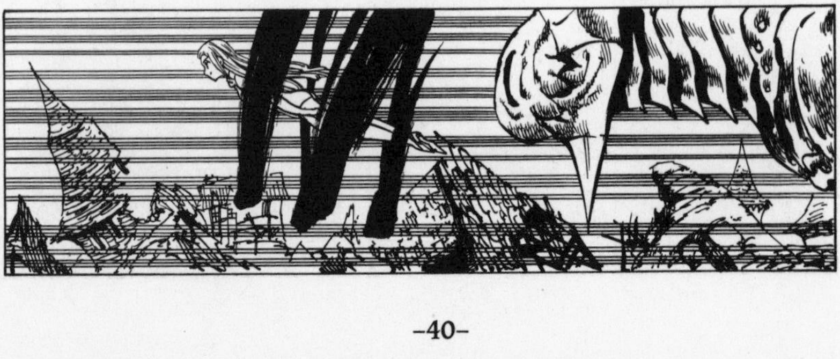

Chapter 147 - The Chase of Death

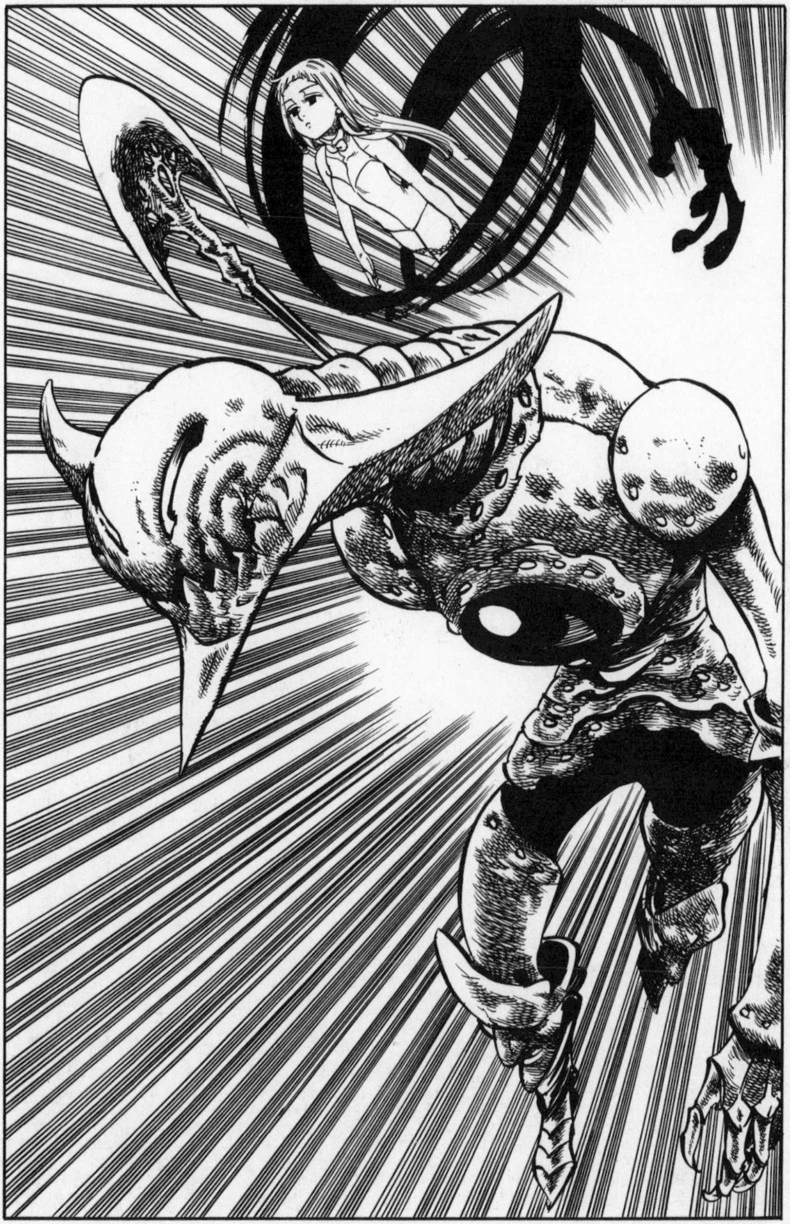

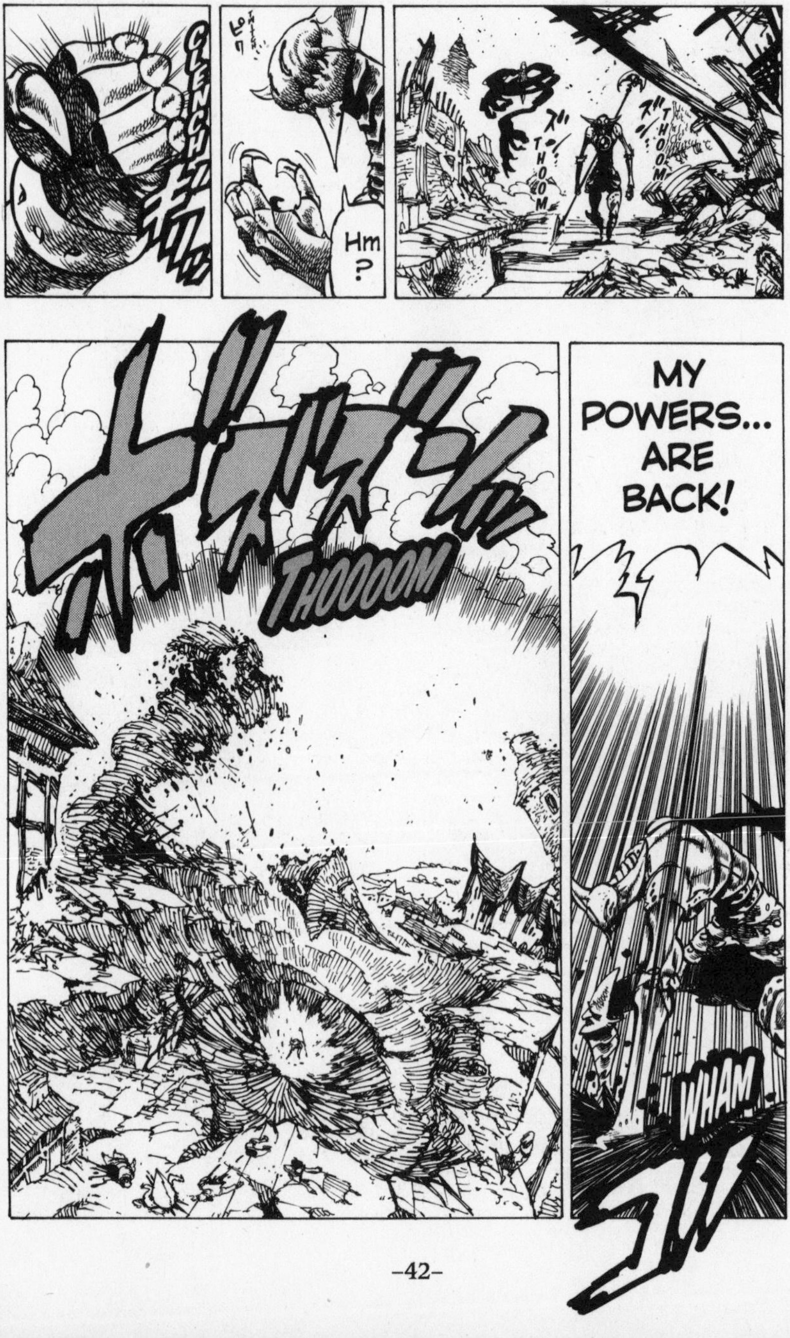
THOOM
THOOM
Hm?
CLENCH
MY POWERS... ARE BACK!
WHAM
THOOOOM

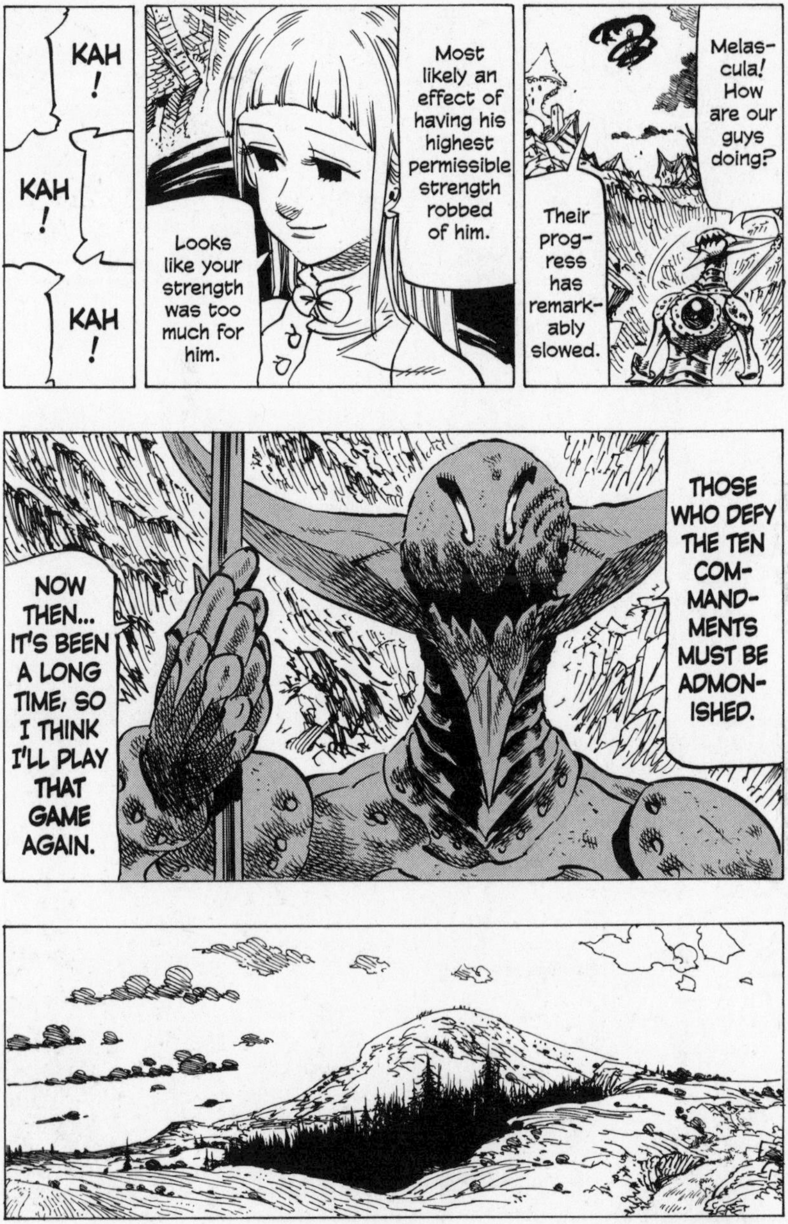
Melascula! How are our guys doing?
Their progress has remarkably slowed.
Most likely an effect of having his highest permissible strength robbed of him.
Looks like your strength was too much for him.
KAH!
KAH!
KAH!
THOSE WHO DEFY THE TEN COMMANDMENTS MUST BE ADMONISHED.
NOW THEN... IT'S BEEN A LONG TIME, SO I THINK I'LL PLAY THAT GAME AGAIN.

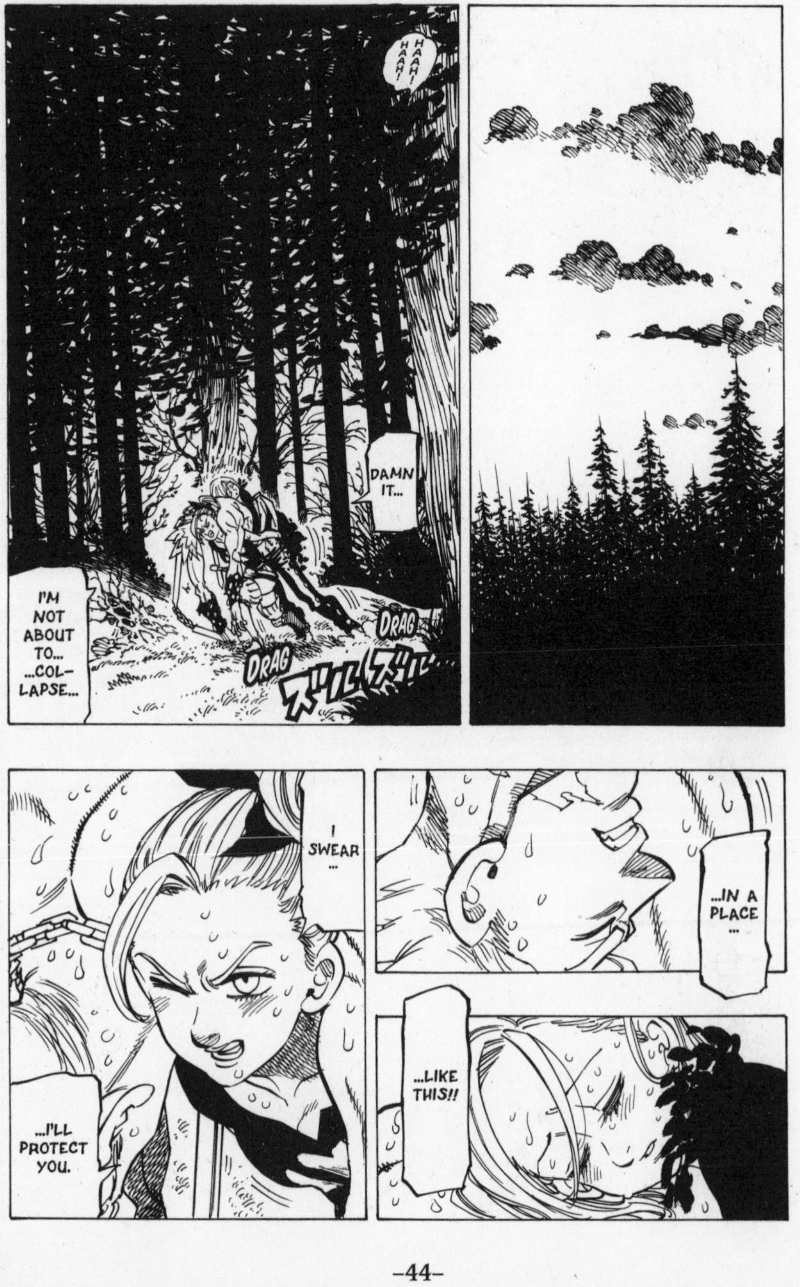
HAAH! HAAH!
DAMN IT...
DRAG
DRAG
I'M NOT ABOUT TO... ...COL-LAPSE...
...IN A PLACE ...
...LIKE THIS!!
I SWEAR ...
...I'LL PROTECT YOU.

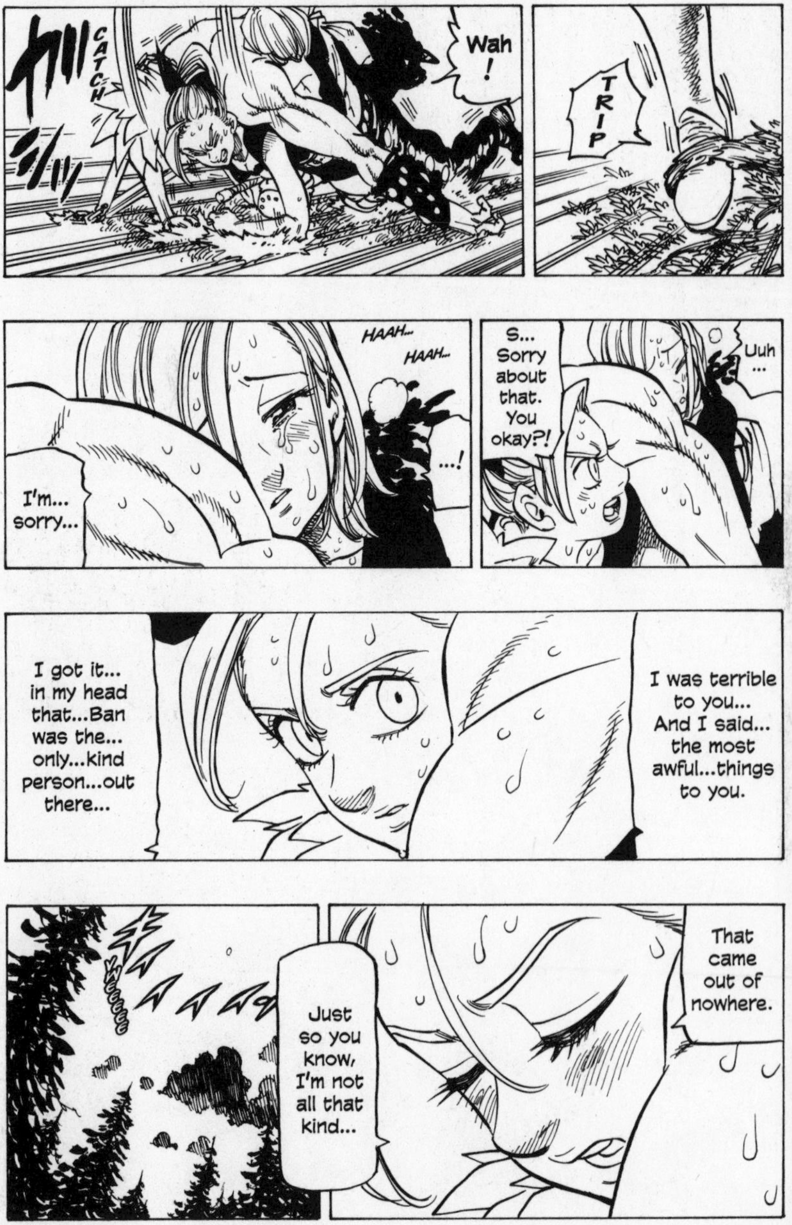
TRIP
Wah!
CATCH
Uuh...
S... Sorry about that. You okay?!
HAAH... HAAH...
...!
I'm... sorry...
I was terrible to you... And I said... the most awful...things to you.
I got it... in my head that...Ban was the... only...kind person...out there...
That came out of nowhere.
Just so you know, I'm not all that kind...

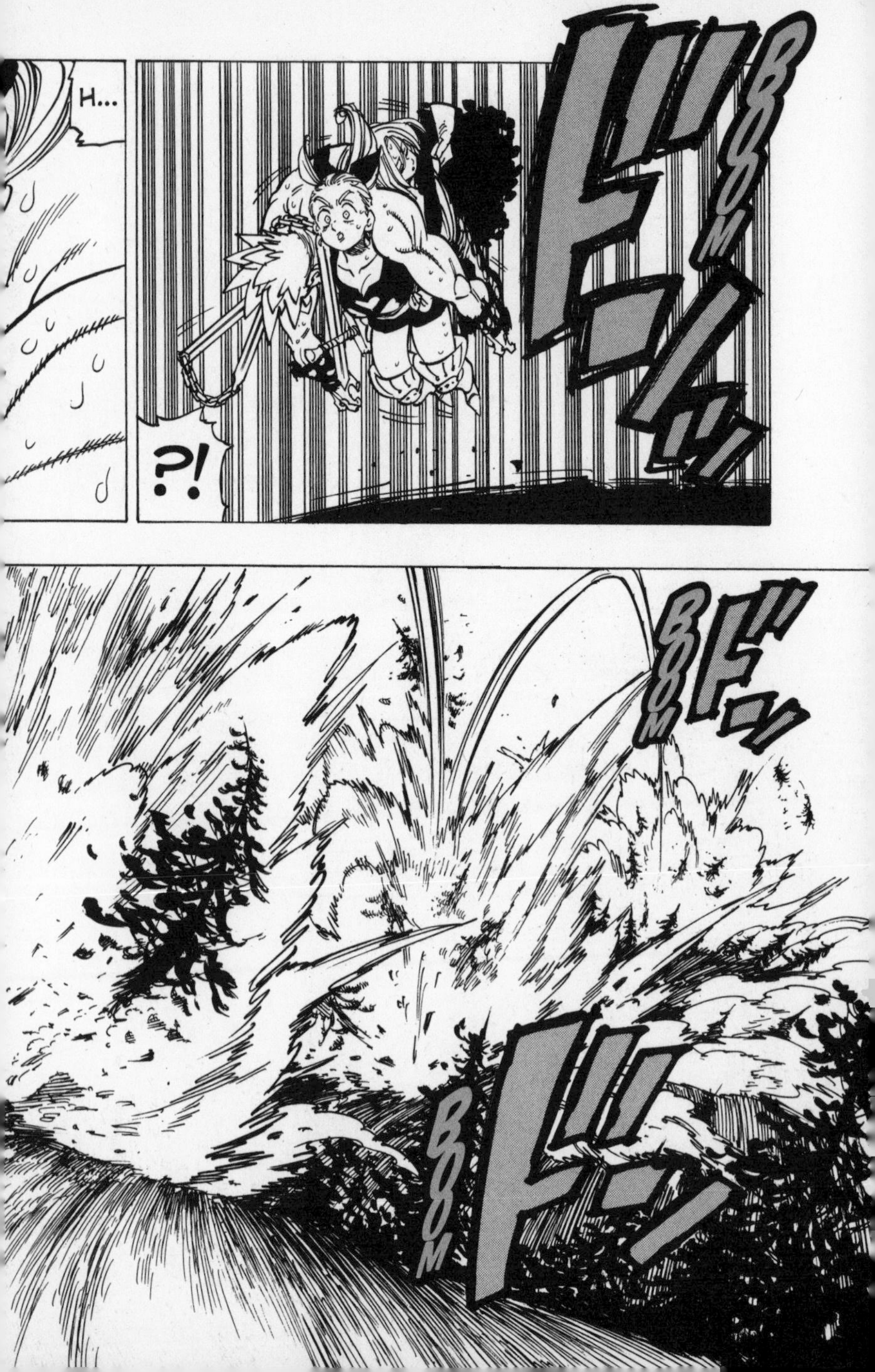
BOOM
?!
H...
BOOM
BOOM

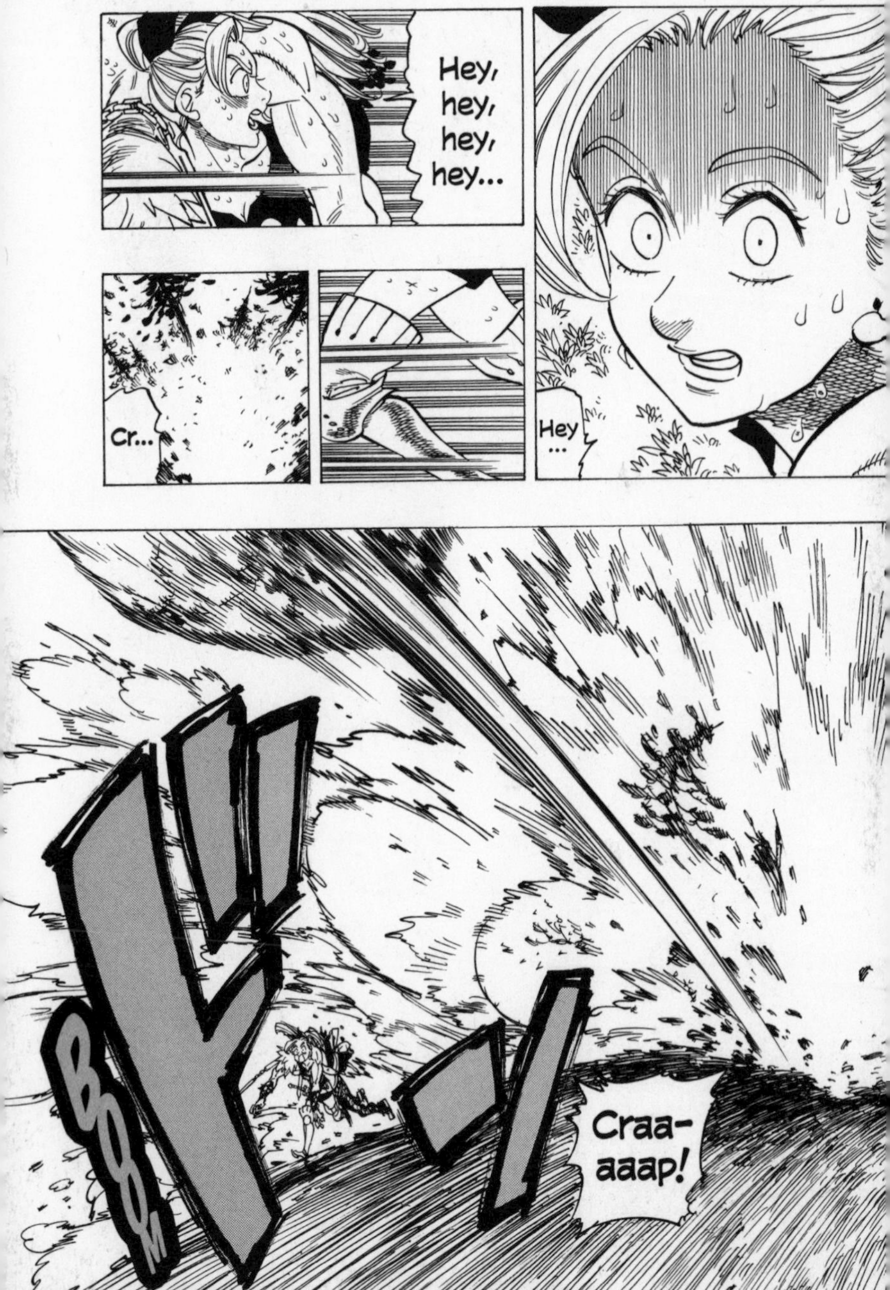
Hey
...
Hey,
hey,
hey,
hey...
Cr...
Craa-
aaap!
BOOM

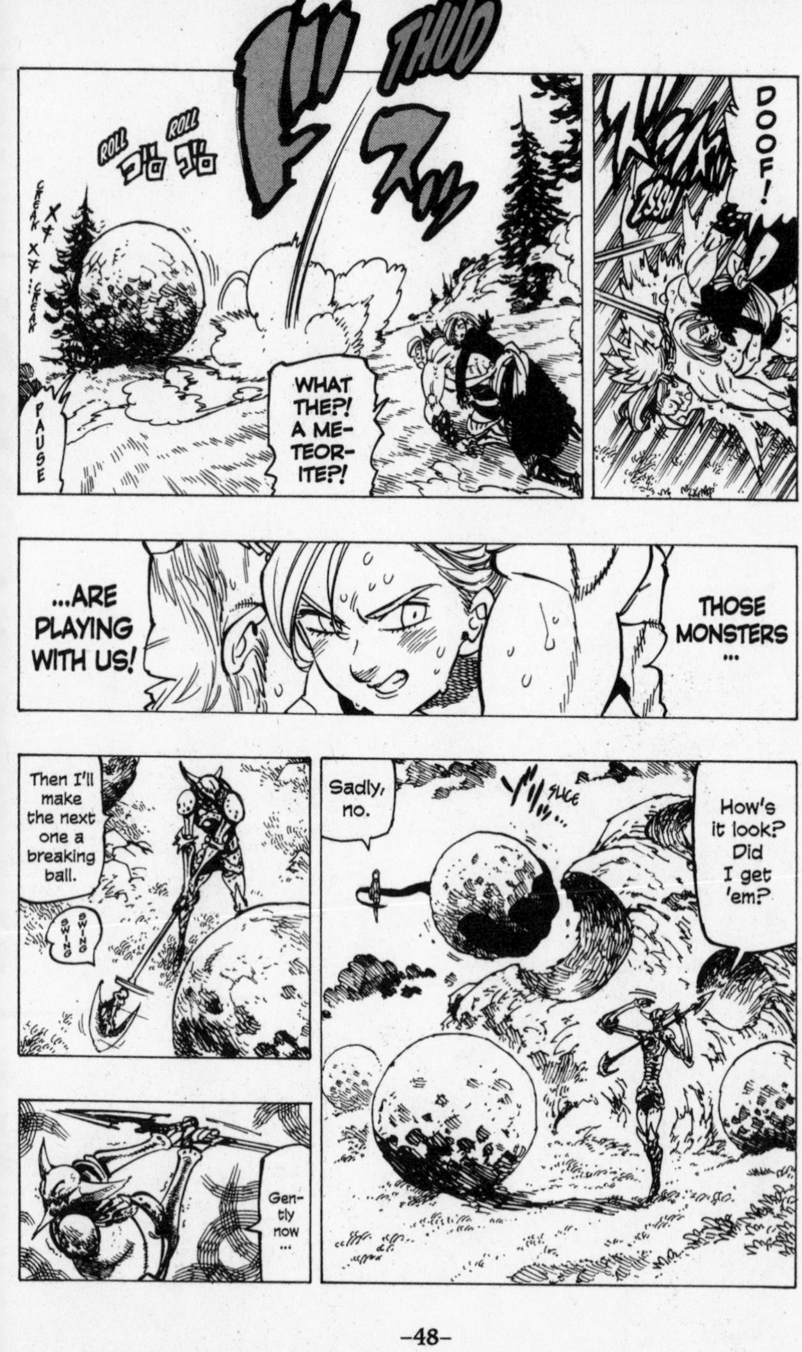
DOOF!
TSSH
THUD
ROLL ROLL
CREAK CREAK
PAUSE
WHAT THE?! A METEORITE?!
THOSE MONSTERS...
...ARE PLAYING WITH US!
How's it look? Did I get 'em?
SLICE
Sadly, no.
Then I'll make the next one a breaking ball.
SWING SWING
Gently now...

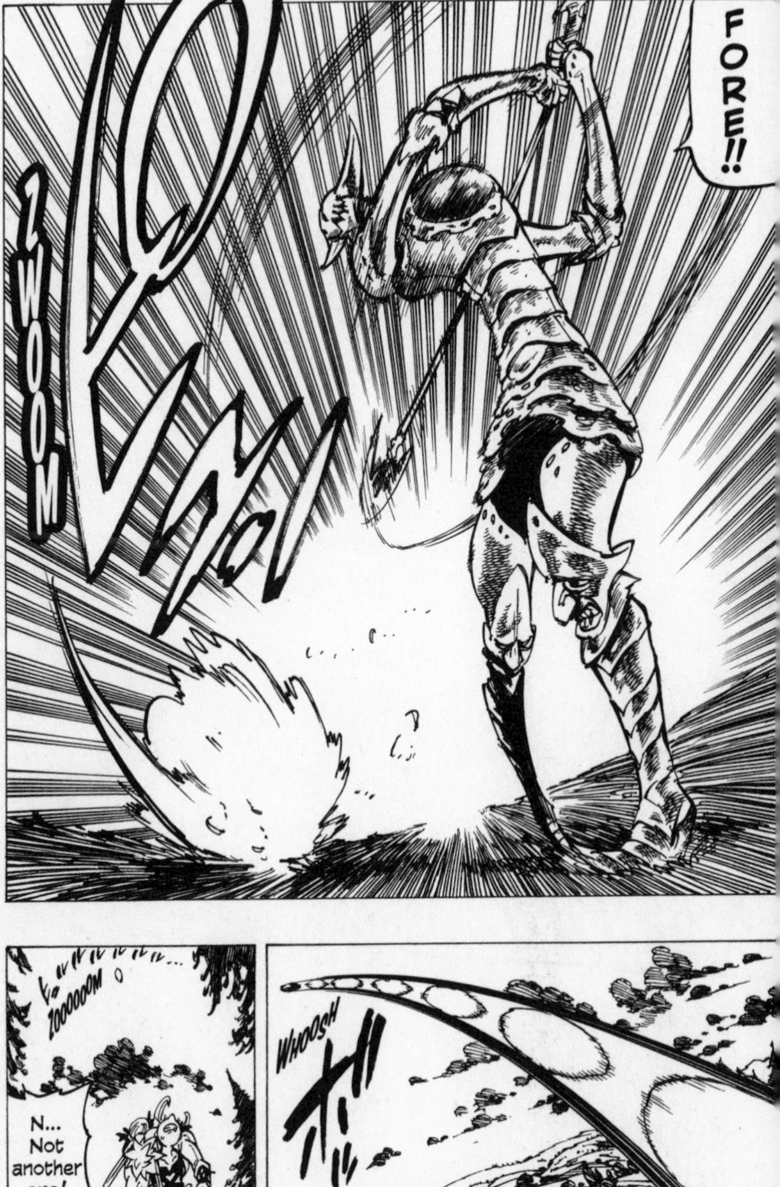
FORE!!
ZWOOOM
WHOOSH
ZOOOOOOM
N... Not another one!

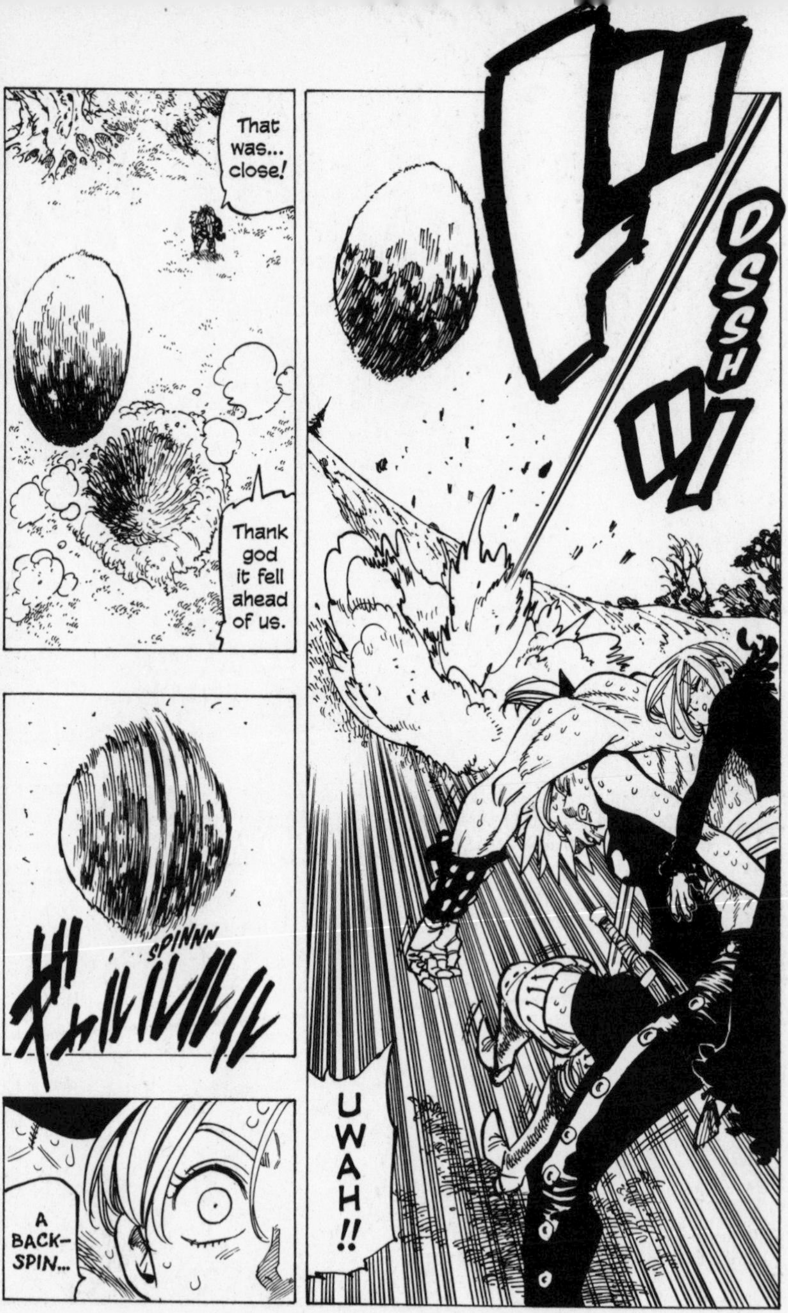
DOSSH
UWAH!!
That was... close!
Thank god it fell ahead of us.
SPINNN
A BACK-SPIN...

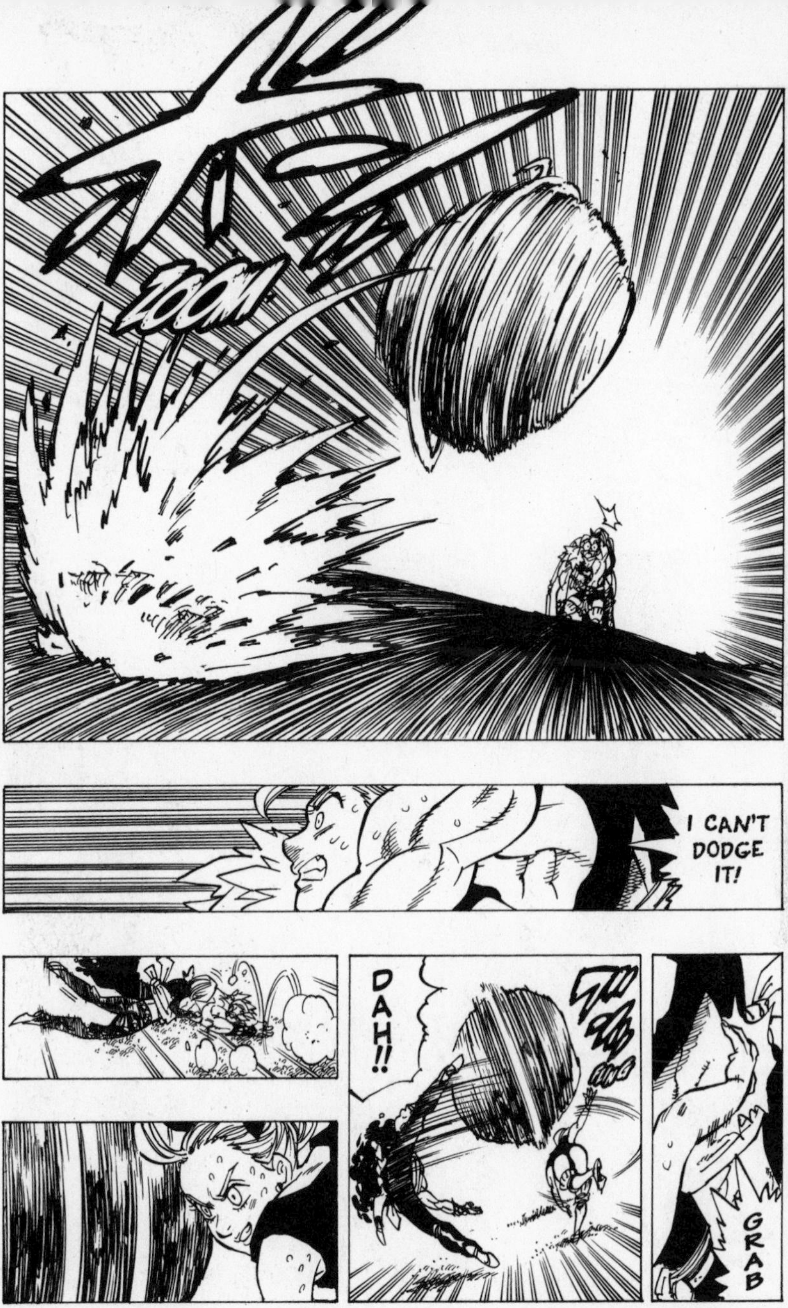
I CAN'T DODGE IT!
GRAB
DAH!!

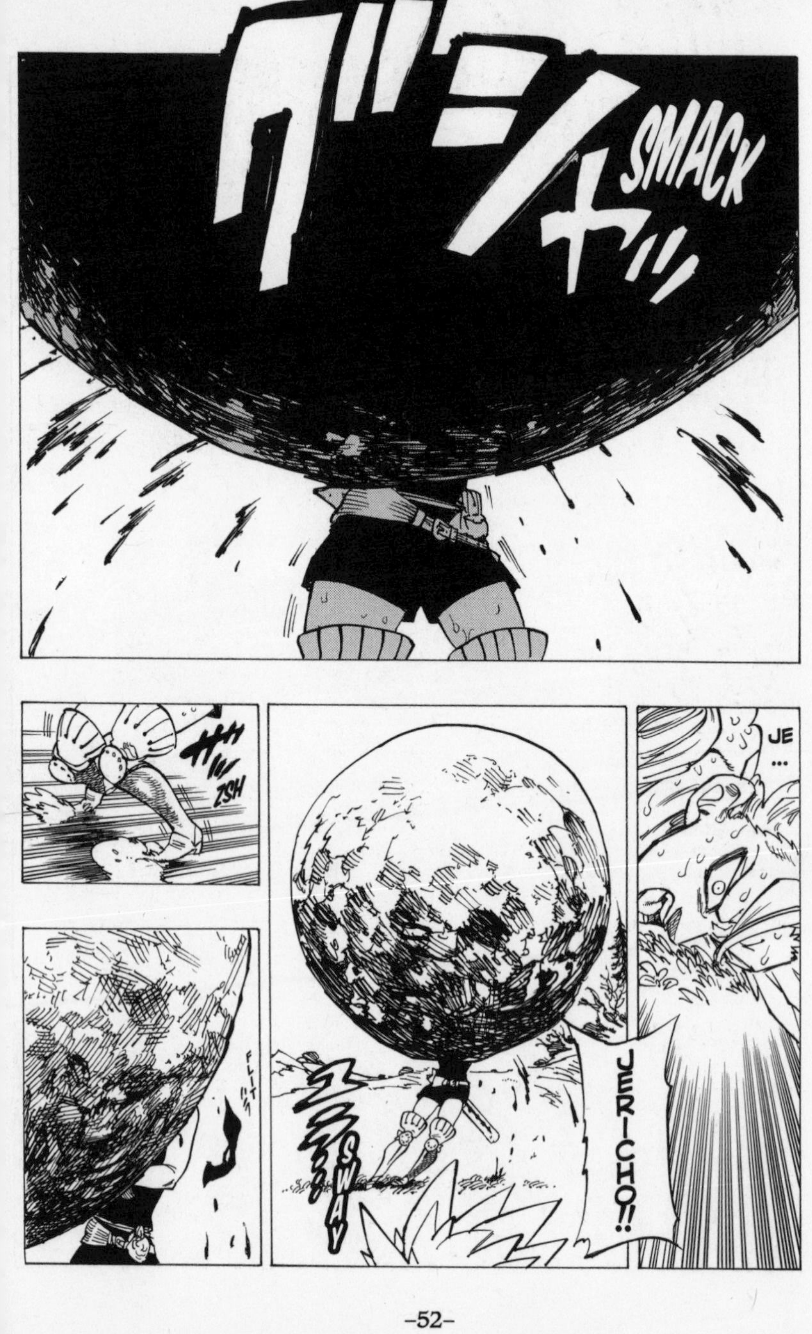
SMACK
JE
...
JERICHO!!
SWAY
ZSH
FLIT

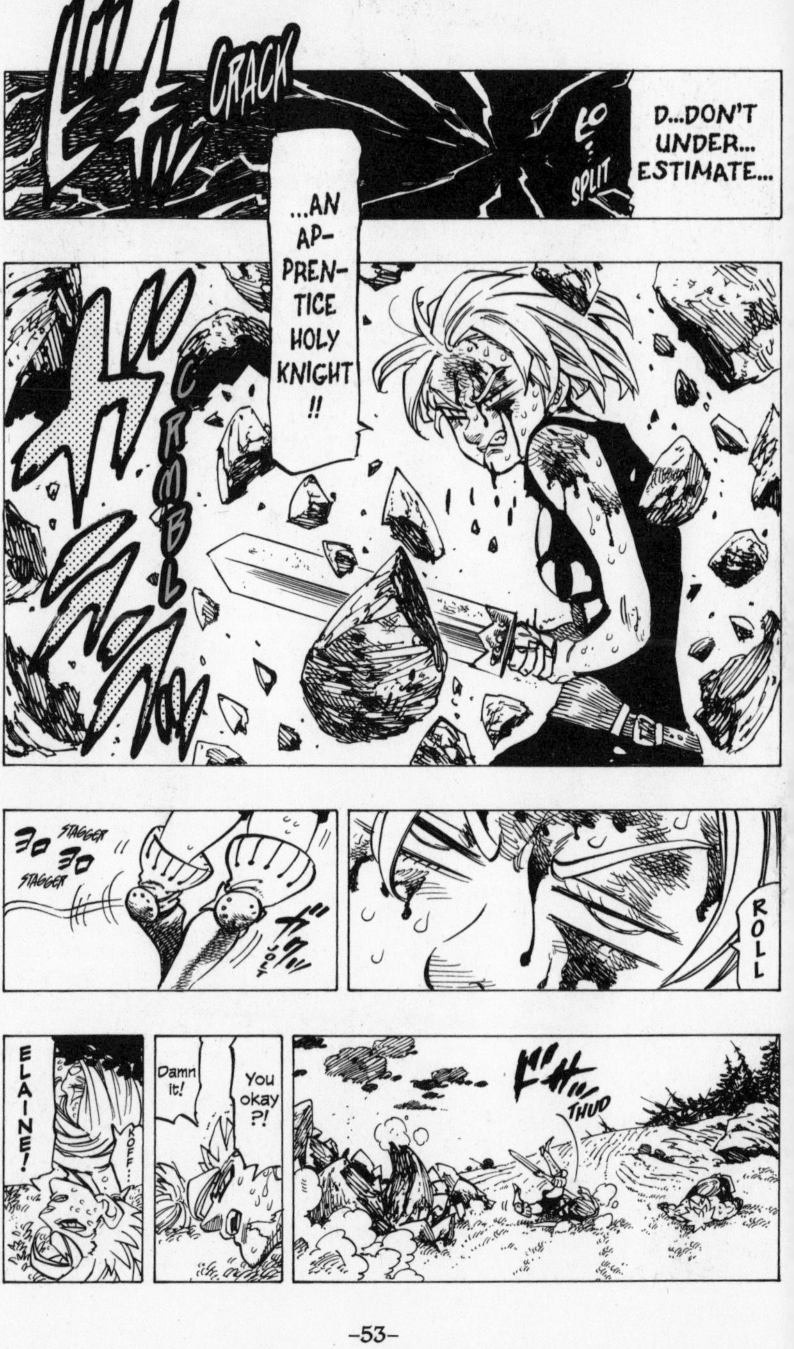
D...DON'T UNDER... ESTIMATE...
SPLIT
CRACK
...AN AP-PREN-TICE HOLY KNIGHT !!
CRMBL
ROLL
STAGGER
STAGGER
JOLT
THUD
You okay ?!
Damn it!
KOFF...
ELAINE!

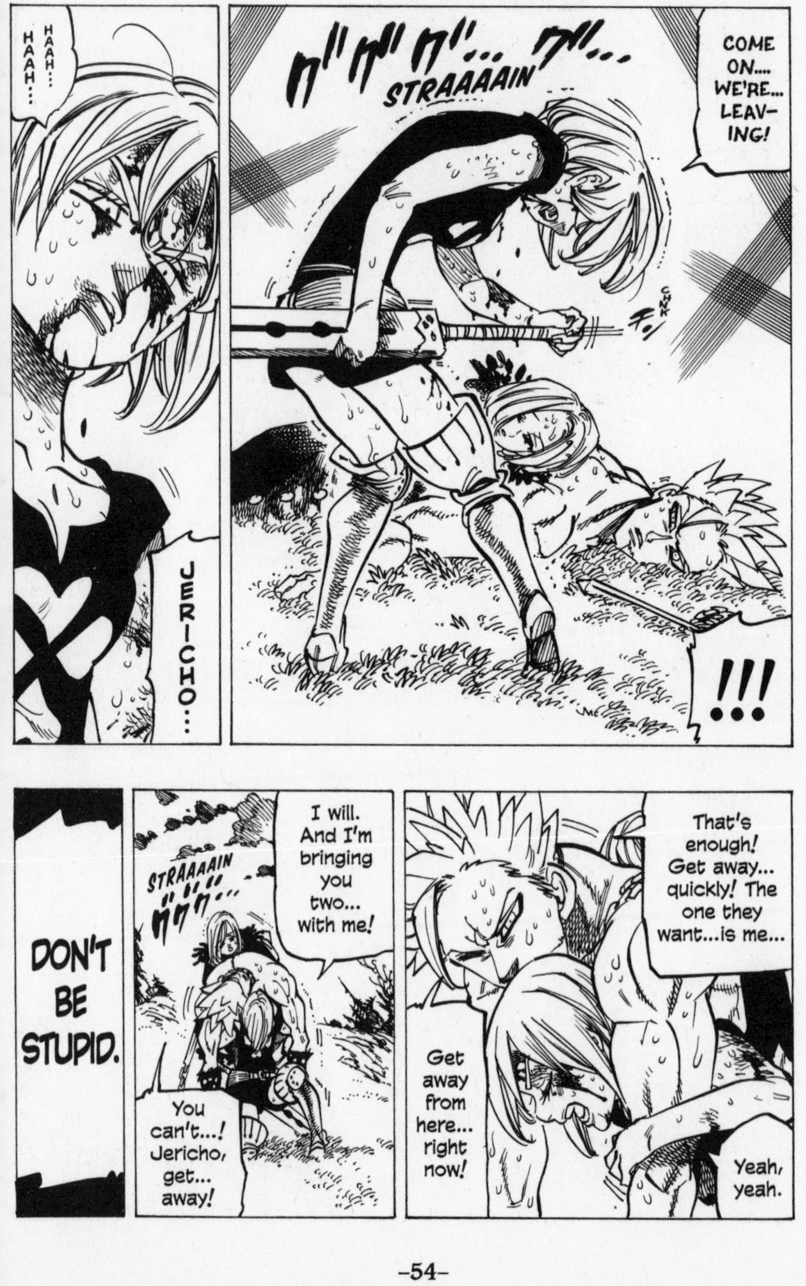
COME ON.... WE'RE... LEAV-ING!
STRAAAAIN
CHNK
!!!
HAAH... HAAH...
JERICHO...
That's enough! Get away... quickly! The one they want...is me...
Get away from here... right now!
Yeah, yeah.
I will. And I'm bringing you two... with me!
STRAAAAIN
You can't...! Jericho, get... away!
DON'T BE STUPID.

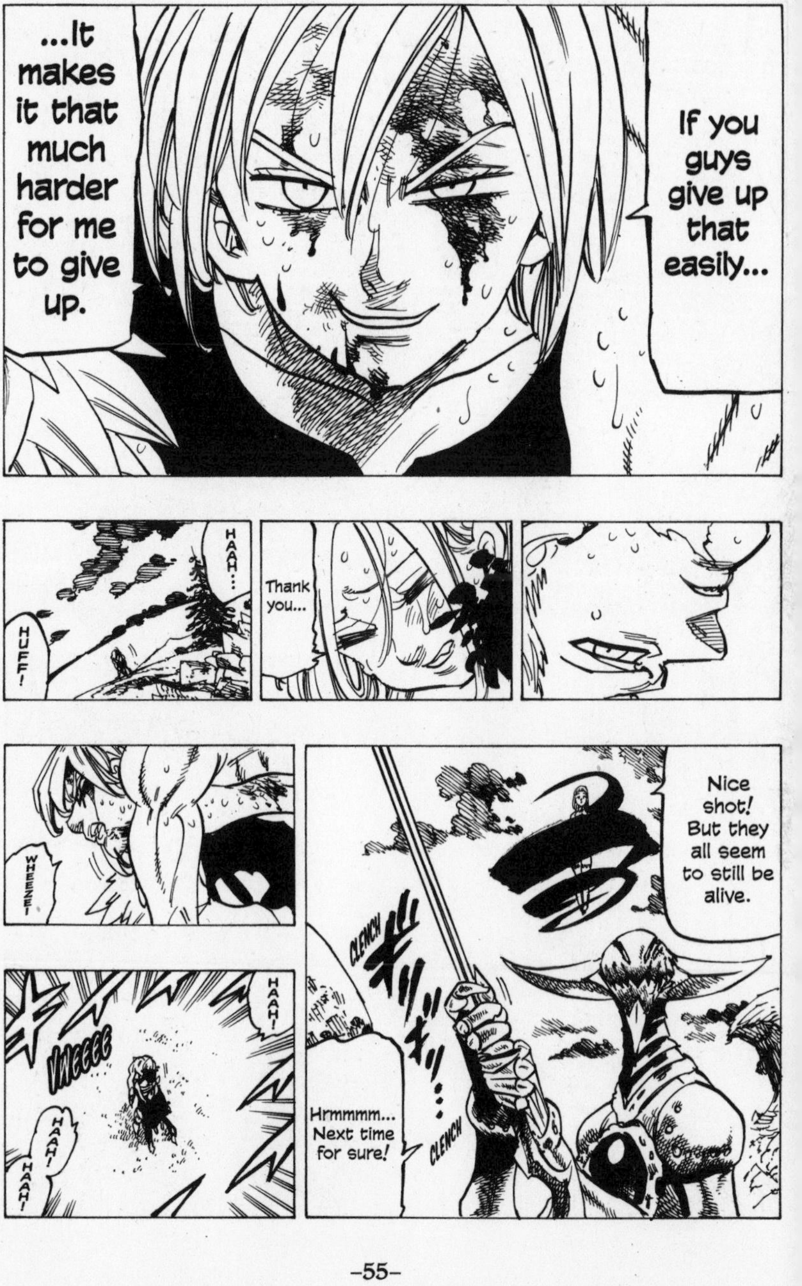
If you guys give up that easily...
...It makes it that much harder for me to give up.
Thank you...
HAAH...
HUFF!
Nice shot! But they all seem to still be alive.
CLENCH
Hrmmmm... Next time for sure!
CLENCH
WHEEZE!
HAAH!
VHEEEE
HAAH!
HAAH!

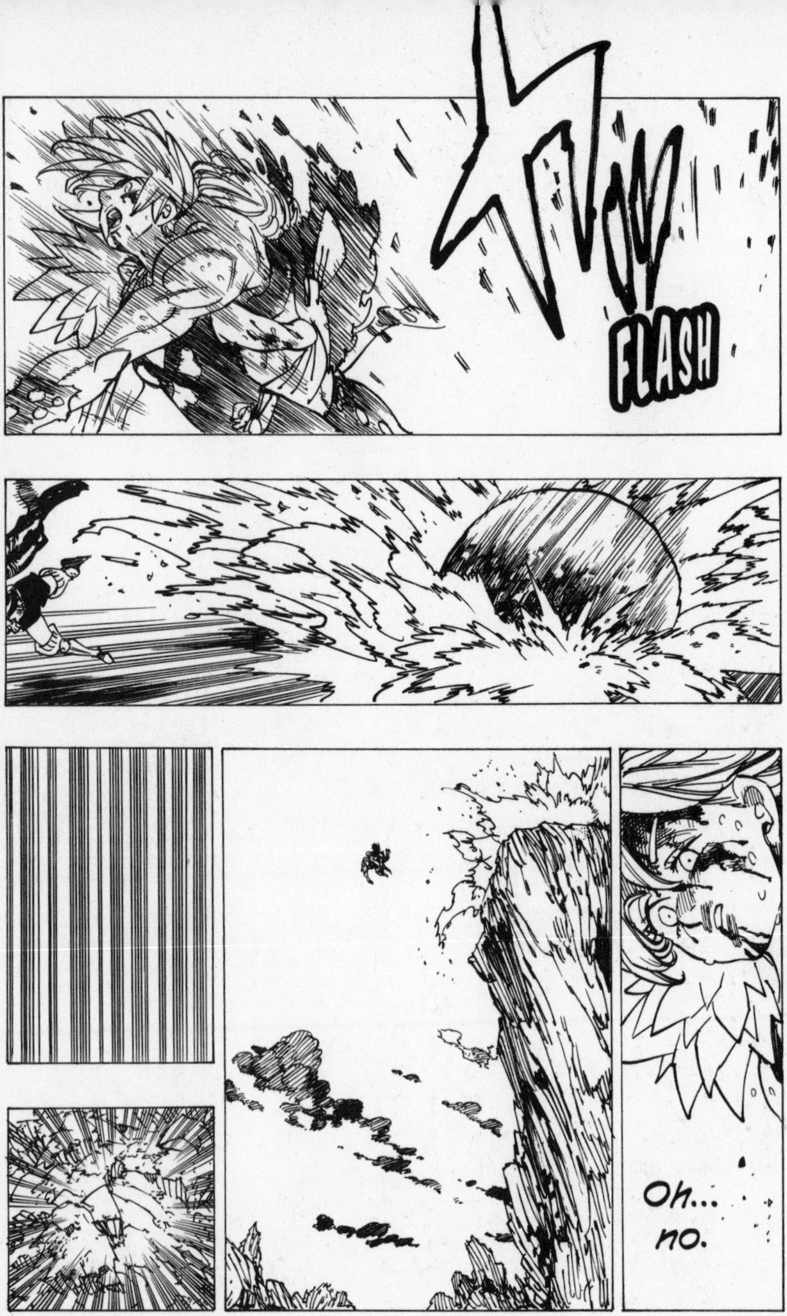
FLASH
Oh... no.

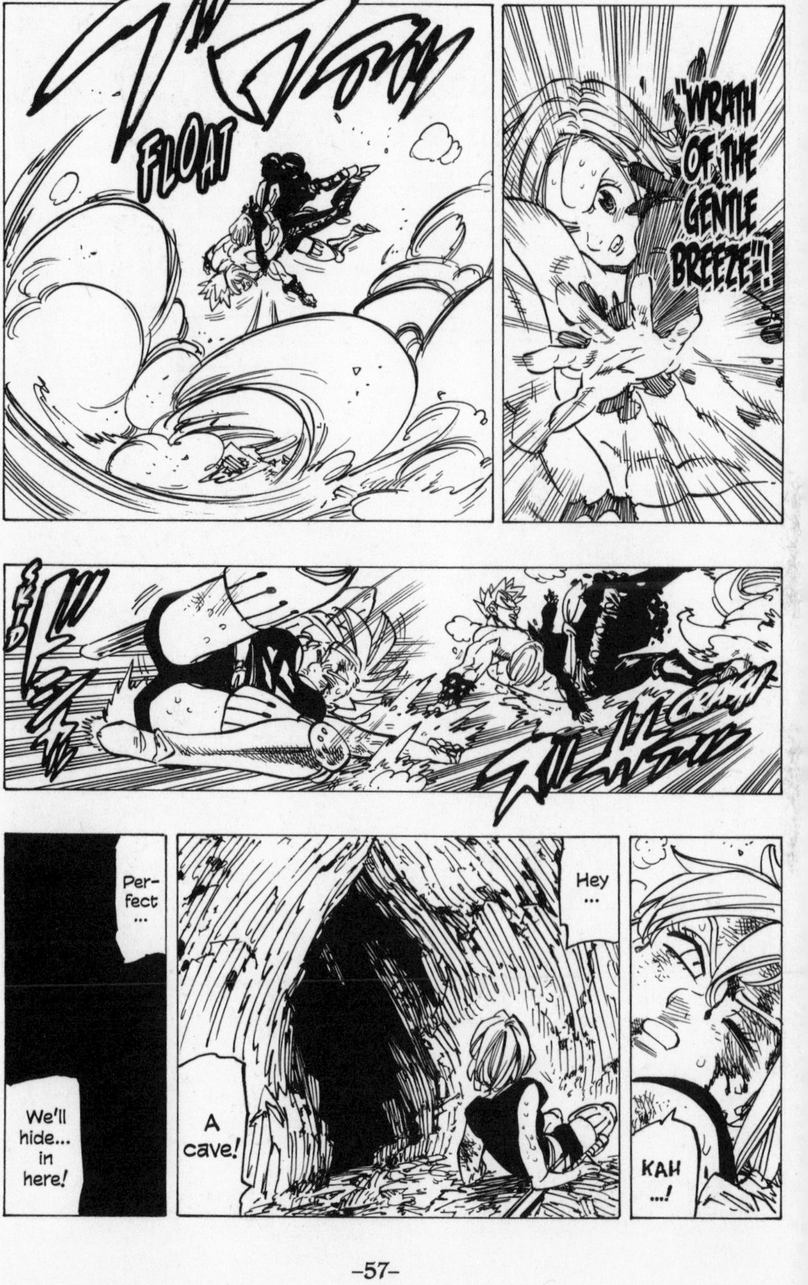
"WRATH OF THE GENTLE BREEZE"!
FLOAT
CRASH
SKID
KAH ...!
Hey ...
A cave!
Per-fect ...
We'll hide... in here!

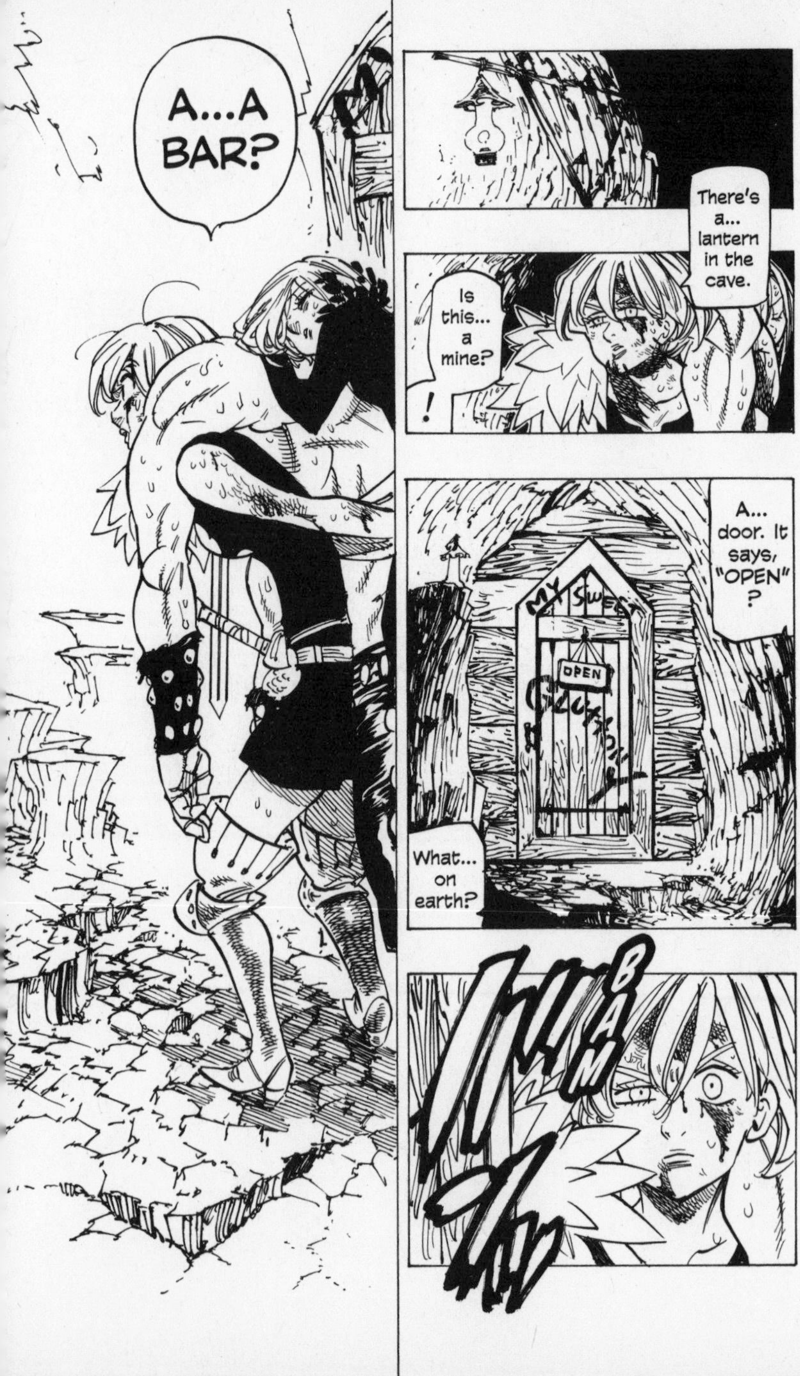
There's a... lantern in the cave.
Is this... a mine?
!
A... door. It says, "OPEN"?
MY SWEET
OPEN
What... on earth?
BAM
A...A BAR?

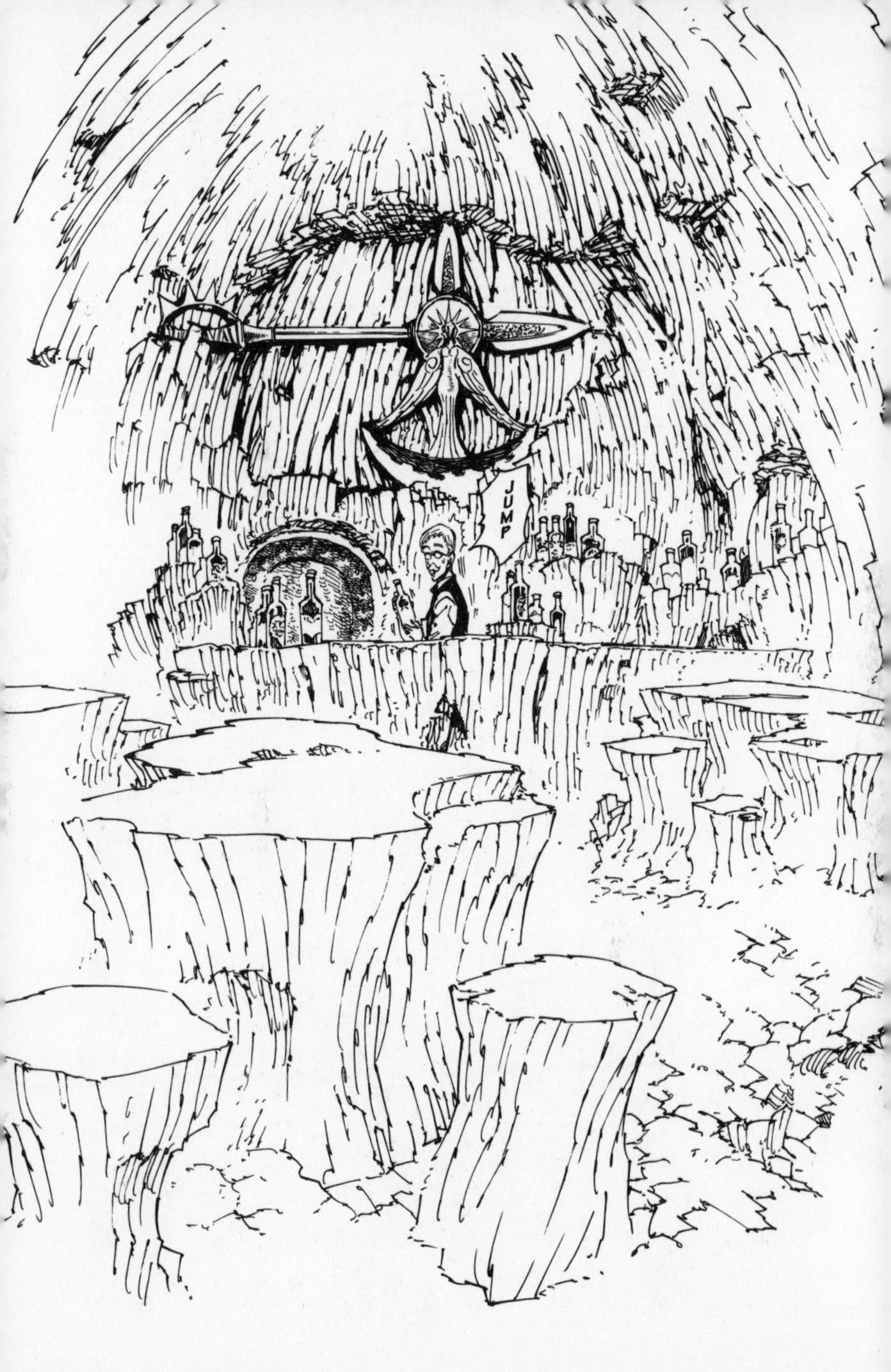
JUMP

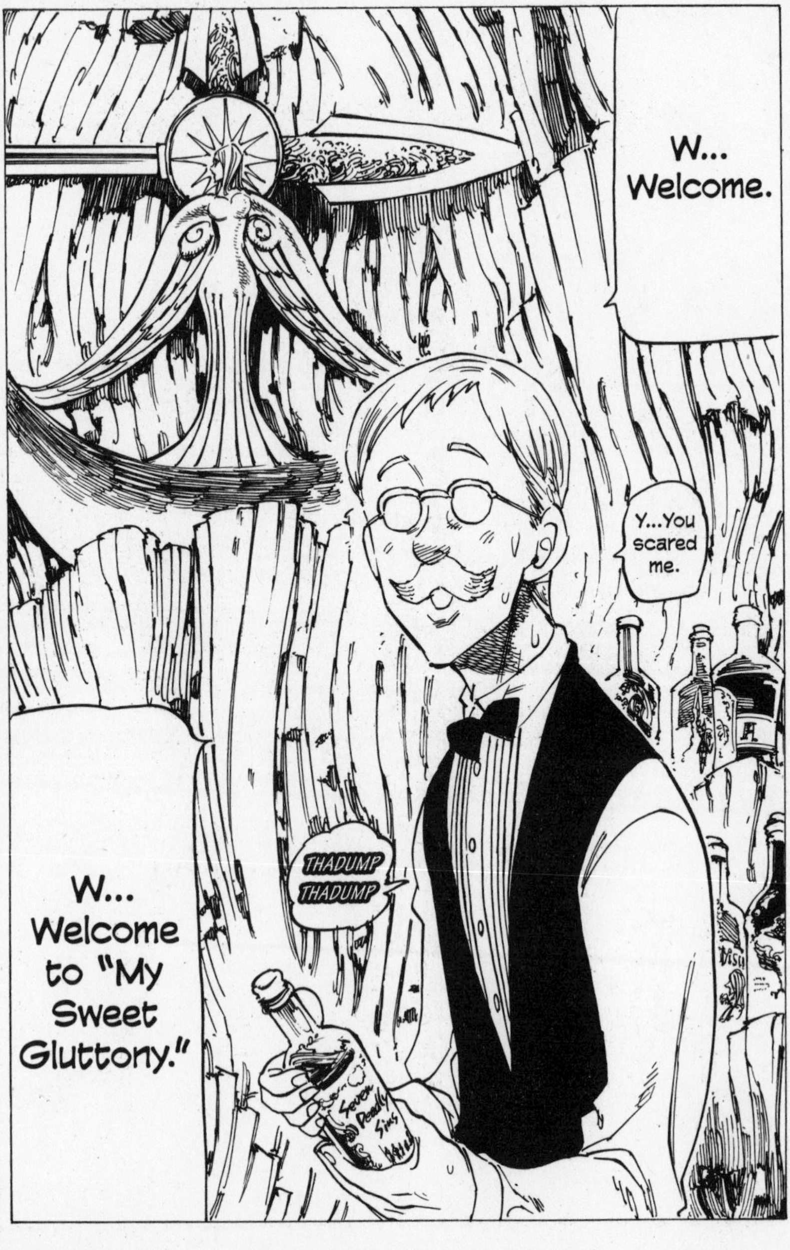
W... Welcome.
Y...You scared me.
THADUMP THADUMP
Seven Deadly Sins
W... Welcome to "My Sweet Gluttony."

Chapter 148 - Galland's Game

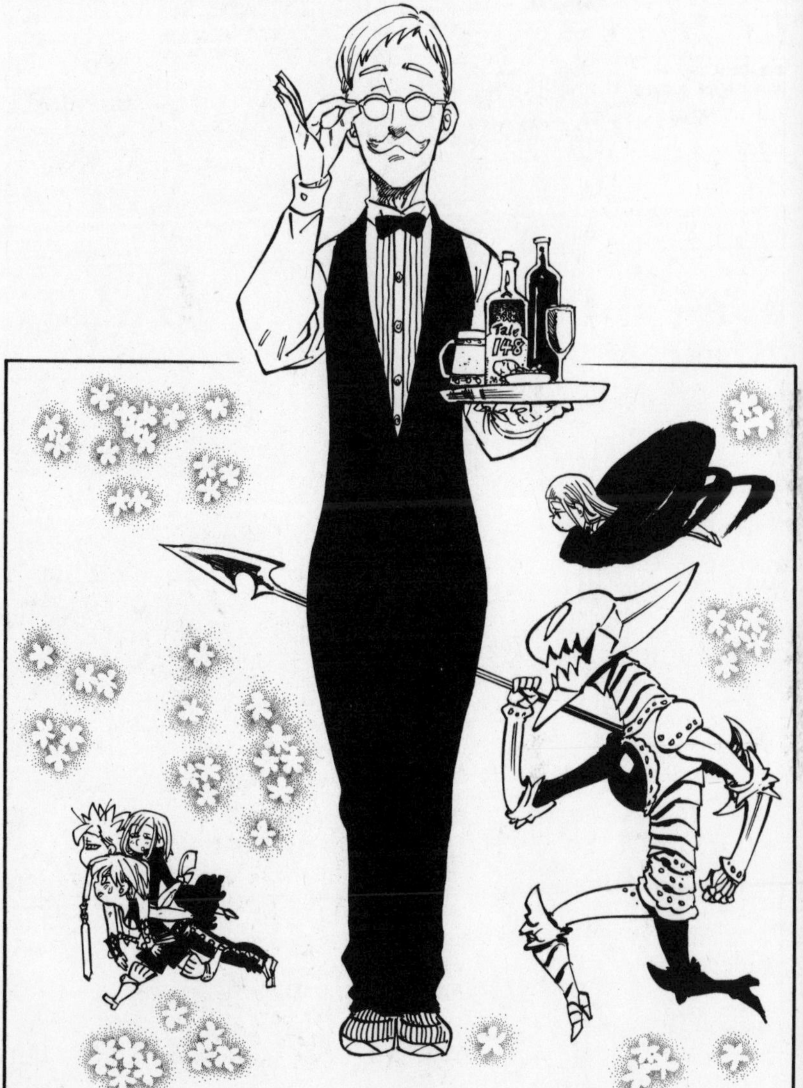
Tale 148

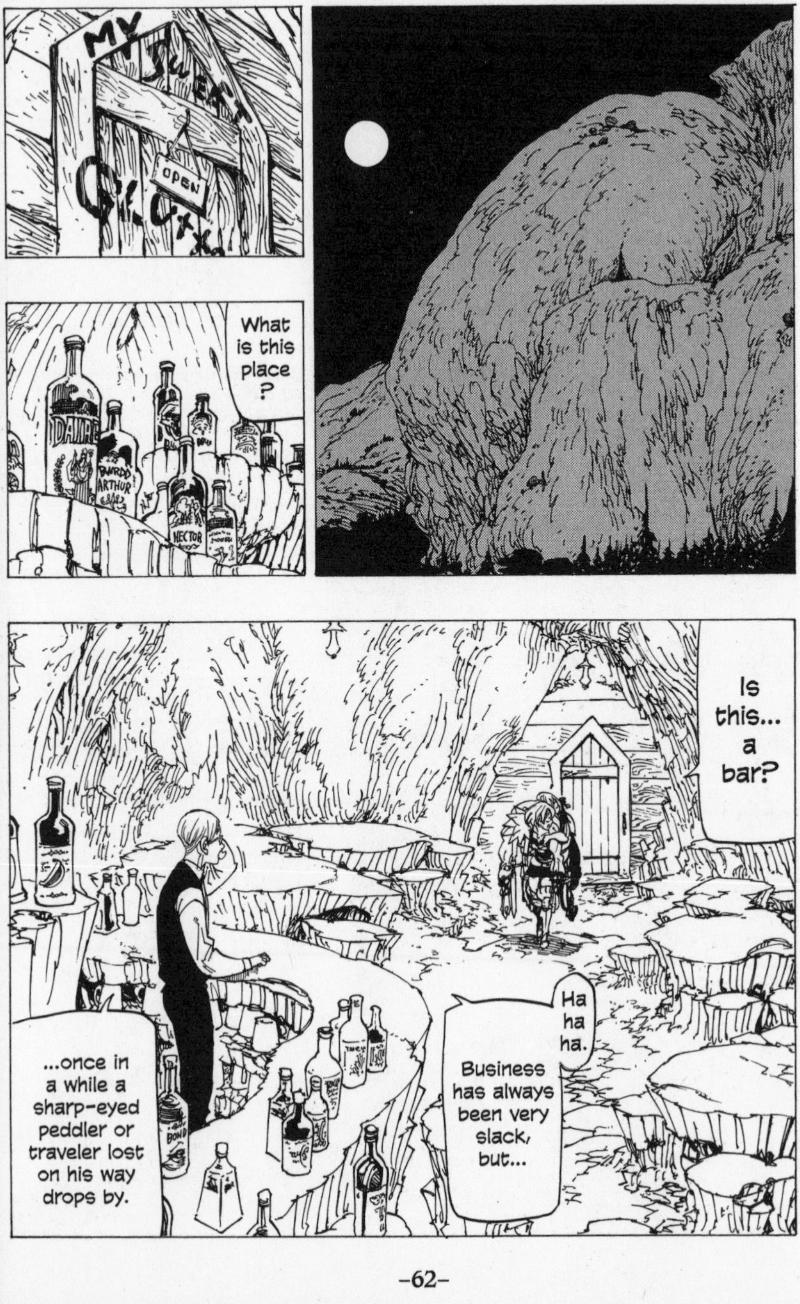
OPEN
What is this place?
Is this... a bar?
Ha ha ha.
Business has always been very slack, but...
...once in a while a sharp-eyed peddler or traveler lost on his way drops by.

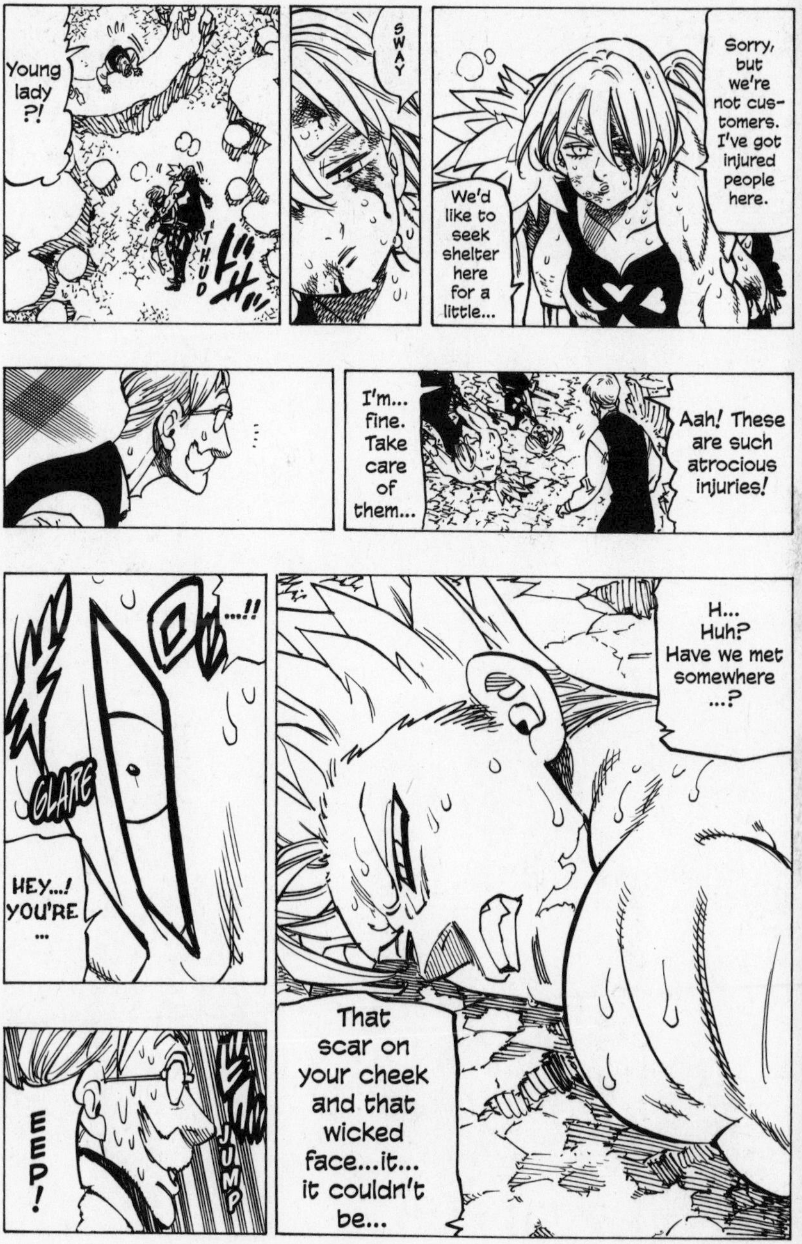
Sorry, but we're not customers. I've got injured people here.
We'd like to seek shelter here for a little...
SWAY
Young lady ?!
THUD
Aah! These are such atrocious injuries!
I'm... fine. Take care of them...
...
H... Huh? Have we met somewhere ...?
That scar on your cheek and that wicked face...it... it couldn't be...
...!!
GLARE
HEY...! YOU'RE ...
JUMP
EEP!

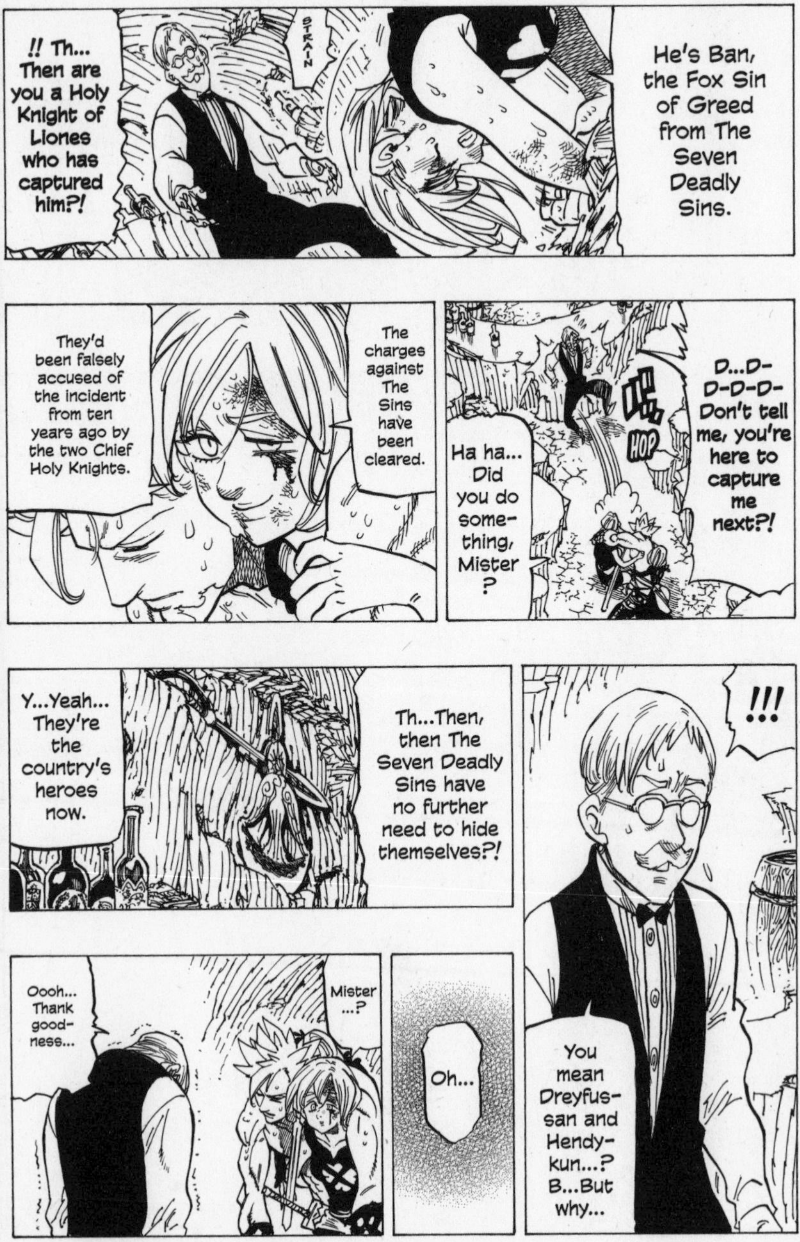
He's Ban, the Fox Sin of Greed from The Seven Deadly Sins.
STRAIN
!! Th... Then are you a Holy Knight of Liones who has captured him?!
D...D-D-D-D-Don't tell me, you're here to capture me next?!
HOP
Ha ha... Did you do something, Mister?
The charges against The Sins have been cleared.
They'd been falsely accused of the incident from ten years ago by the two Chief Holy Knights.
!!!
You mean Dreyfus-san and Hendy-kun...? B...But why...
Th...Then, then The Seven Deadly Sins have no further need to hide themselves?!
Y...Yeah... They're the country's heroes now.
Oh...
Mister...?
Oooh... Thank goodness...

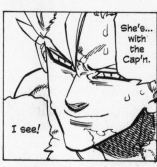

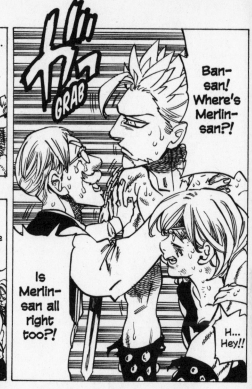

GRAB
Ban-san! Where's Merlin-san?!
Is Merlin-san all right too?!
H... Hey!!
She's... with the Cap'n.
I see!
You've gone and grown yourself a little mustache since I last saw you.♪
W...Well. I thought it might make me look...a little dignified!
TAH HA HA!
...Do you guys know each other?
More importantly, we're being chased right now!
Chased? By whom?
There's no time to explain! You gotta help us, Mister!
V... V-V-V-Very well.
Hide yourselves in this stock room behind the counter!
CREAK
CREAK
You have our thanks.
BOOM
CLUNK
WAH?!

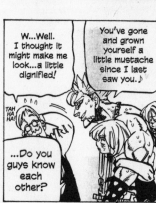

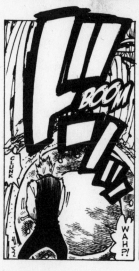

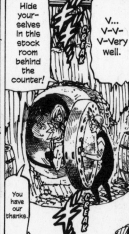

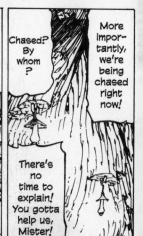

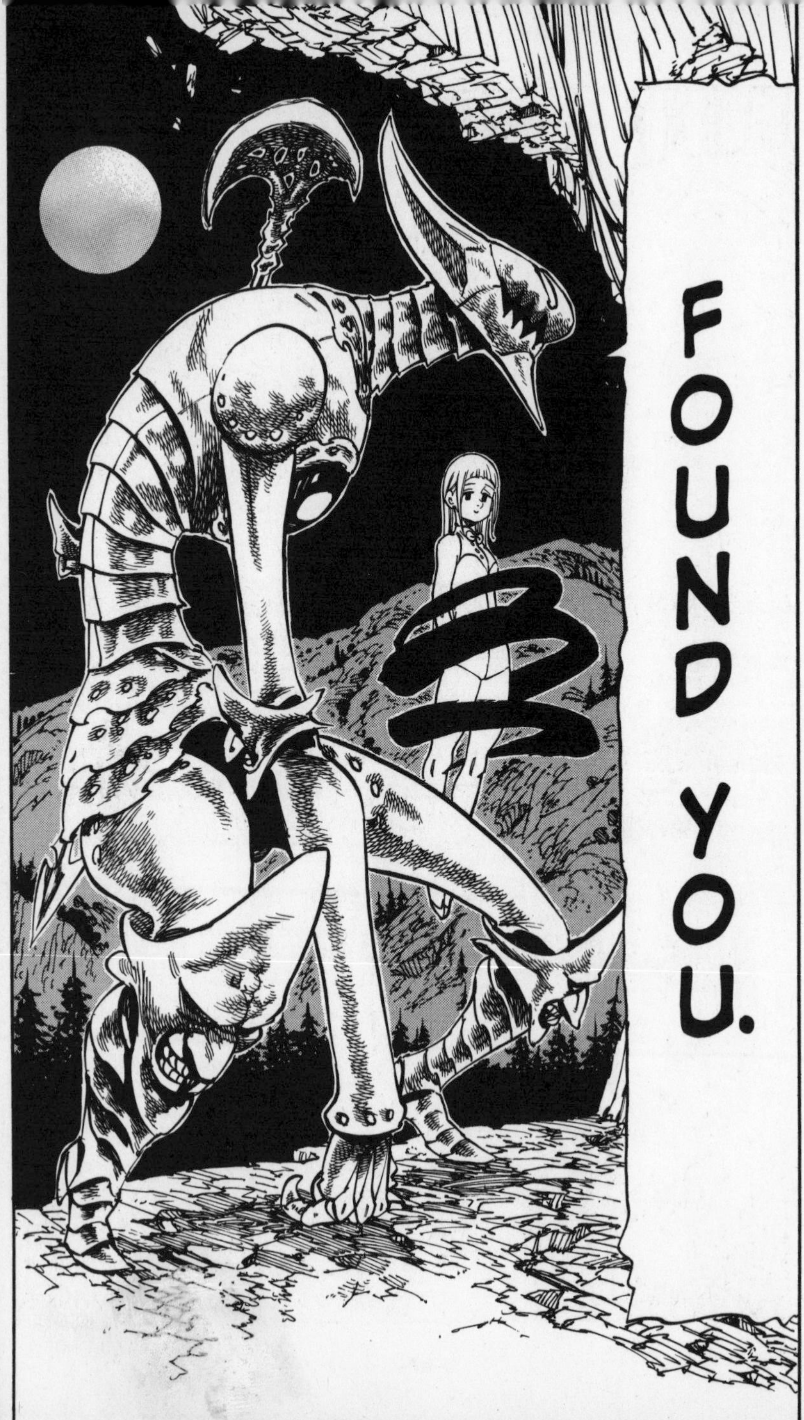
FOUND YOU.

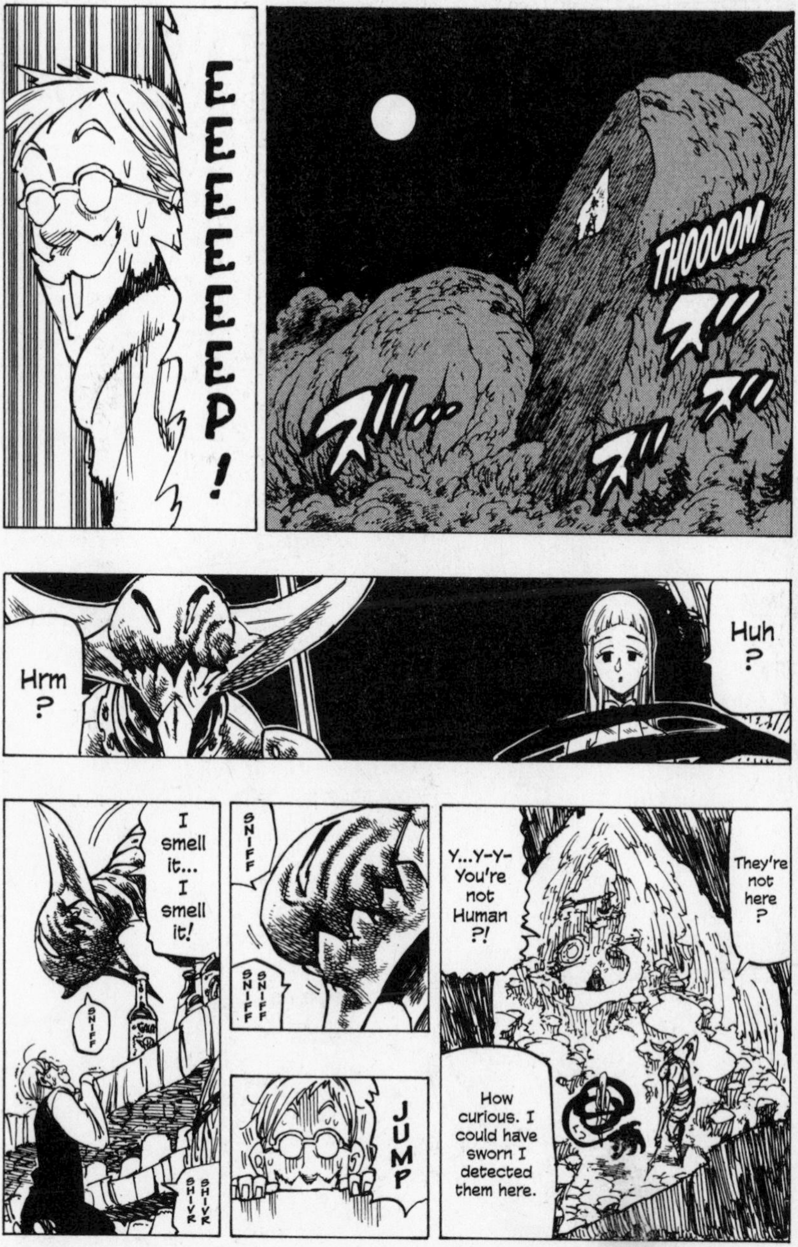
THOOOOM
EEEEEEP!
Huh?
Hrm?
They're not here?
Y...Y-Y- You're not Human?!
How curious. I could have sworn I detected them here.
SNIFF
SNIFF SNIFF
JUMP
I smell it... I smell it!
SNIFF
SHIVR SHIVR

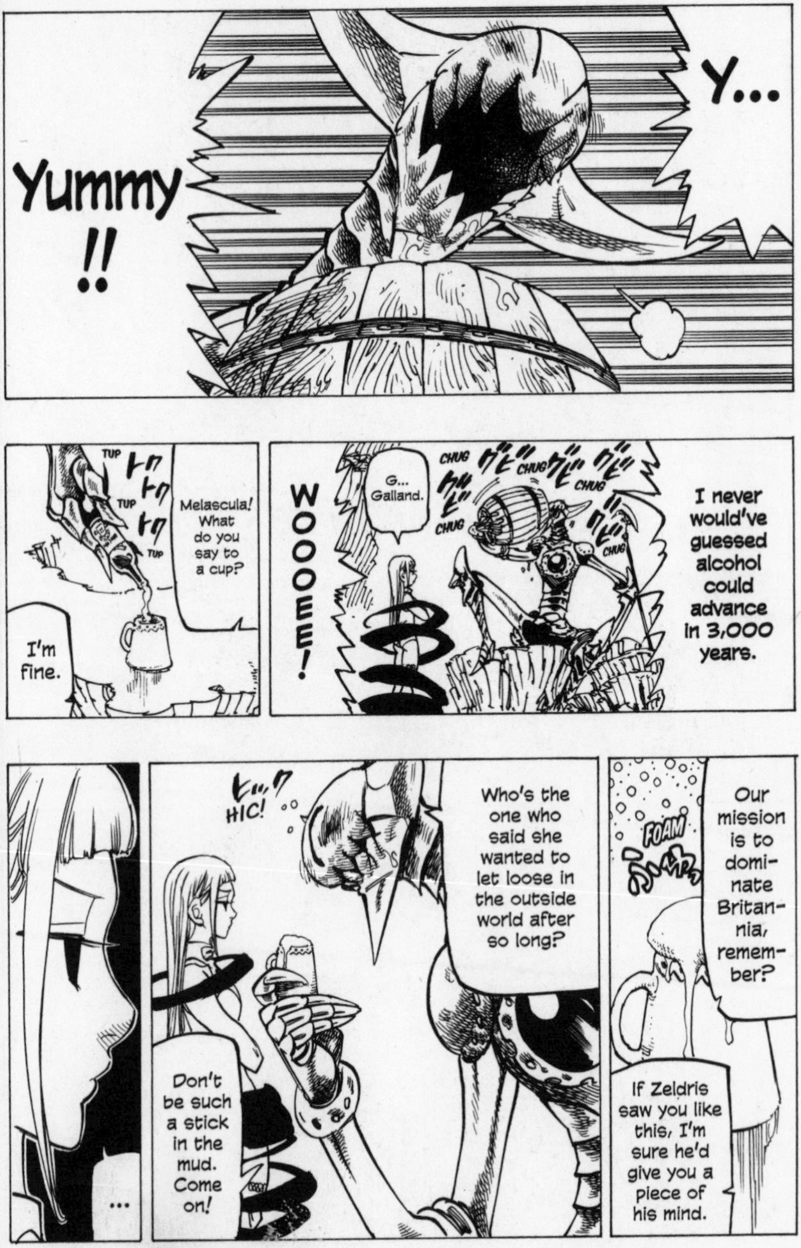
Y...
Yummy!!
I never would've guessed alcohol could advance in 3,000 years.
CHUG
CHUG
CHUG
CHUG
CHUG
G... Galland.
WOOOEE!
TUP
TUP
TUP
TUP
Melascula! What do you say to a cup?
I'm fine.
Our mission is to dominate Britannia, remember?
FOAM
If Zeldris saw you like this, I'm sure he'd give you a piece of his mind.
Who's the one who said she wanted to let loose in the outside world after so long?
HIC!
Don't be such a stick in the mud. Come on!
...

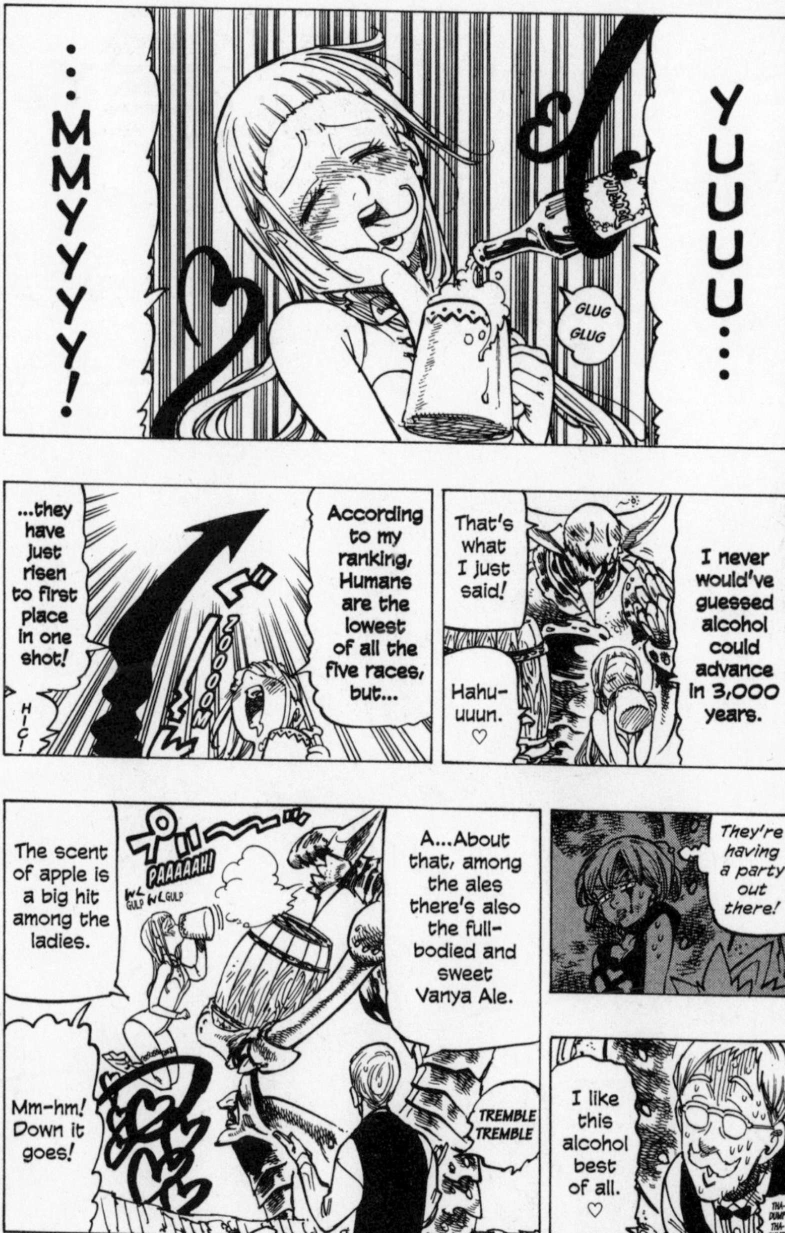
YUUUU...
GLUG GLUG
...MMYYYY!
I never would've guessed alcohol could advance in 3,000 years.
That's what I just said!
Hahu-uuun. ♡
According to my ranking, Humans are the lowest of all the five races, but...
ZOOOOOM
...they have just risen to first place in one shot!
HIC!
They're having a party out there!
I like this alcohol best of all. ♡
THA-DUMP THA-DUMP
A...About that, among the ales there's also the full-bodied and sweet Vanya Ale.
PAAAAAH!
GULP GULP
The scent of apple is a big hit among the ladies.
TREMBLE TREMBLE
Mm-hm! Down it goes!

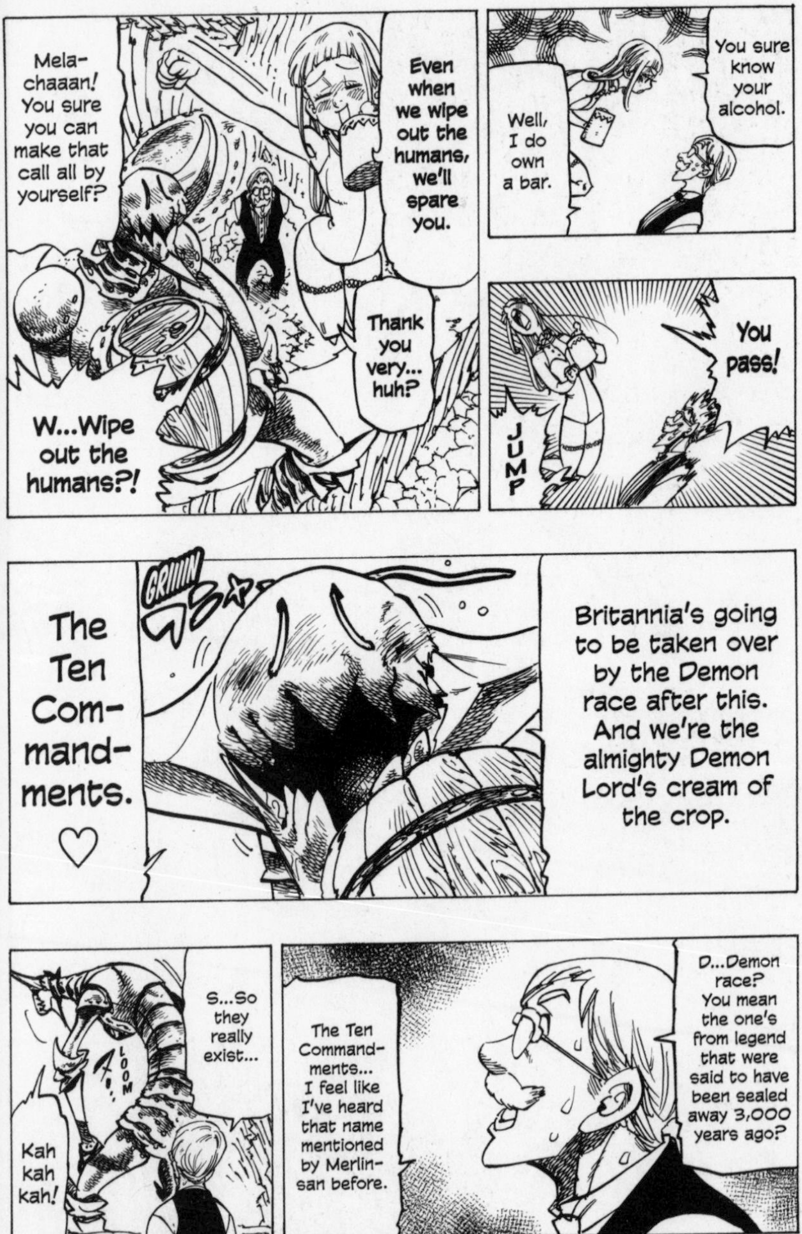

You sure know your alcohol.
Well, I do own a bar.
You pass!
JUMP
Even when we wipe out the humans, we'll spare you.
Mela-chaaan! You sure you can make that call all by yourself?
Thank you very... huh?
W...Wipe out the humans?!
Britannia's going to be taken over by the Demon race after this. And we're the almighty Demon Lord's cream of the crop.
GRIIIIN
The Ten Commandments. ♡
D...Demon race? You mean the one's from legend that were said to have been sealed away 3,000 years ago?
The Ten Commandments... I feel like I've heard that name mentioned by Merlin-san before.
S...So they really exist...
LOOM
Kah kah kah!

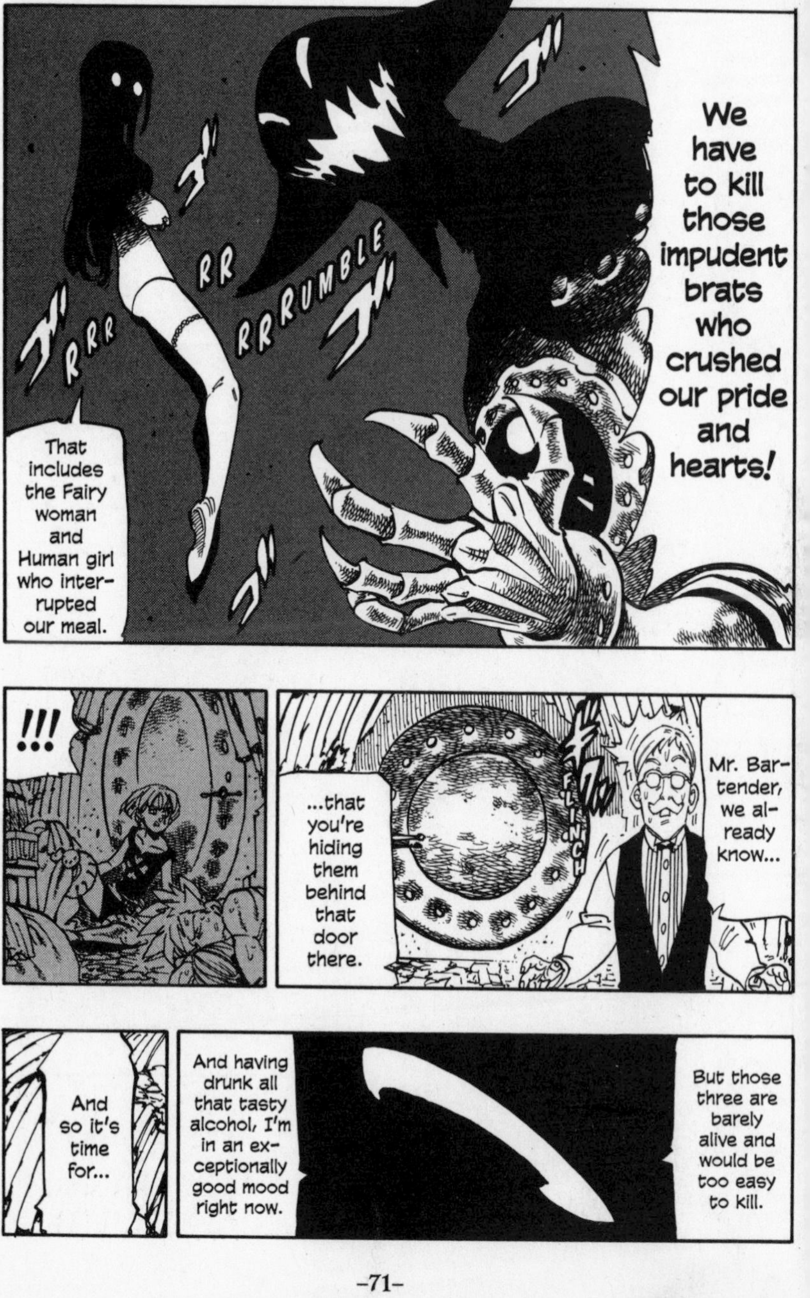
We have to kill those impudent brats who crushed our pride and hearts!
RR
RRRUMBLE
RRR
That includes the Fairy woman and Human girl who interrupted our meal.
Mr. Bartender, we already know...
FLINCH
...that you're hiding them behind that door there.
!!!
But those three are barely alive and would be too easy to kill.
And having drunk all that tasty alcohol, I'm in an exceptionally good mood right now.
And so it's time for...

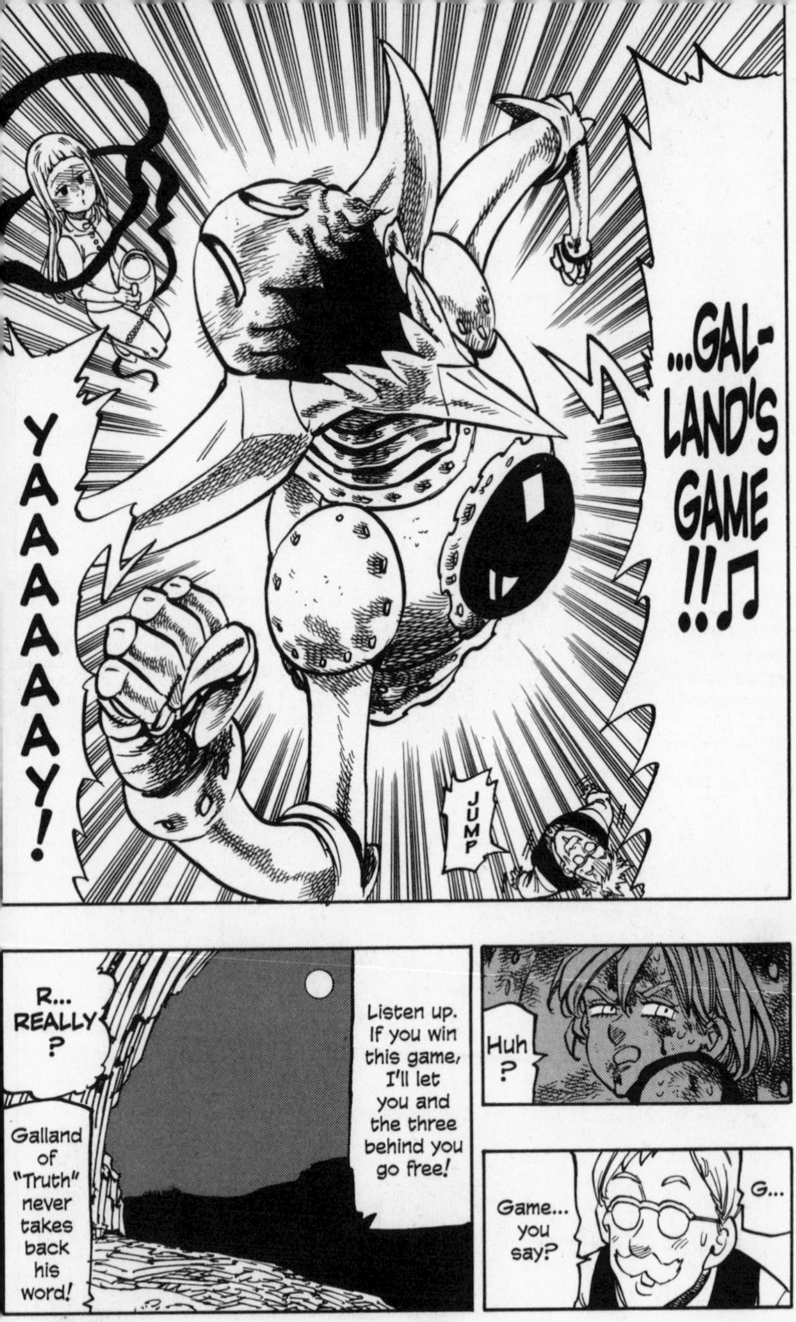
...GAL-LAND'S GAME!!♫
JUMP
YAAAAAAAY!
Huh?
G...
Game... you say?
Listen up. If you win this game, I'll let you and the three behind you go free!
R... REALLY?
Galland of "Truth" never takes back his word!

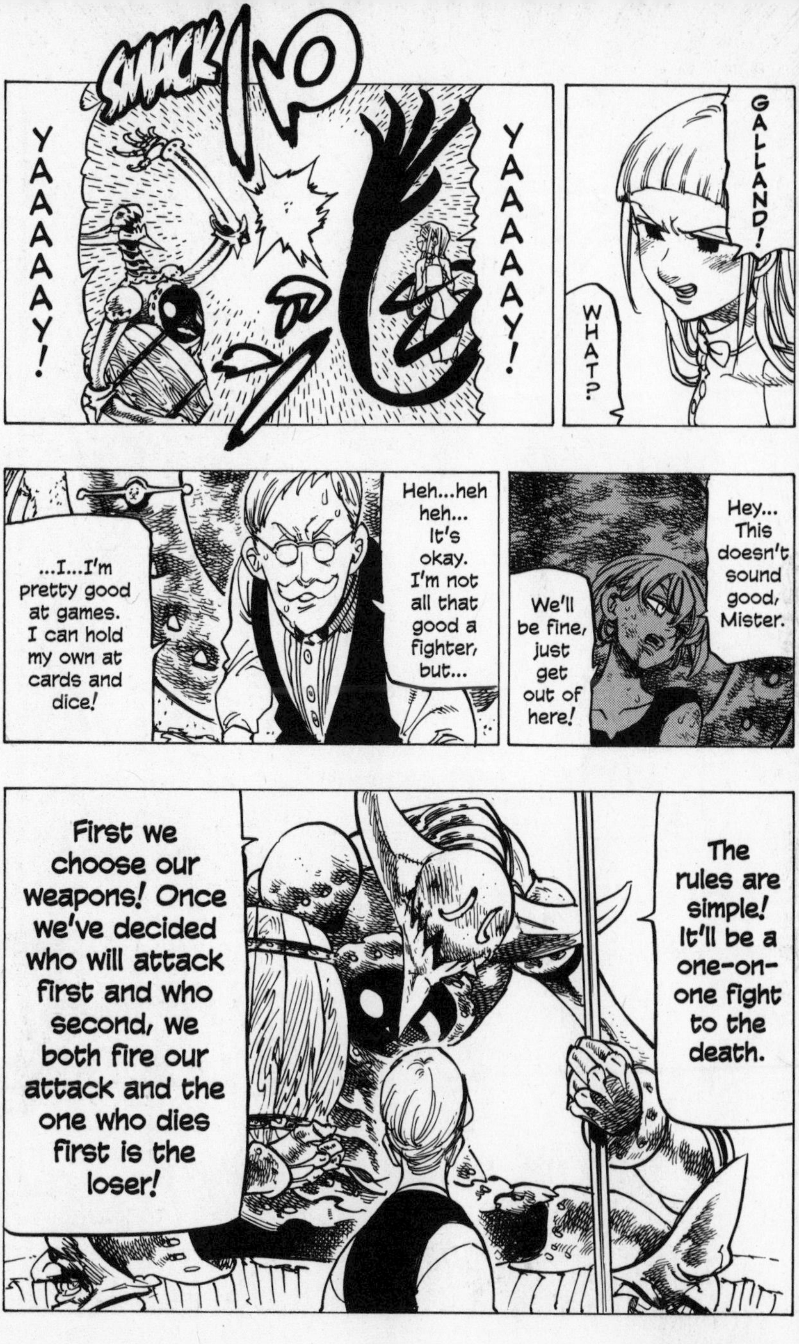
GALLAND!
WHAT?
SMACK
YAAAAAAY!
YAAAAAAY!
Hey... This doesn't sound good, Mister.
We'll be fine, just get out of here!
Heh...heh heh... It's okay. I'm not all that good a fighter, but...
...I...I'm pretty good at games. I can hold my own at cards and dice!
The rules are simple! It'll be a one-on-one fight to the death.
First we choose our weapons! Once we've decided who will attack first and who second, we both fire our attack and the one who dies first is the loser!

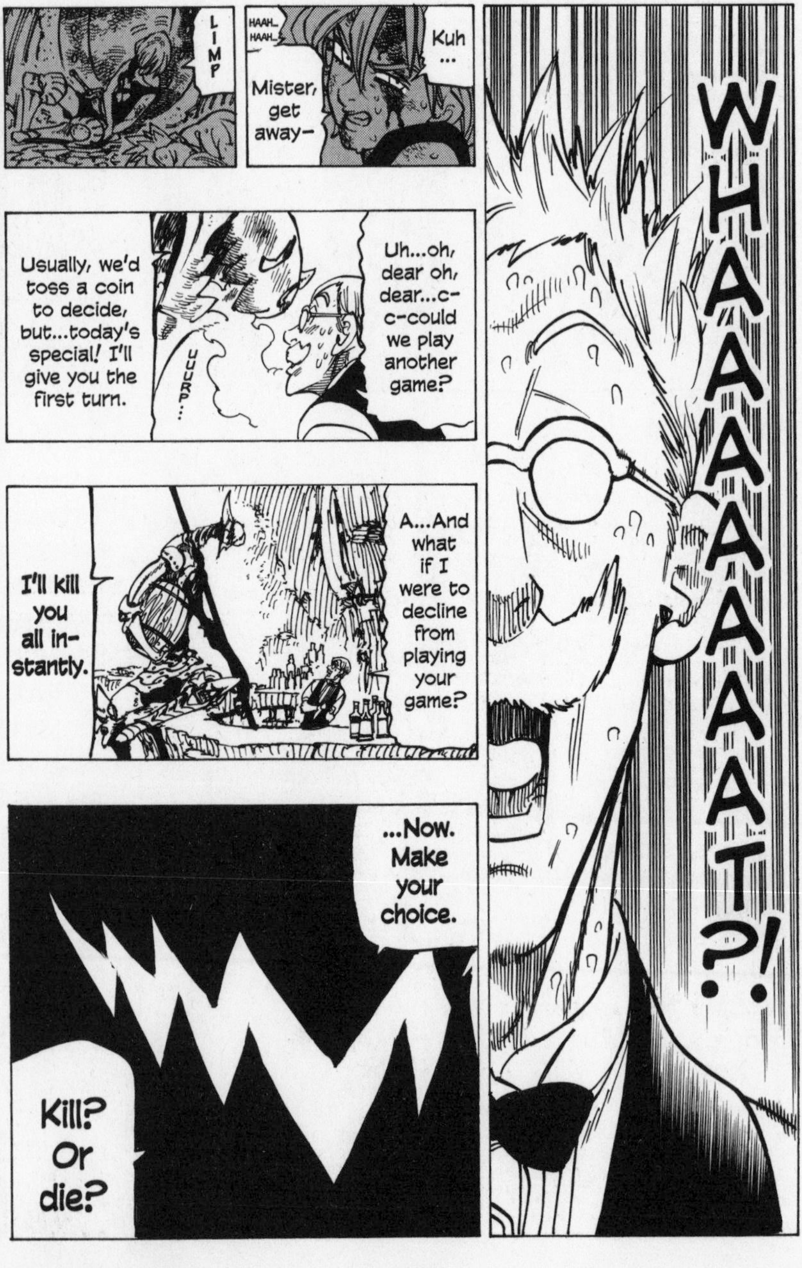
WHAAAAAT?!
HAAH... HAAH...
Kuh ...
Mister, get away-
LIMP
Uh...oh, dear oh, dear...c-c-could we play another game?
UUURP...
Usually, we'd toss a coin to decide, but...today's special! I'll give you the first turn.
A...And what if I were to decline from playing your game?
I'll kill you all in-stantly.
...Now. Make your choice.
Kill? Or die?

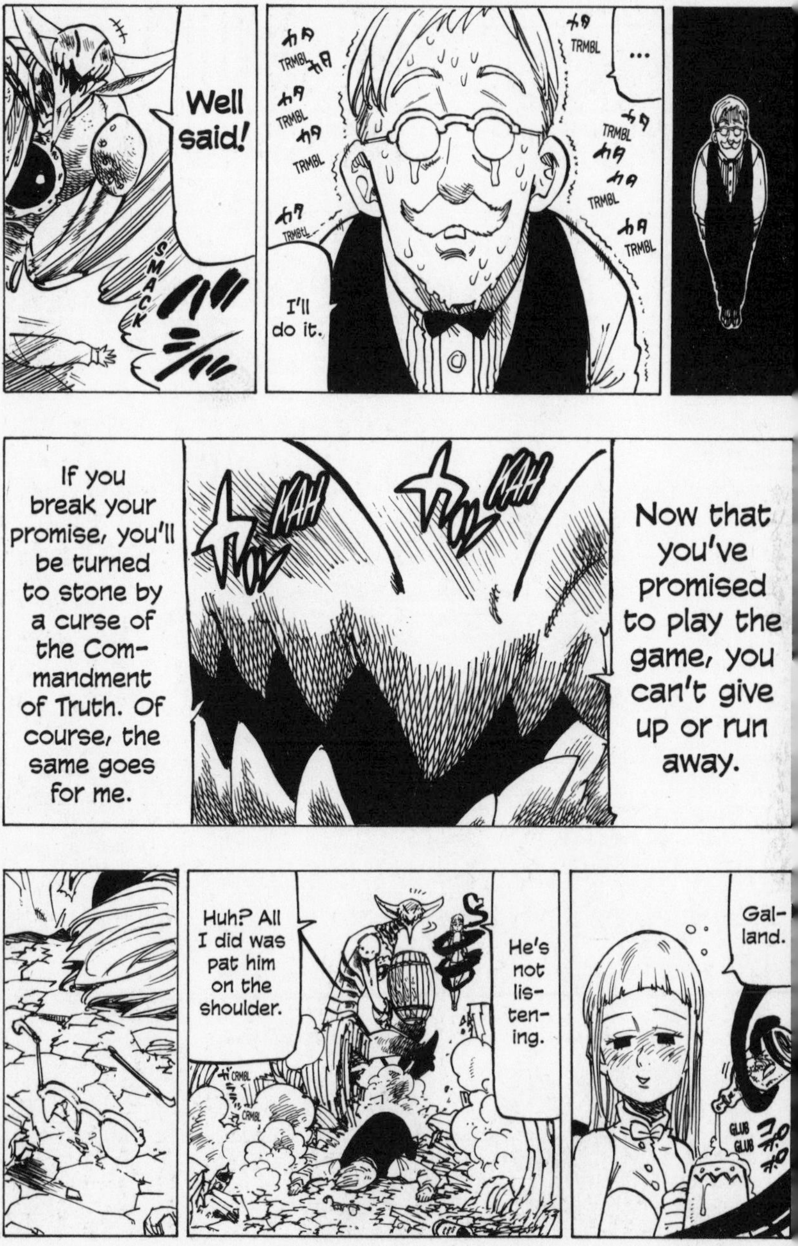
...
TRMBL
TRMBL
TRMBL
TRMBL
TRMBL
TRMBL
TRMBL
TRMBL
I'll do it.
Well said!
SMACK
Now that you've promised to play the game, you can't give up or run away.
KAH
KAH
If you break your promise, you'll be turned to stone by a curse of the Commandment of Truth. Of course, the same goes for me.
Galland.
GLUB GLUB
He's not listening.
Huh? All I did was pat him on the shoulder.
CRMBL
CRMBL

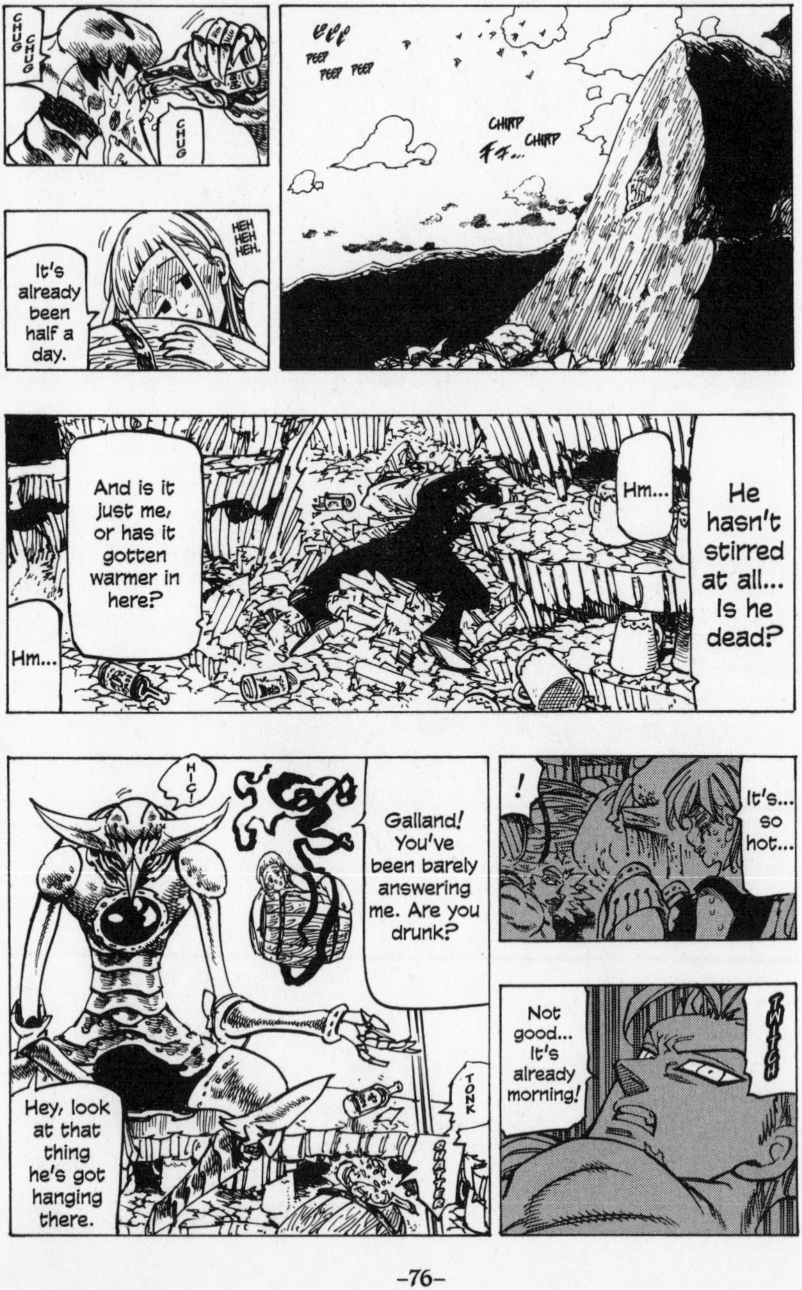

PEEP PEEP PEEP
CHIRP CHIRP
CHUG CHUG
CHUG
HEH HEH HEH.
It's already been half a day.
He hasn't stirred at all... Is he dead?
Hm...
And is it just me, or has it gotten warmer in here?
Hm...
!
It's... so hot...
TWITCH
Not good... It's already morning!
HIC!
Galland! You've been barely answering me. Are you drunk?
TONK
SHATTER
Hey, look at that thing he's got hanging there.

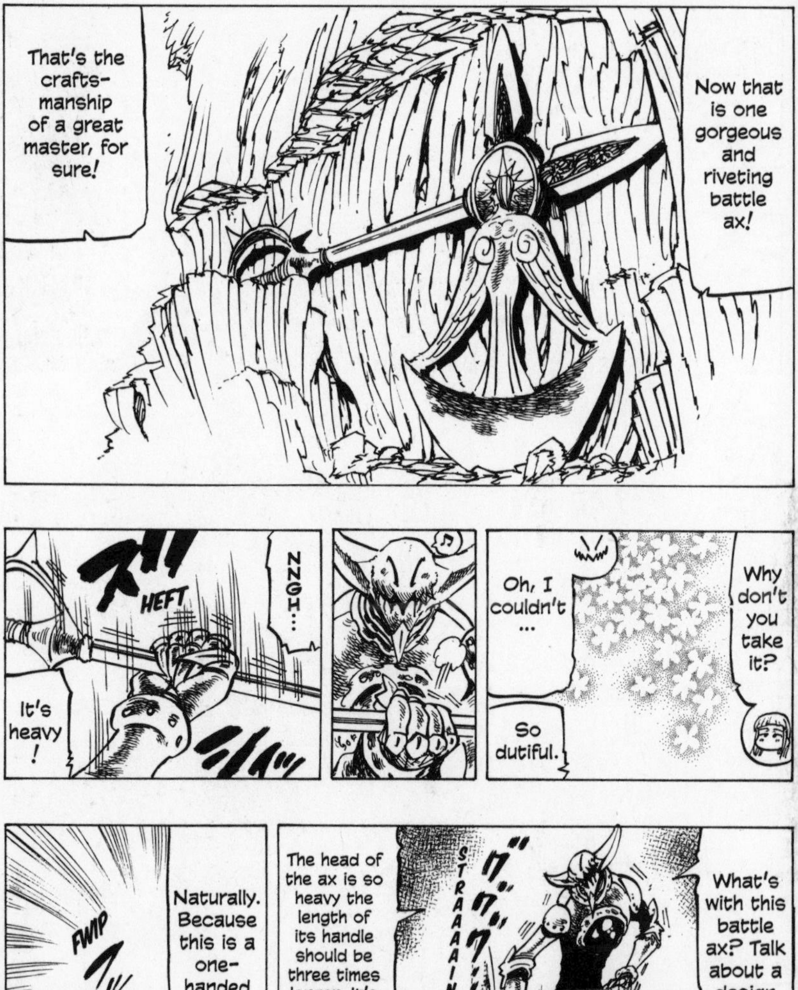
Now that is one gorgeous and riveting battle ax!
That's the crafts-manship of a great master, for sure!
Why don't you take it?
Oh, I couldn't ...
So dutiful.
NNGH...
HEFT
It's heavy!
What's with this battle ax? Talk about a design flaw.
The head of the ax is so heavy the length of its handle should be three times longer. It's too short as it is now to be held with two hands.
STRAAAAIN
THUNK
Naturally. Because this is a one-handed ax.
FWIP

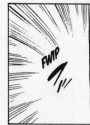

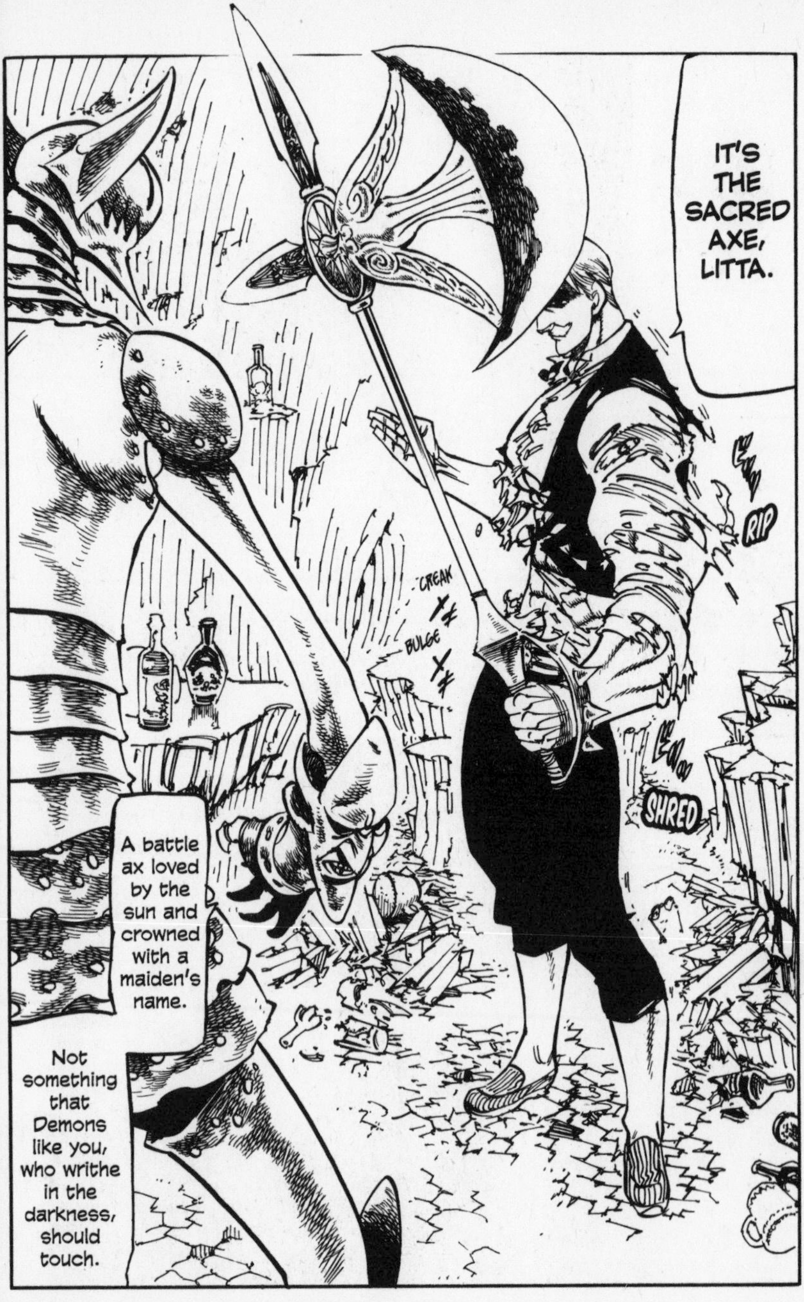
IT'S THE SACRED AXE, LITTA.
RIP
CREAK
BULGE
SHRED
A battle ax loved by the sun and crowned with a maiden's name.
Not something that Demons like you, who writhe in the darkness, should touch.

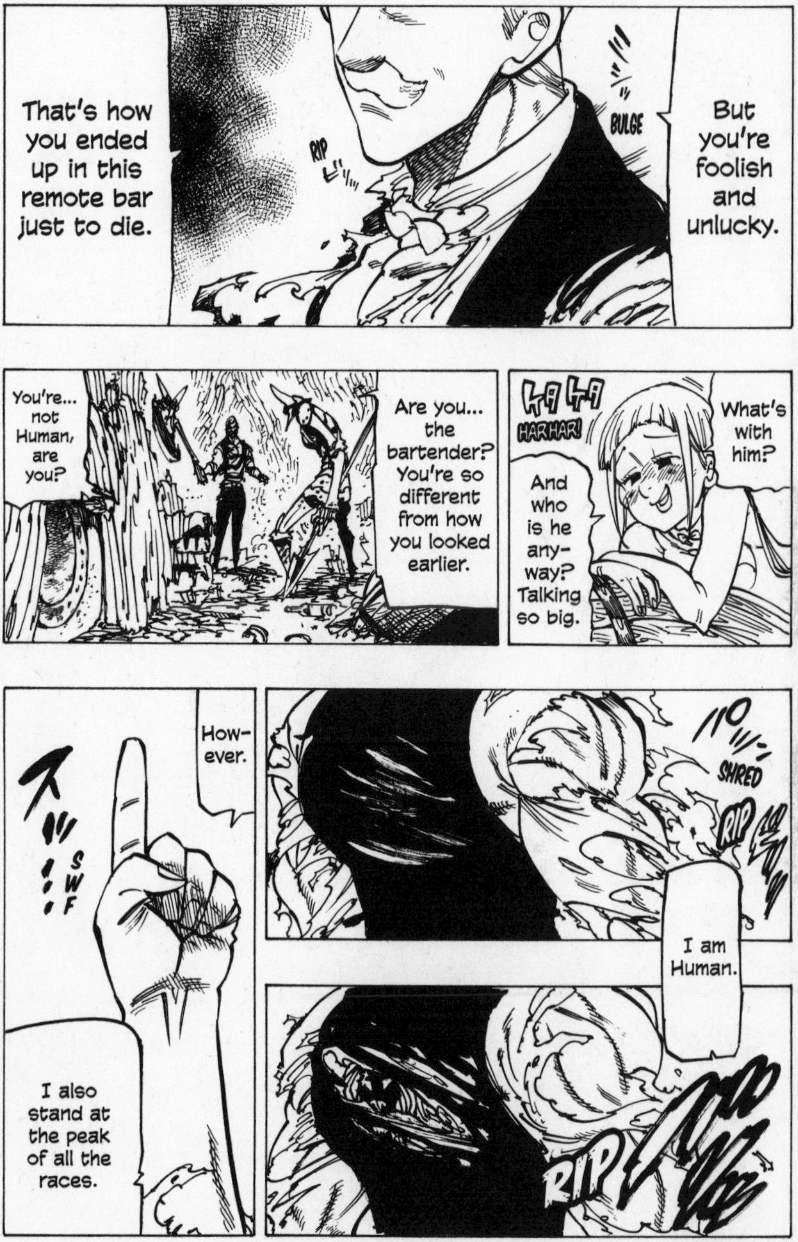
BULGE
But you're foolish and unlucky.
RIP
That's how you ended up in this remote bar just to die.
What's with him?
HAR HAR!
And who is he anyway? Talking so big.
Are you... the bartender? You're so different from how you looked earlier.
You're... not Human, are you?
SHRED
RIP
I am Human.
RIP
However.
SWF
I also stand at the peak of all the races.

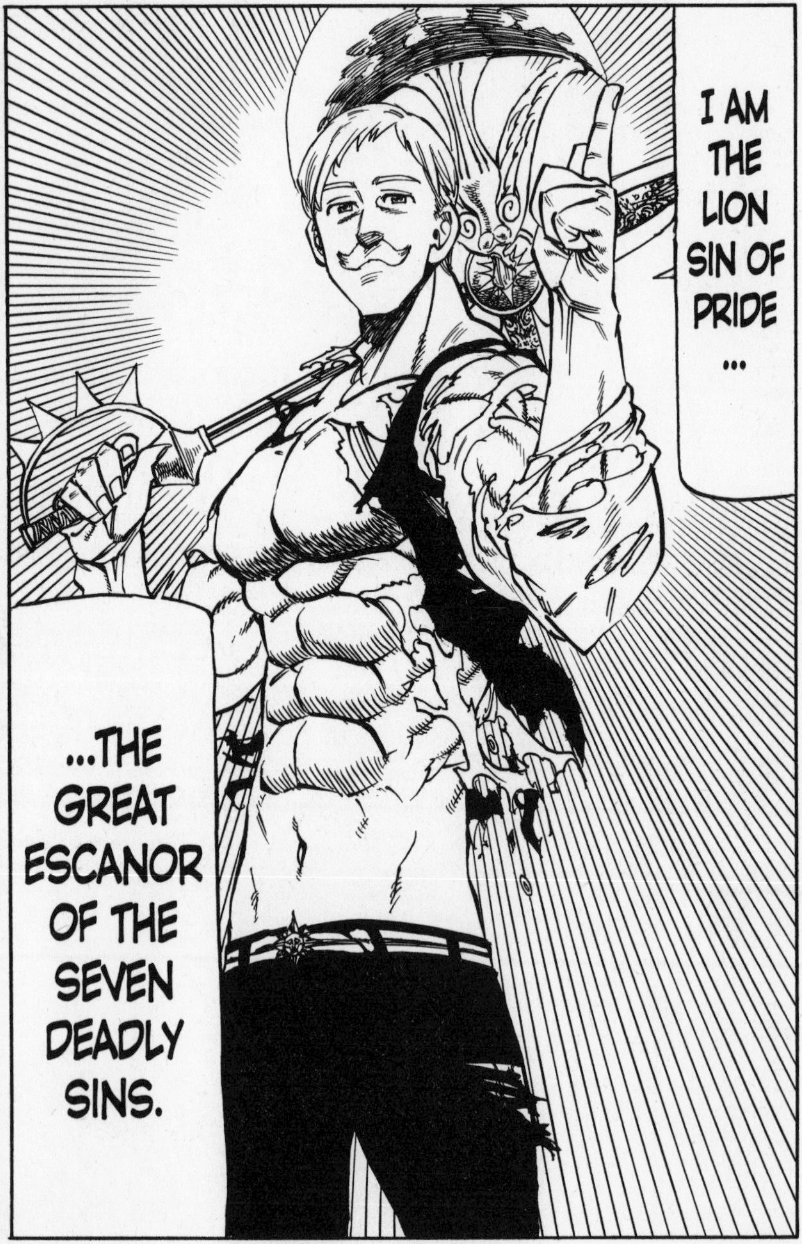
I AM THE LION SIN OF PRIDE ...
...THE GREAT ESCANOR OF THE SEVEN DEADLY SINS.

Chapter 149 - Galland's Magic

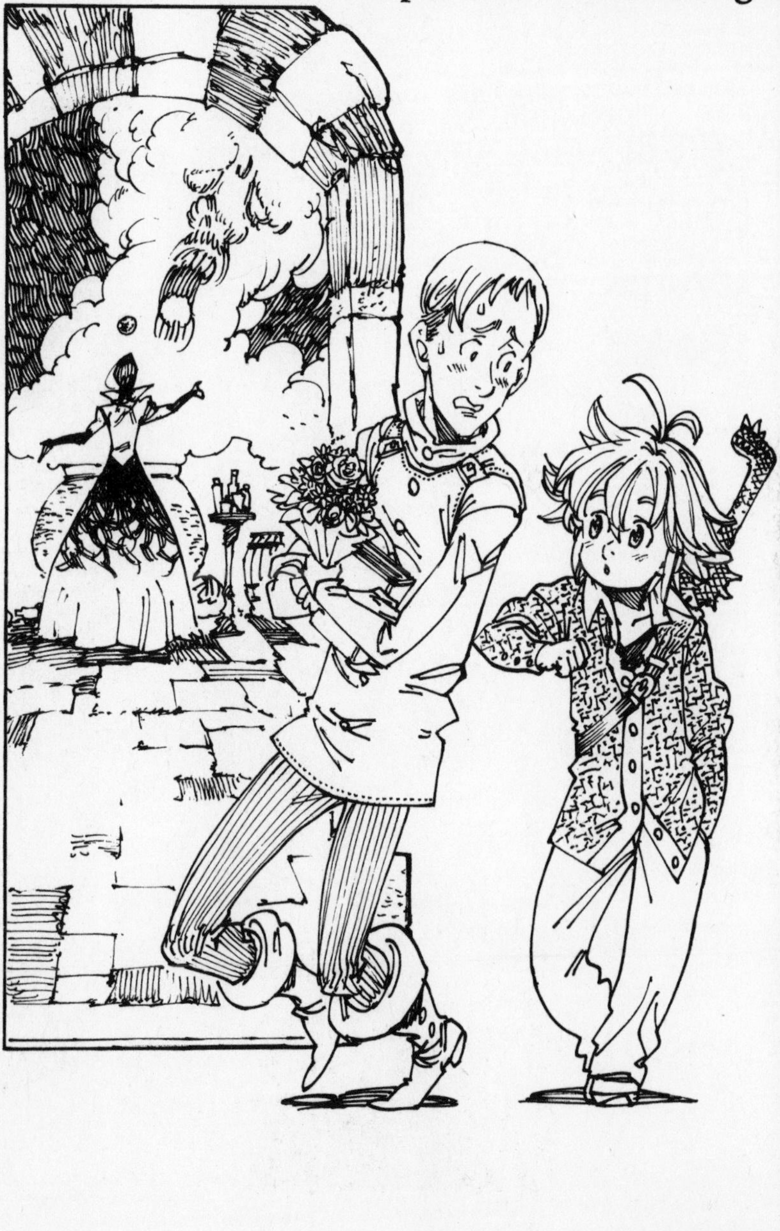

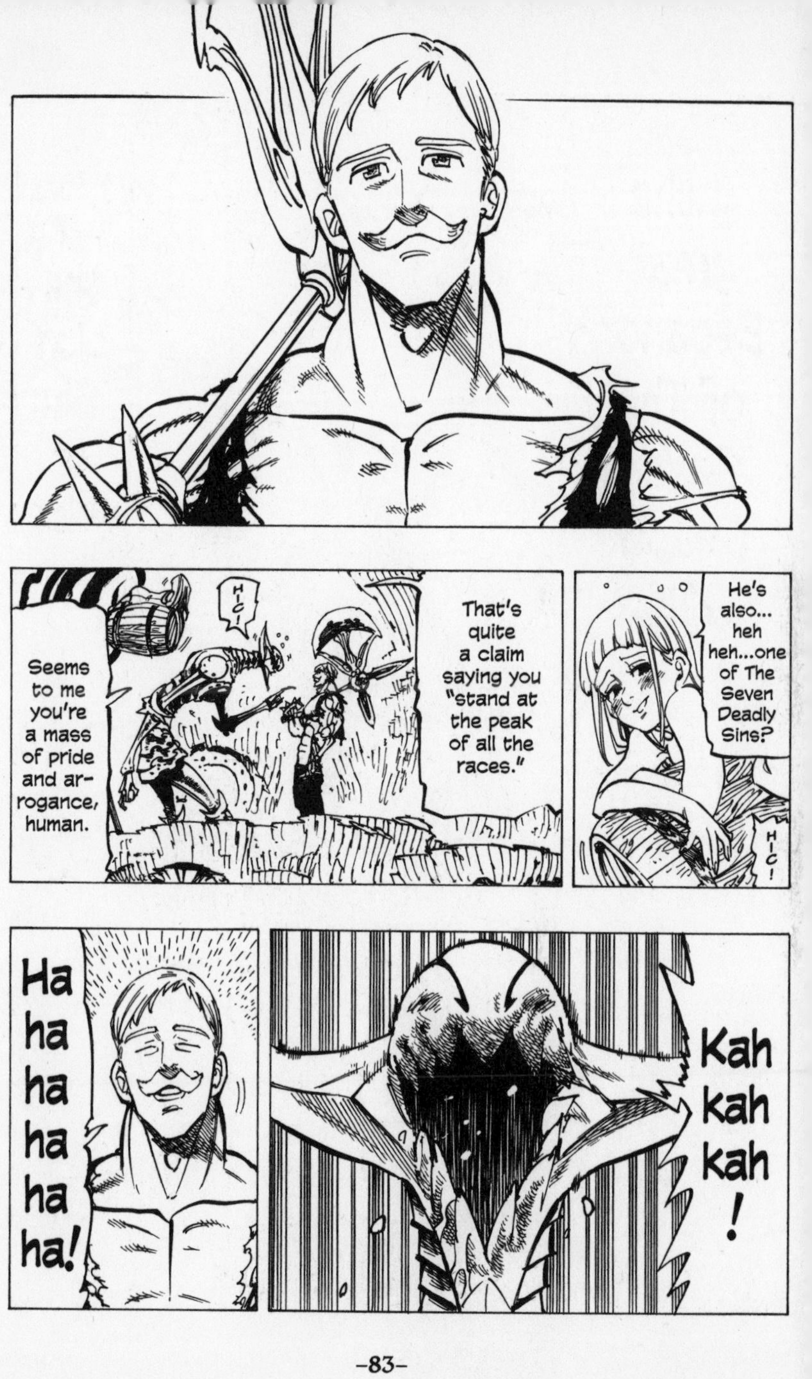
He's also... heh heh...one of The Seven Deadly Sins?
HIC!
That's quite a claim saying you "stand at the peak of all the races."
HIC!
Seems to me you're a mass of pride and ar-rogance, human.
Kah kah kah!
Ha ha ha ha ha ha ha!

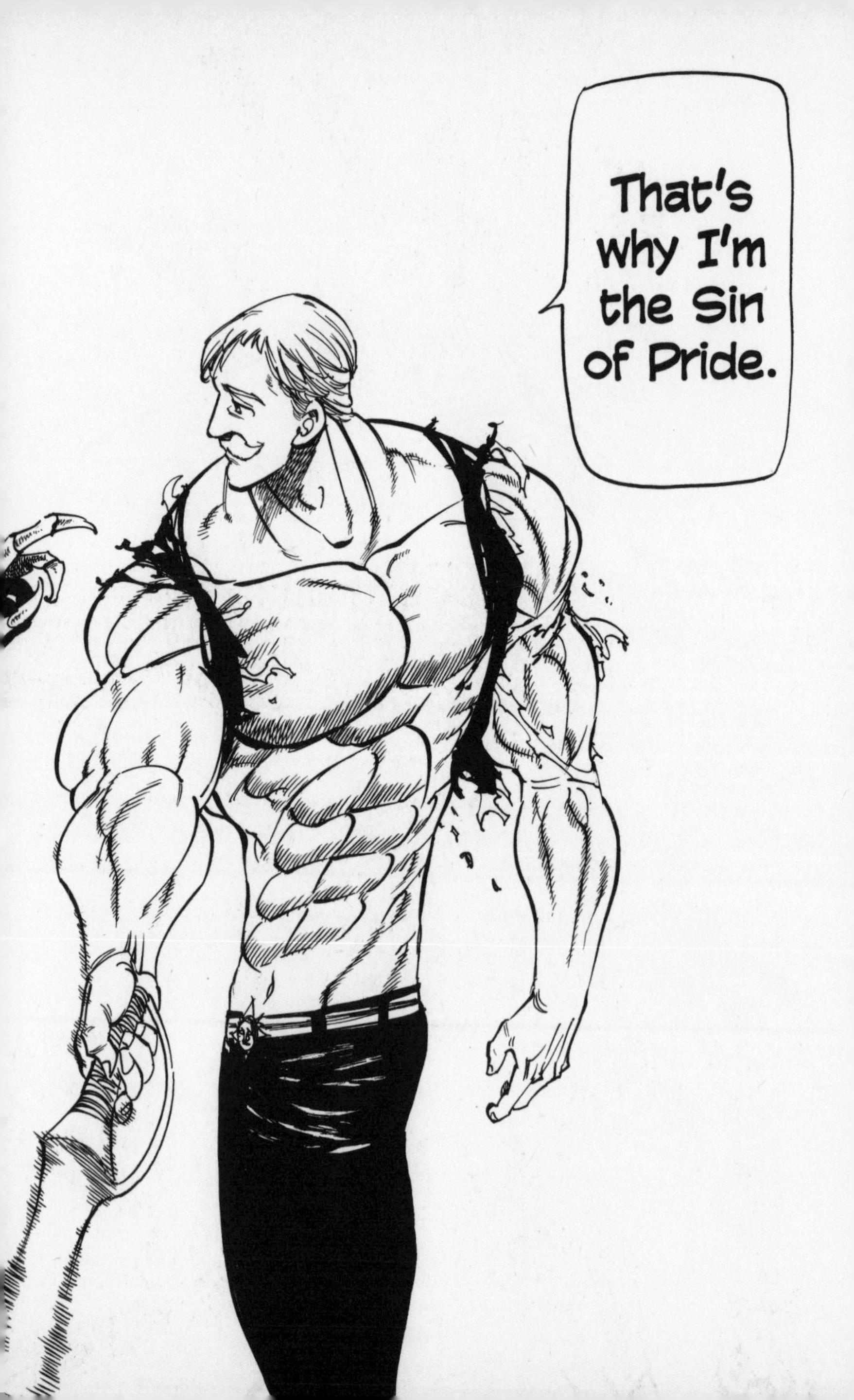
That's why I'm the Sin of Pride.

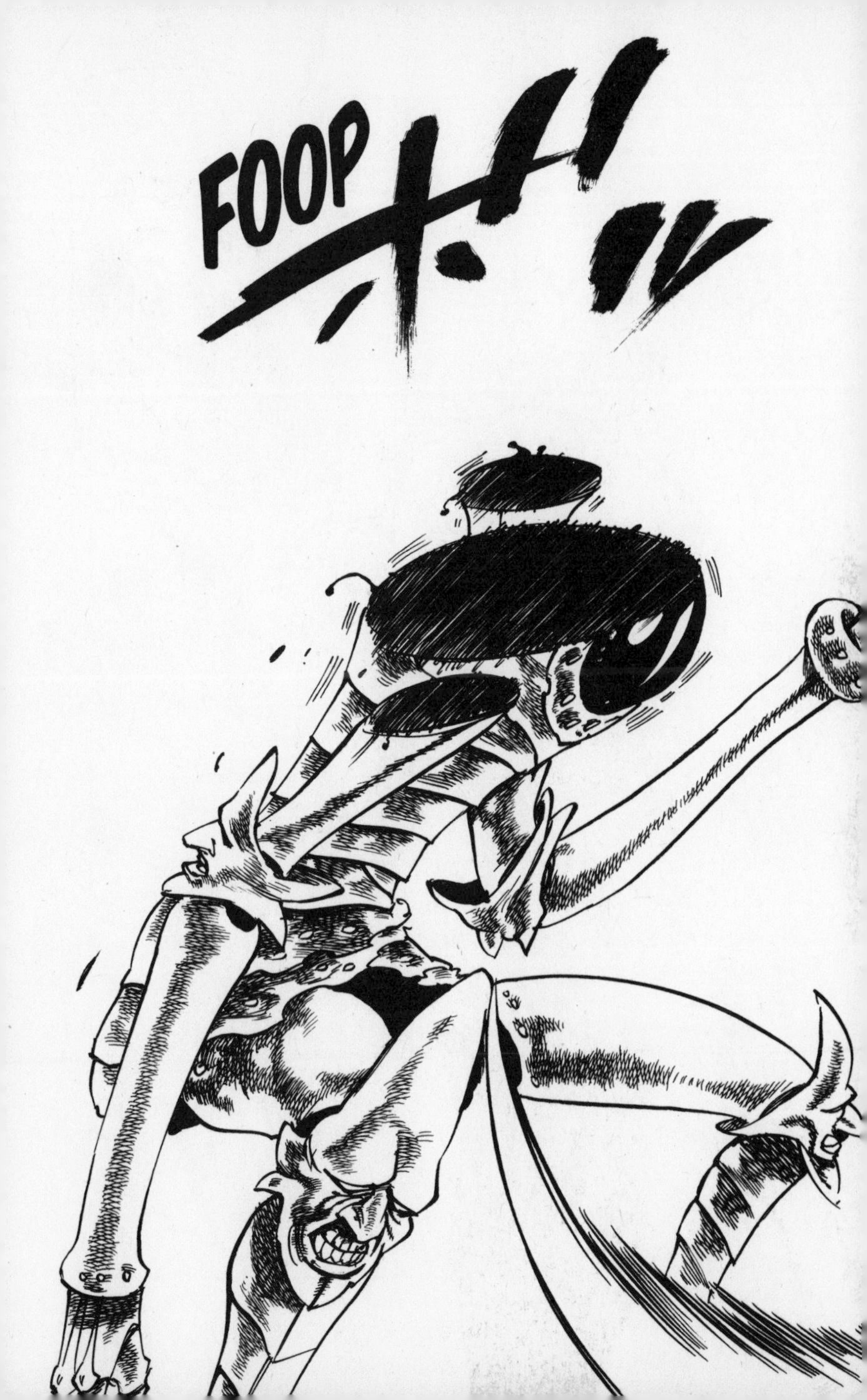
FOOP
ホ!!

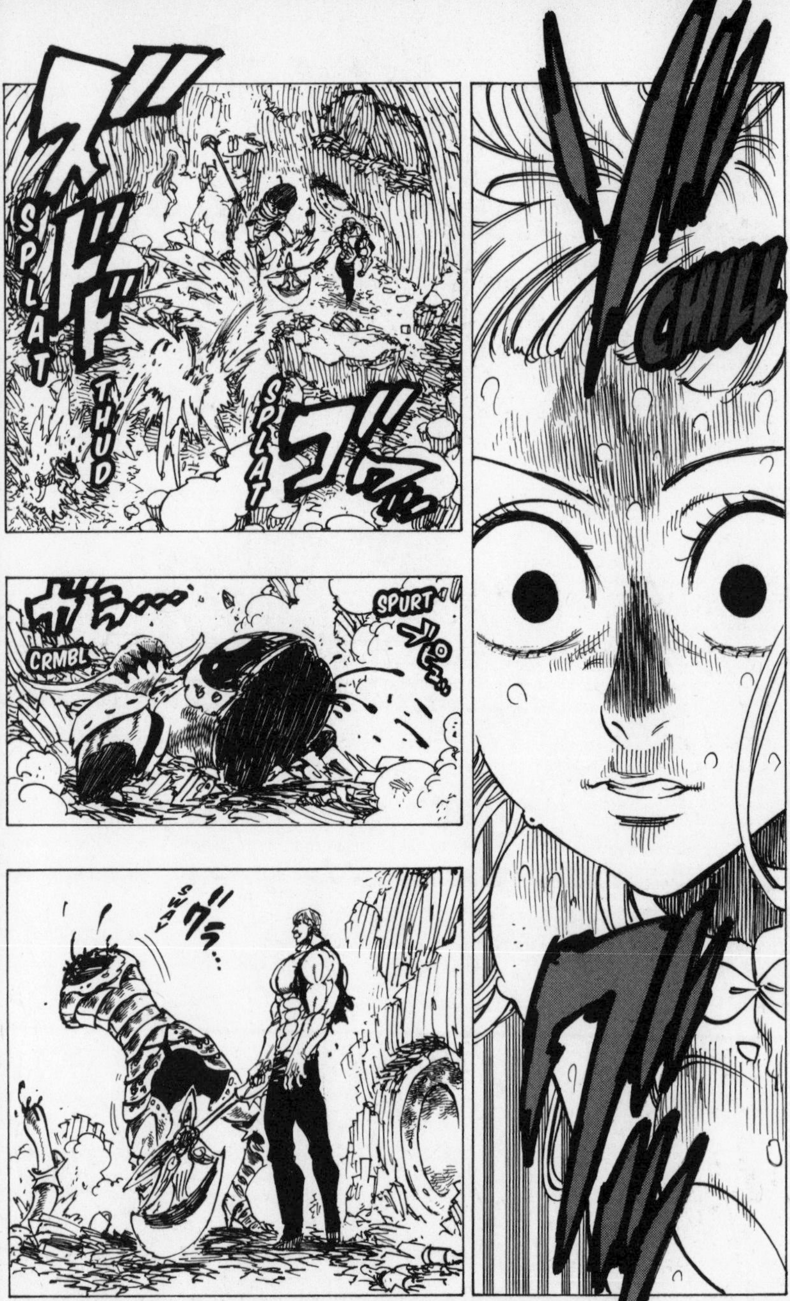
CHILL
SPLAT
THUD
SPLAT
SPURT
CRMBL
SWAY

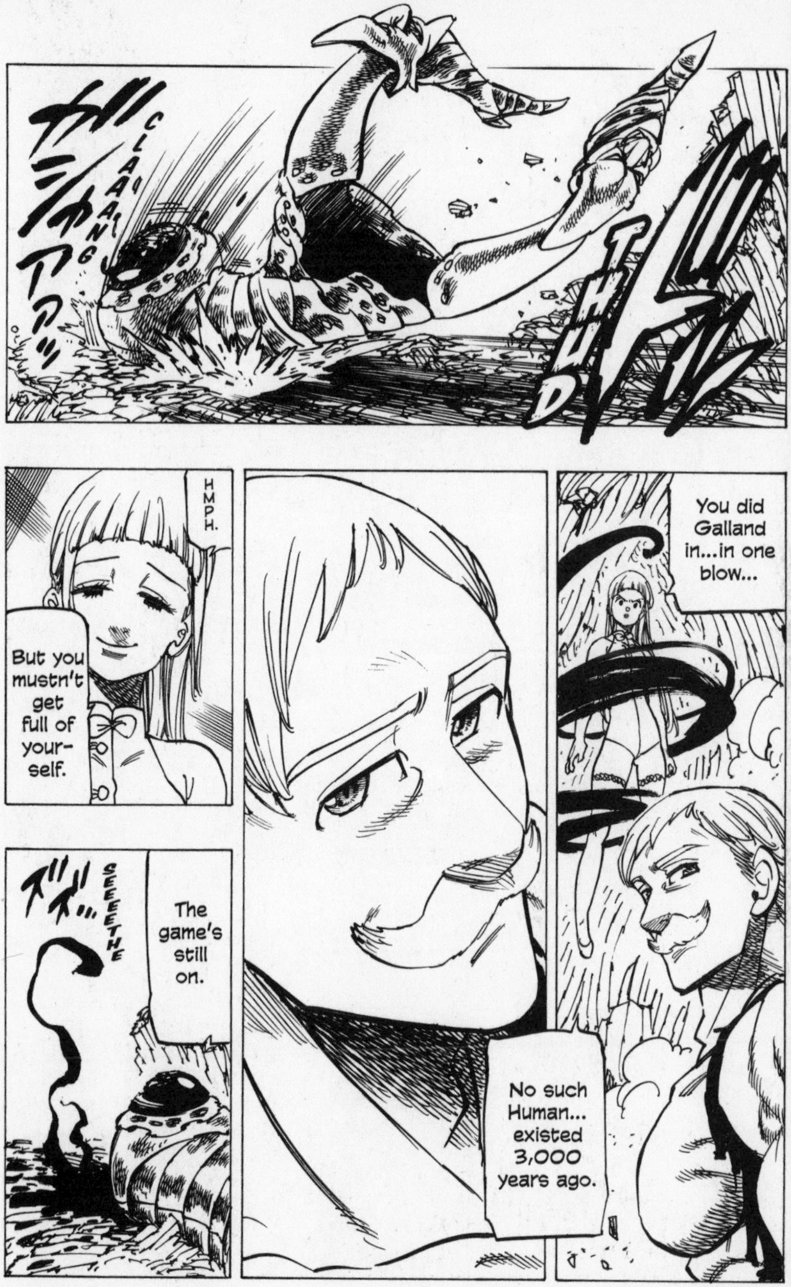
THUD
CLAAANG
You did Galland in...in one blow...
No such Human... existed 3,000 years ago.
HMPH.
But you mustn't get full of yourself.
SEEEETHE
The game's still on.

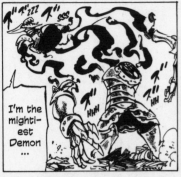

Ggh ...
KAAAAH!
SEETHE
I'm the mightiest Demon ...
SNAP
You think that was enough to kill someone like me?!
Of course, I knew that already.
The game wouldn't be much fun otherwise.

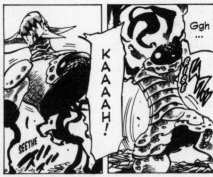

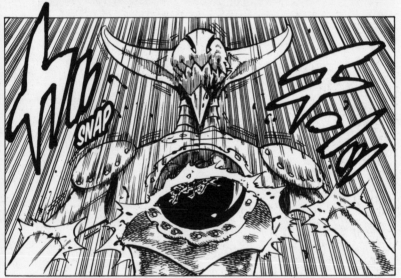

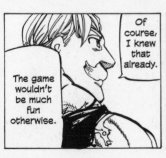

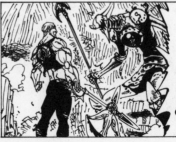

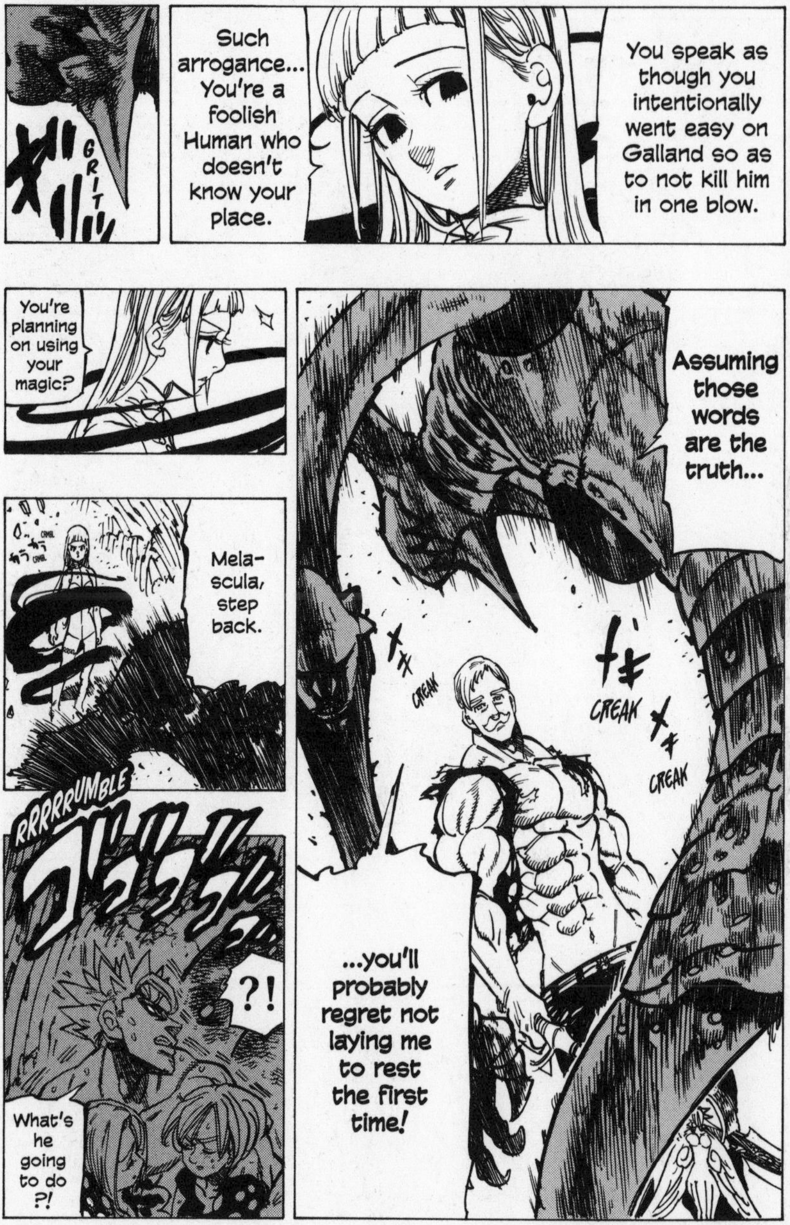
You speak as though you intentionally went easy on Galland so as to not kill him in one blow.
Such arrogance... You're a foolish Human who doesn't know your place.
GRIT
Assuming those words are the truth...
CREAK
CREAK
CREAK
...you'll probably regret not laying me to rest the first time!
You're planning on using your magic?
Mela-scula, step back.
RRRRRUMBLE
?!
What's he going to do ?!

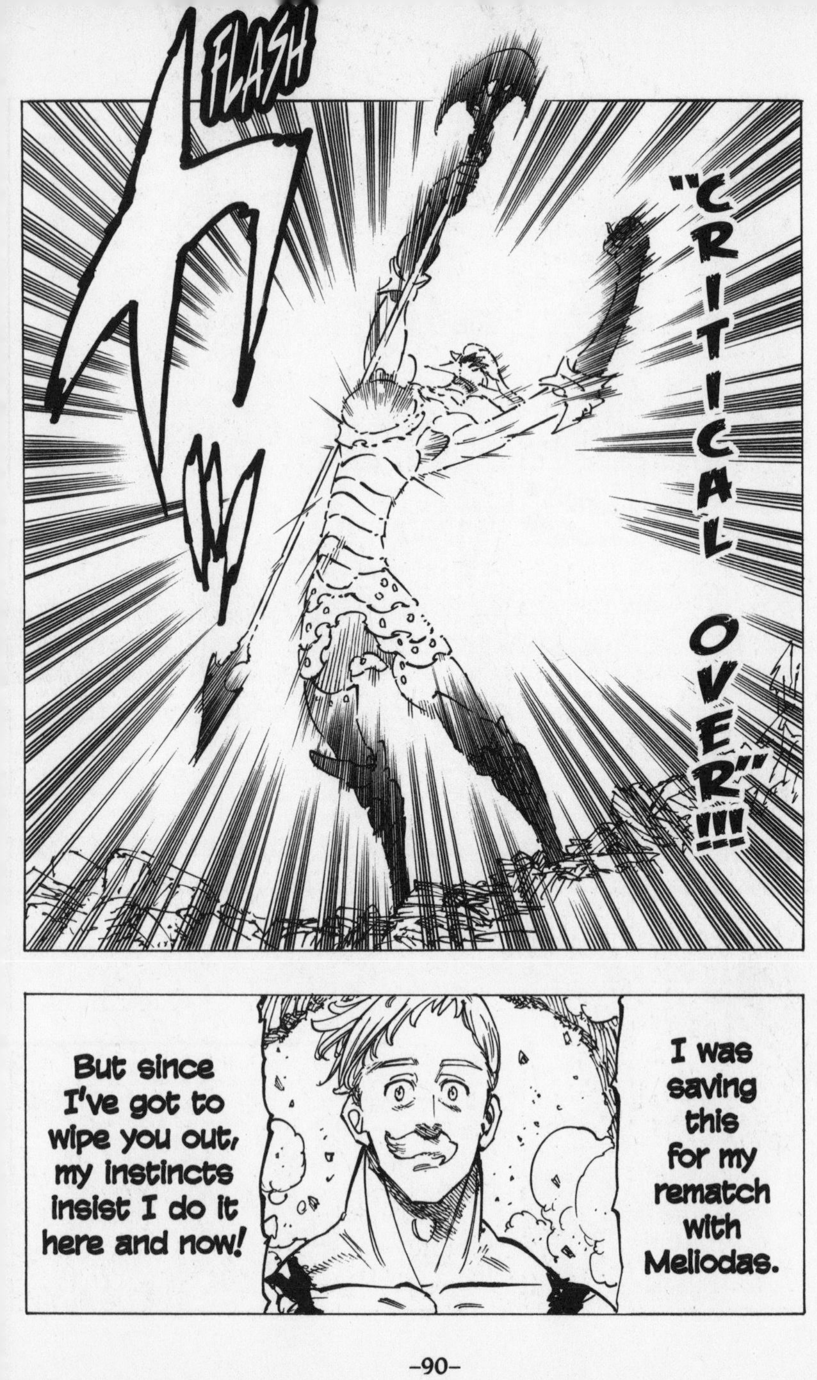
"CRITICAL OVER"!!!
FLASH
I was saving this for my rematch with Meliodas.
But since I've got to wipe you out, my instincts insist I do it here and now!

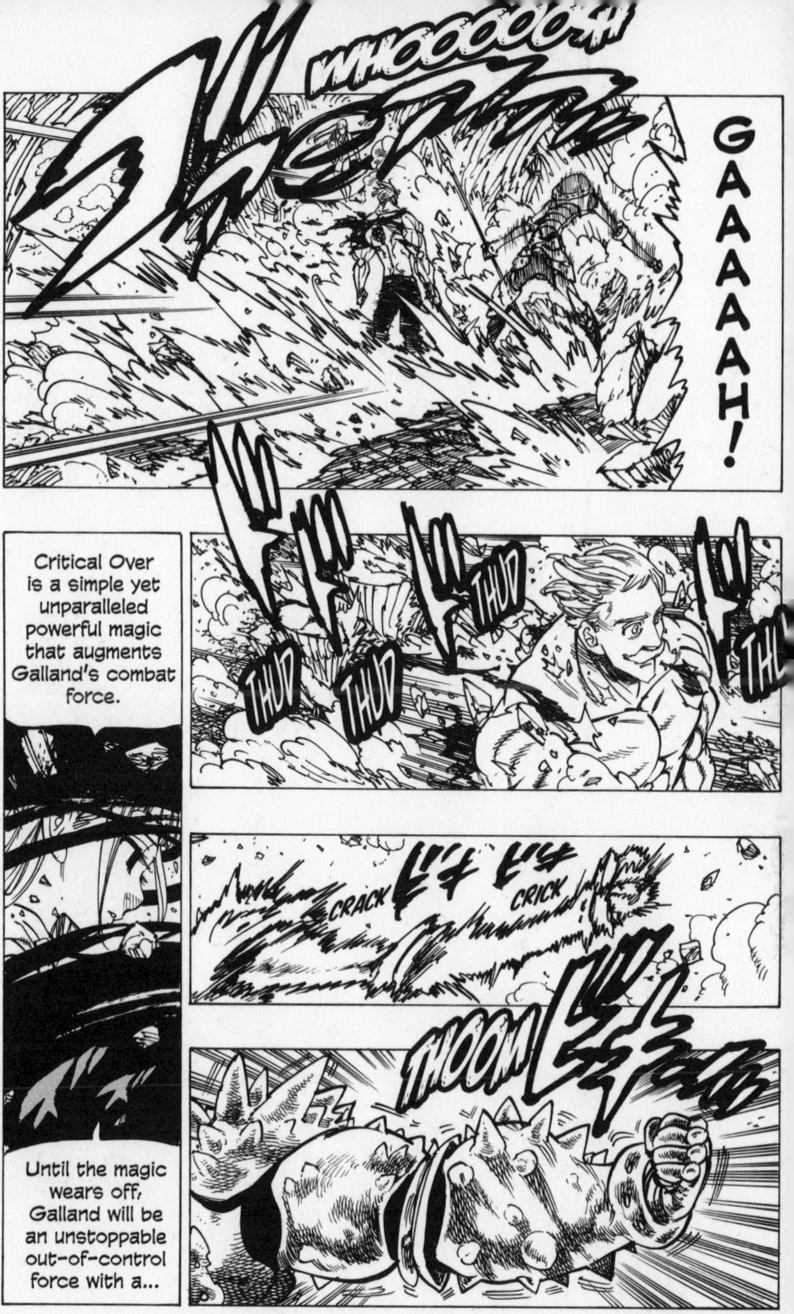

GAAAAAAH!
WHOOOOOSH
THUD
THUD
THUD
THUD
THUD
CRICK
CRACK
THOOM
Critical Over is a simple yet unparalleled powerful magic that augments Galland's combat force.
Until the magic wears off, Galland will be an unstoppable out-of-control force with a...

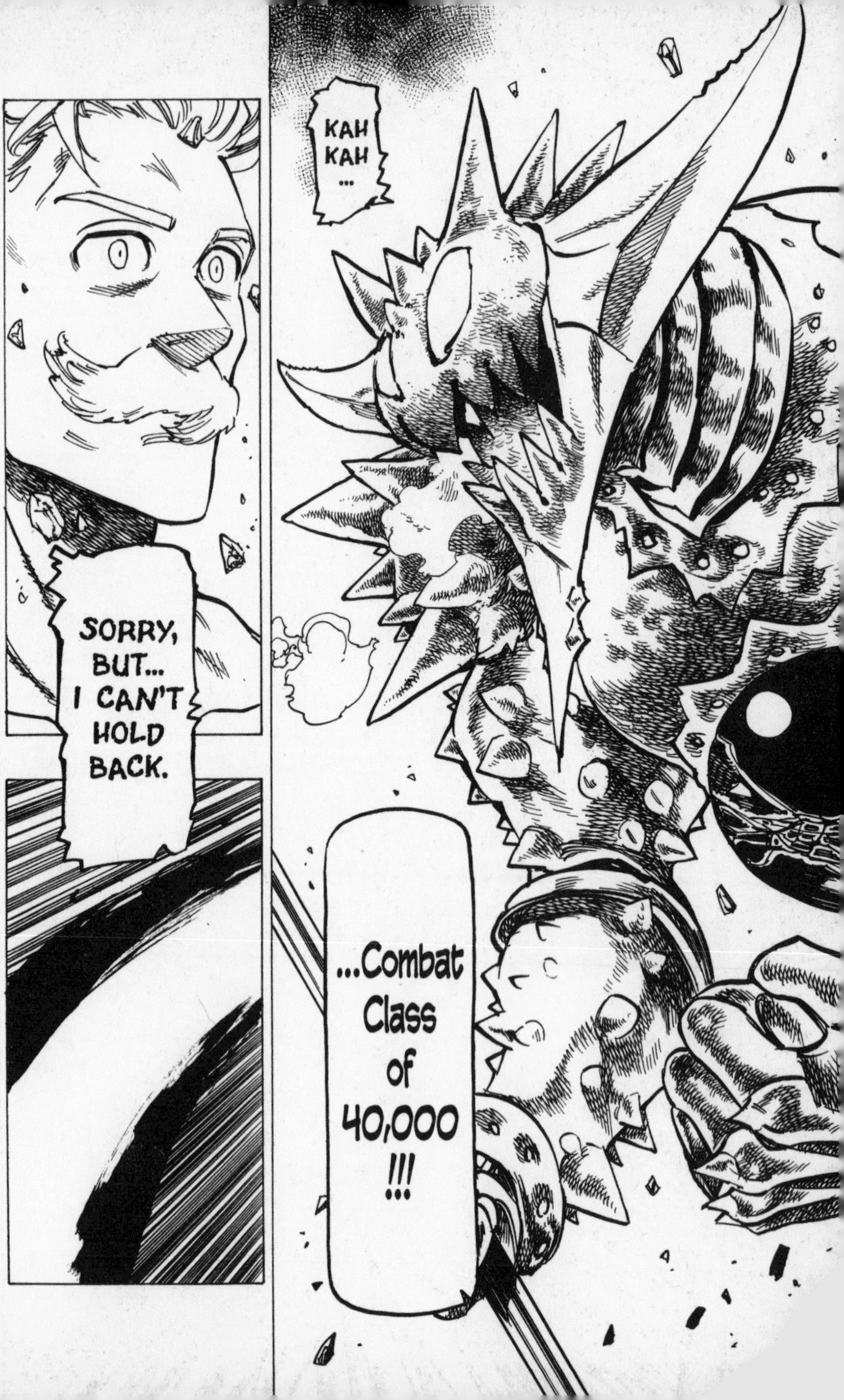
KAH KAH ...
...Combat Class of 40,000 !!!
SORRY, BUT... I CAN'T HOLD BACK.

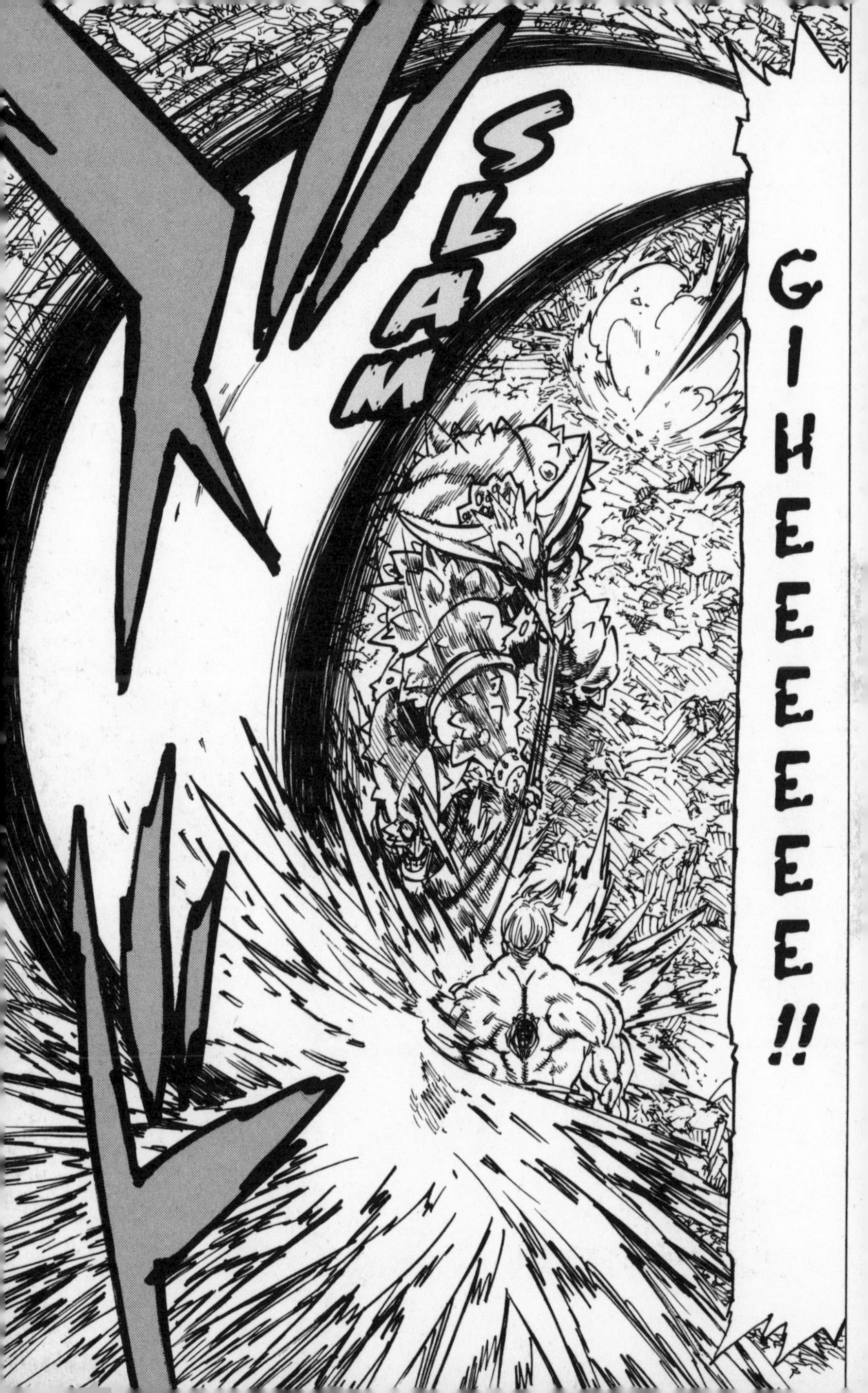
GIHEEEEEE!!
SLAM

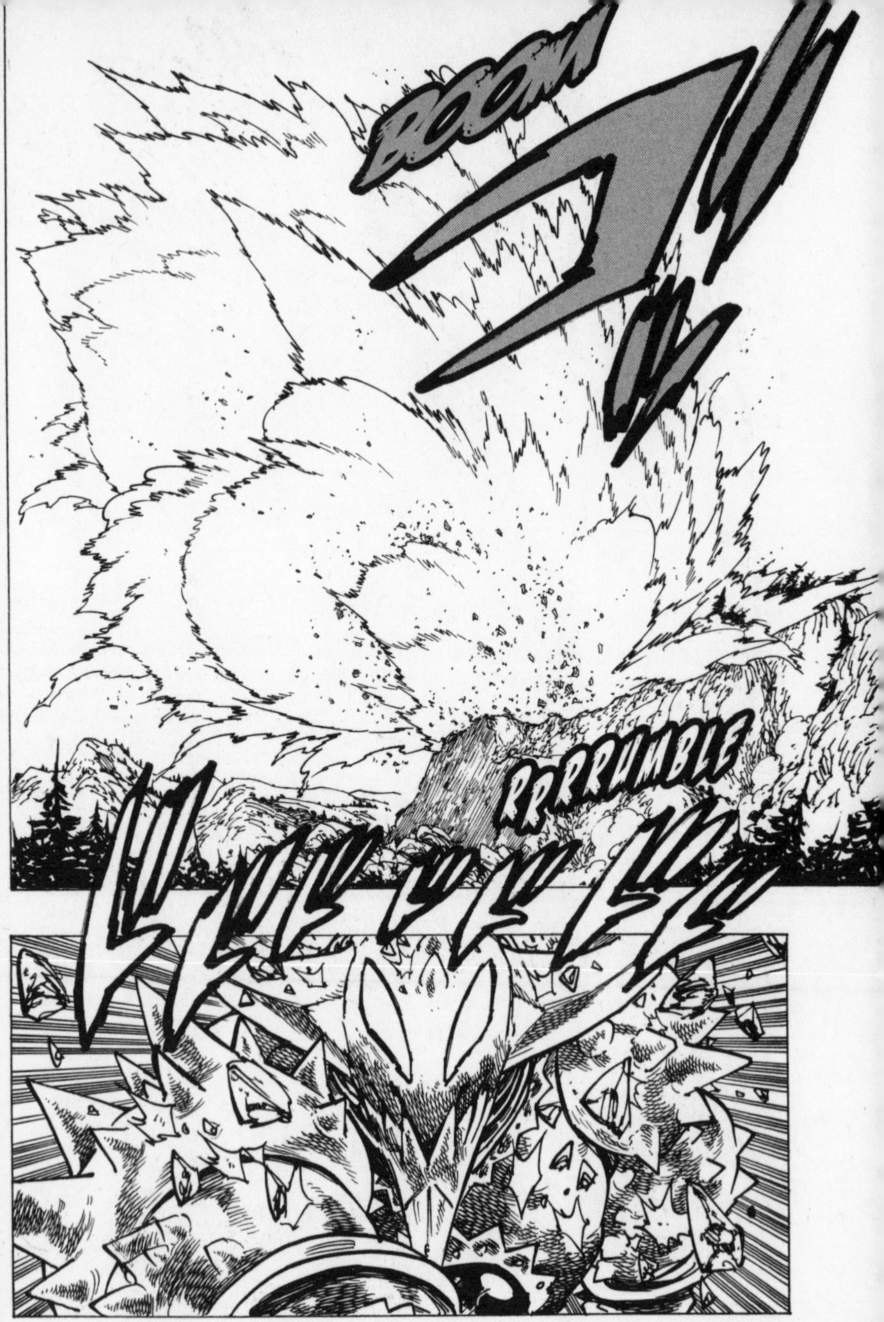
BOOM
RRRRUMBLE

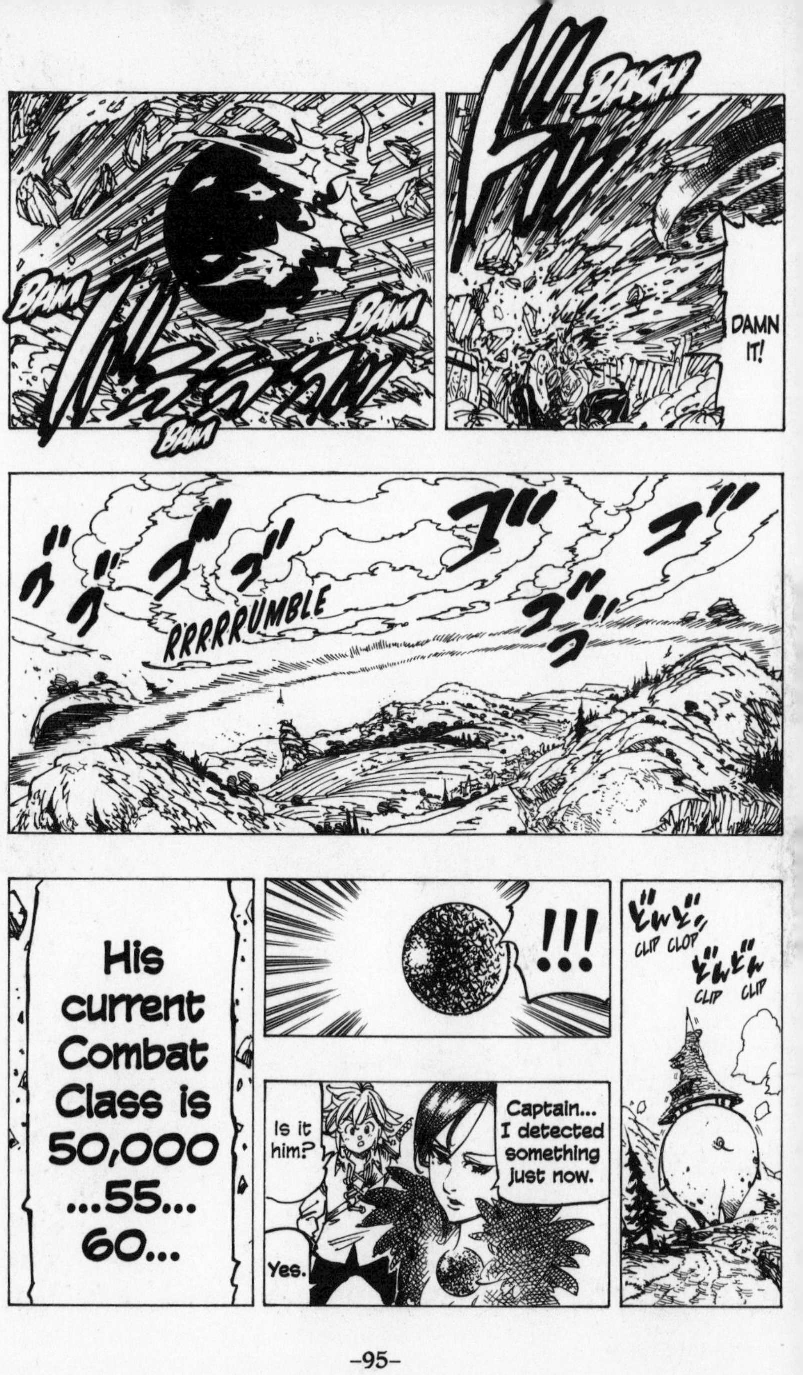
BASH
DAMN IT!
BAM
BAM
BAM
BAM
RRRRRUMBLE
CLIP CLOP
CLIP CLIP
!!!
Captain... I detected something just now.
Is it him?
Yes.
His current Combat Class is 50,000 ...55... 60...

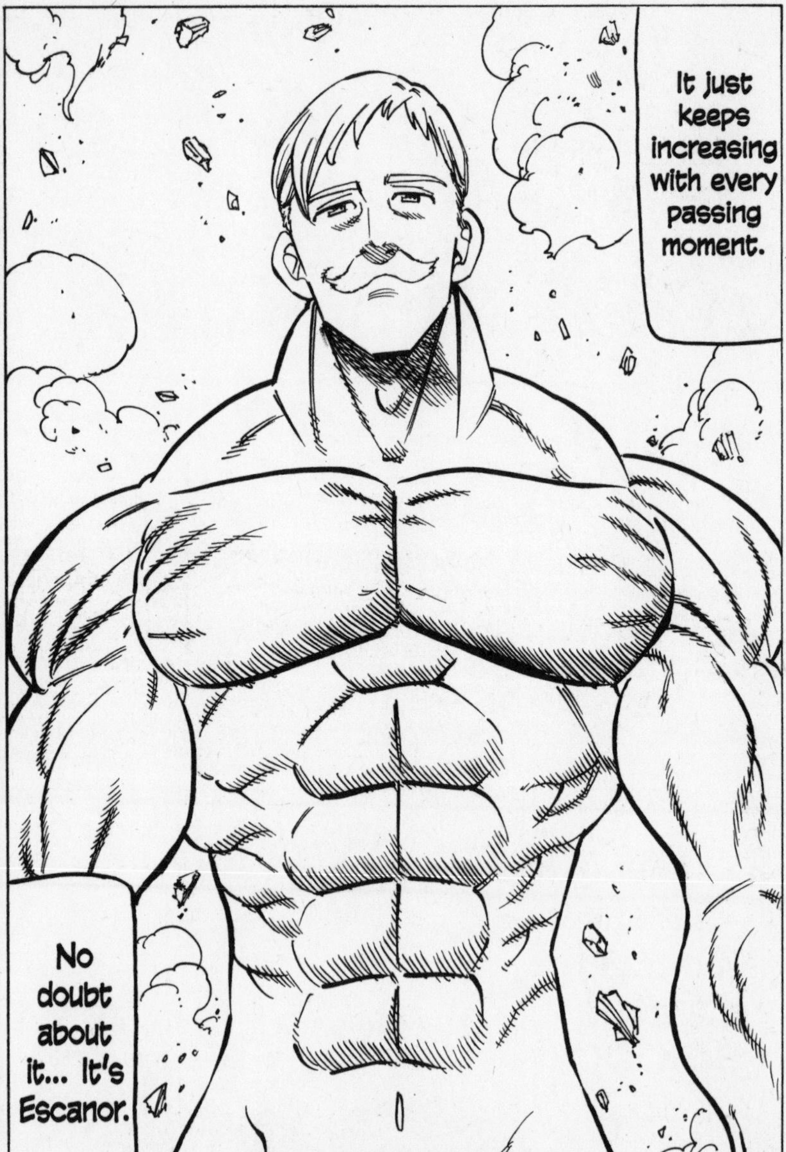
It just keeps increasing with every passing moment.
No doubt about it... It's Escanor.

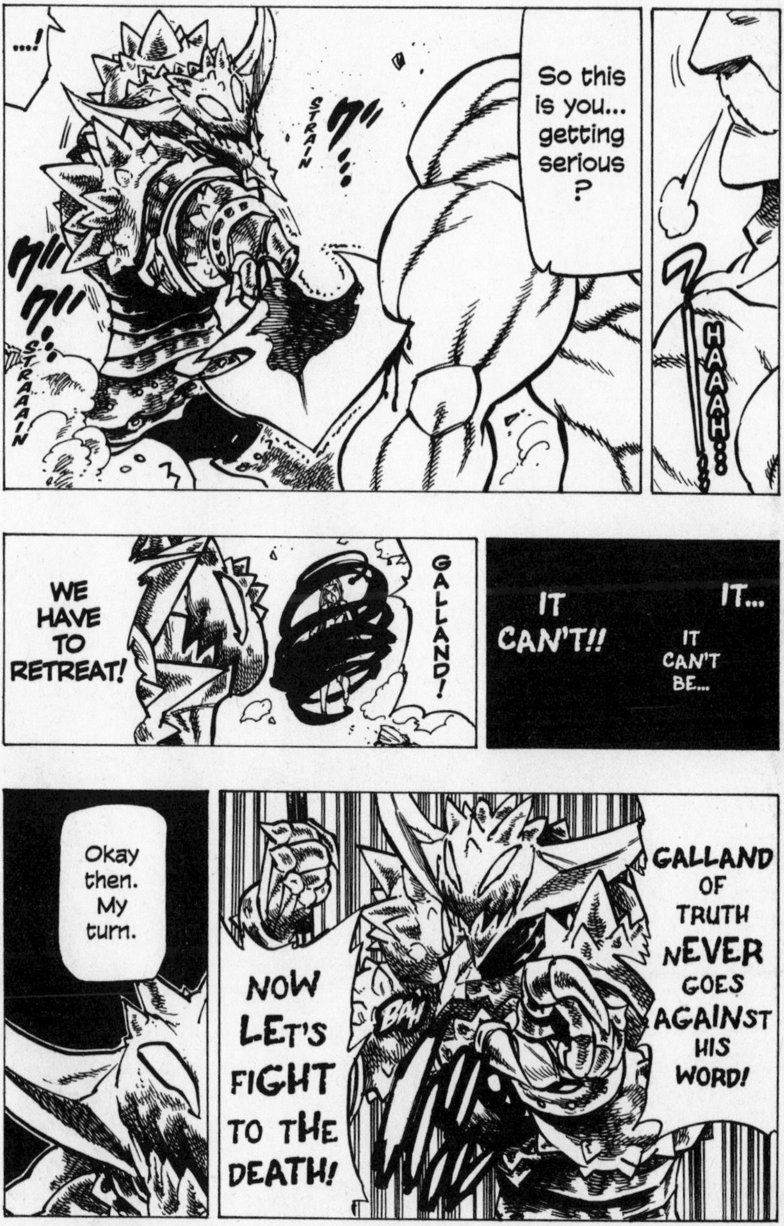
HAAAAH...
So this is you... getting serious?
STRAIN
...!
STRAAAIN
IT...
IT CAN'T BE...
IT CAN'T!!
GALLAND!
WE HAVE TO RETREAT!
GALLAND OF TRUTH NEVER GOES AGAINST HIS WORD!
NOW LET'S FIGHT TO THE DEATH!
Okay then. My turn.

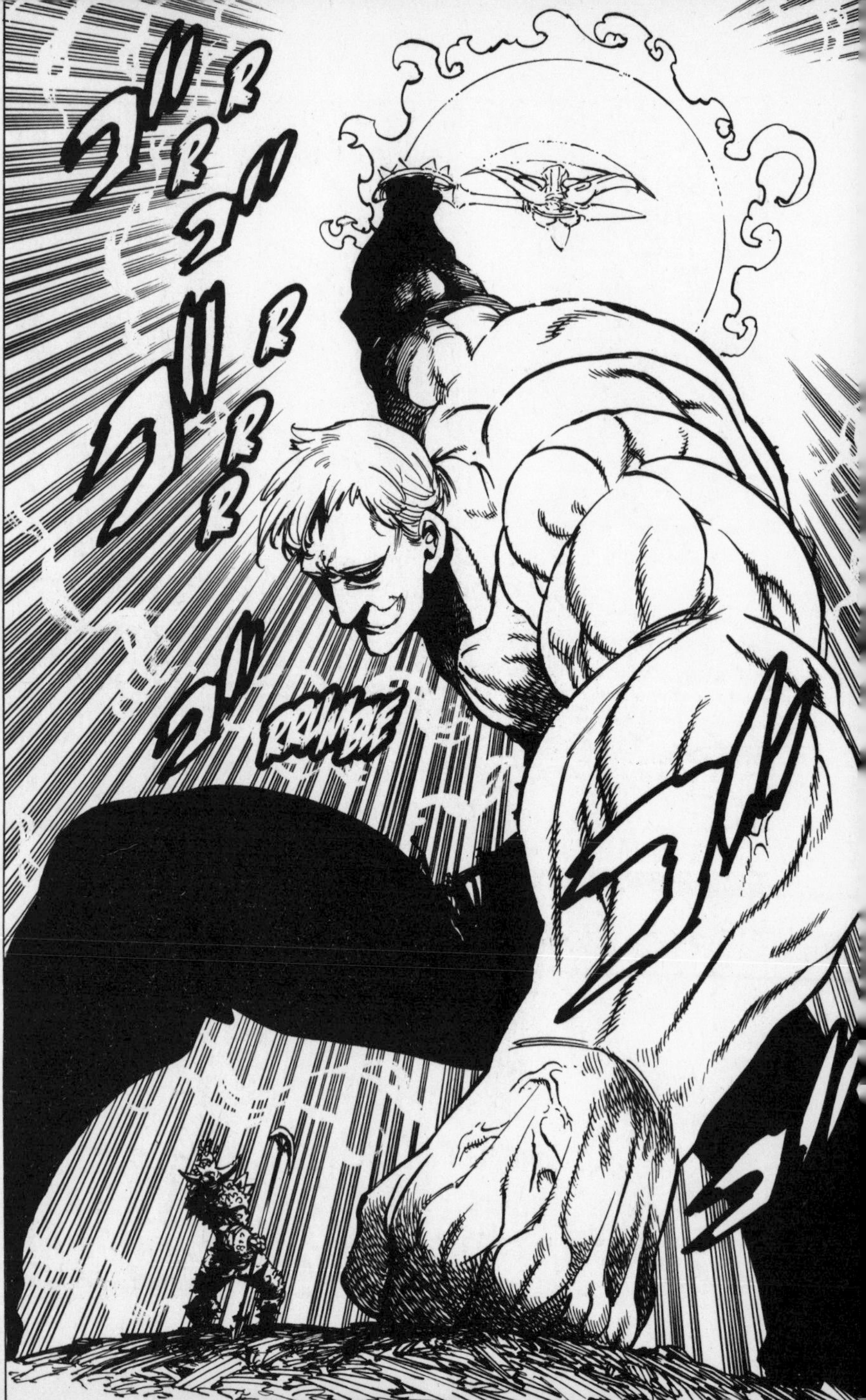
RUMBLE

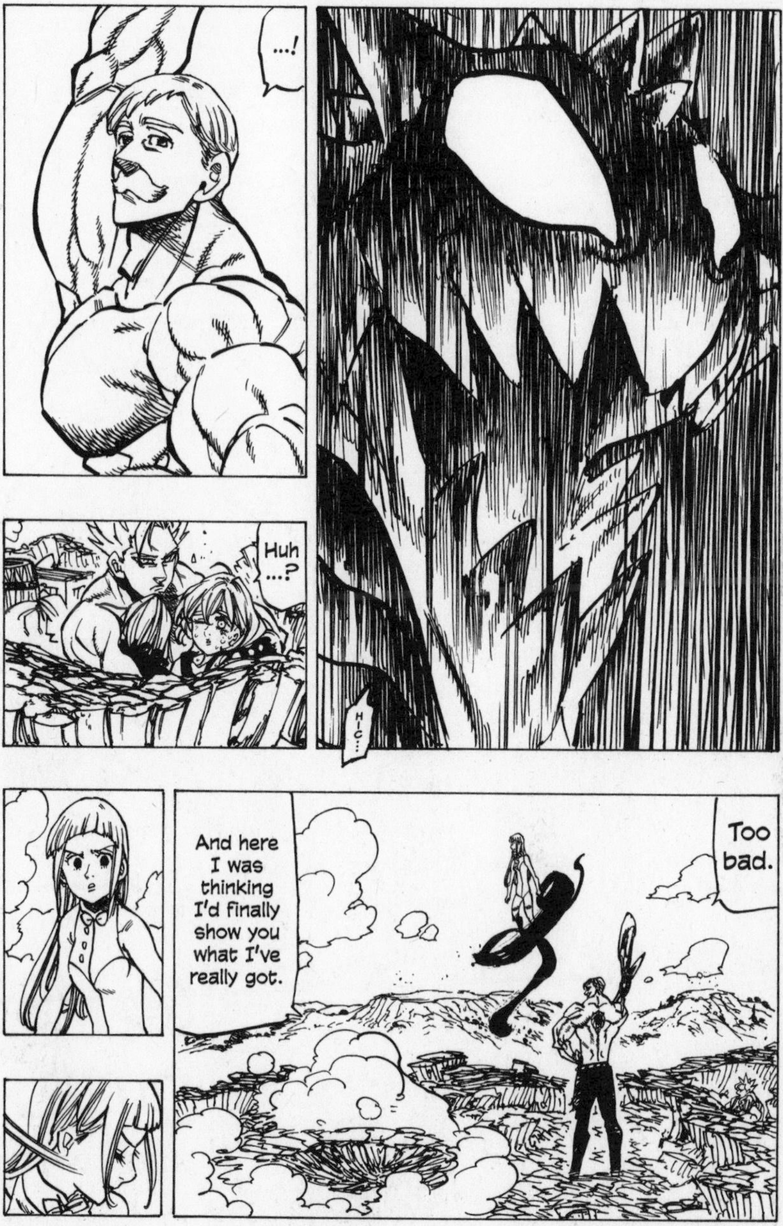
HIC...
...!
Huh ...?
Too bad.
And here I was thinking I'd finally show you what I've really got.

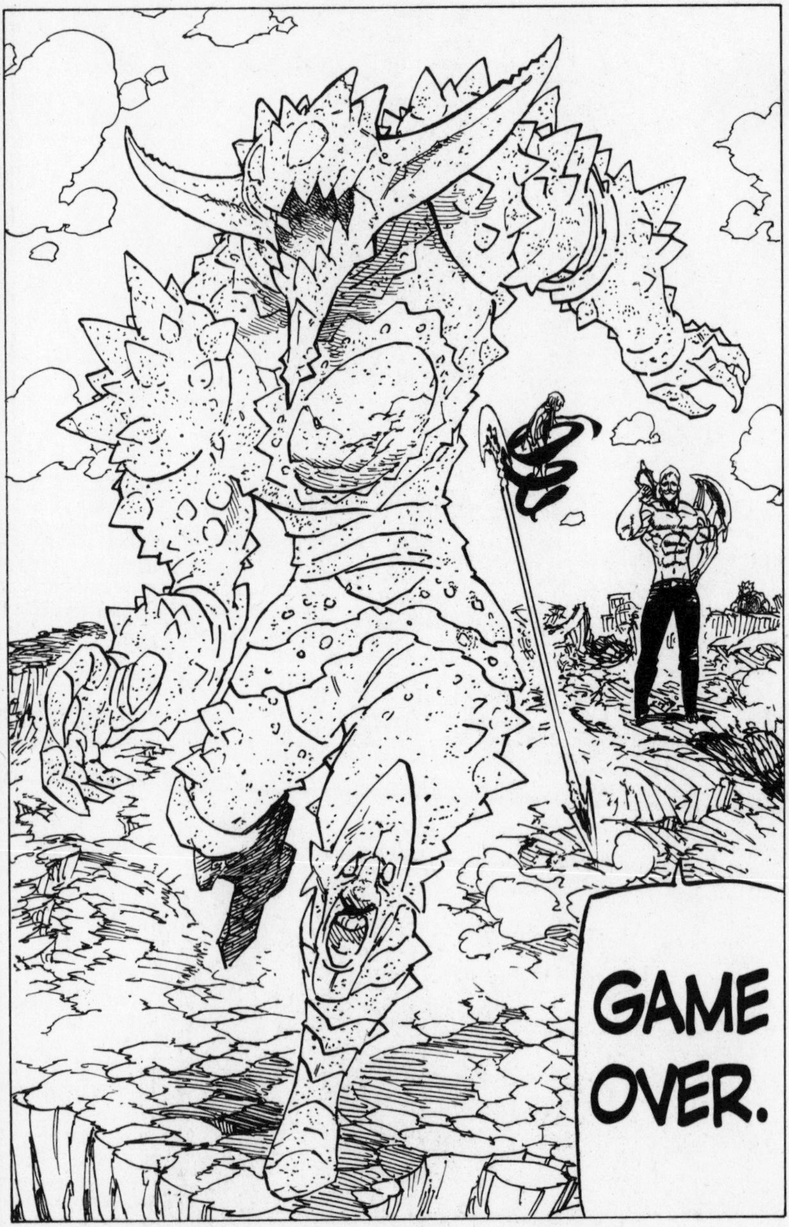
GAME OVER.

Chapter 150 - Master of the Sun

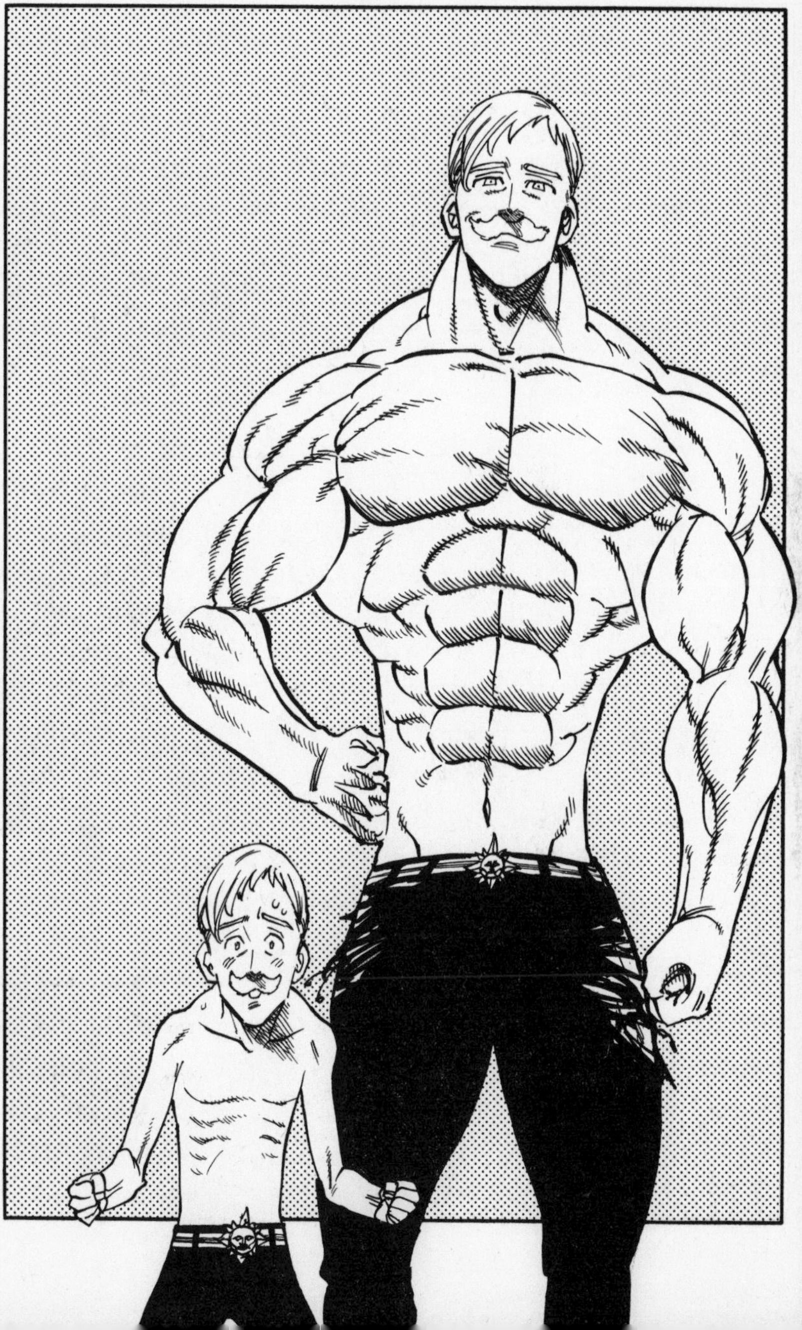

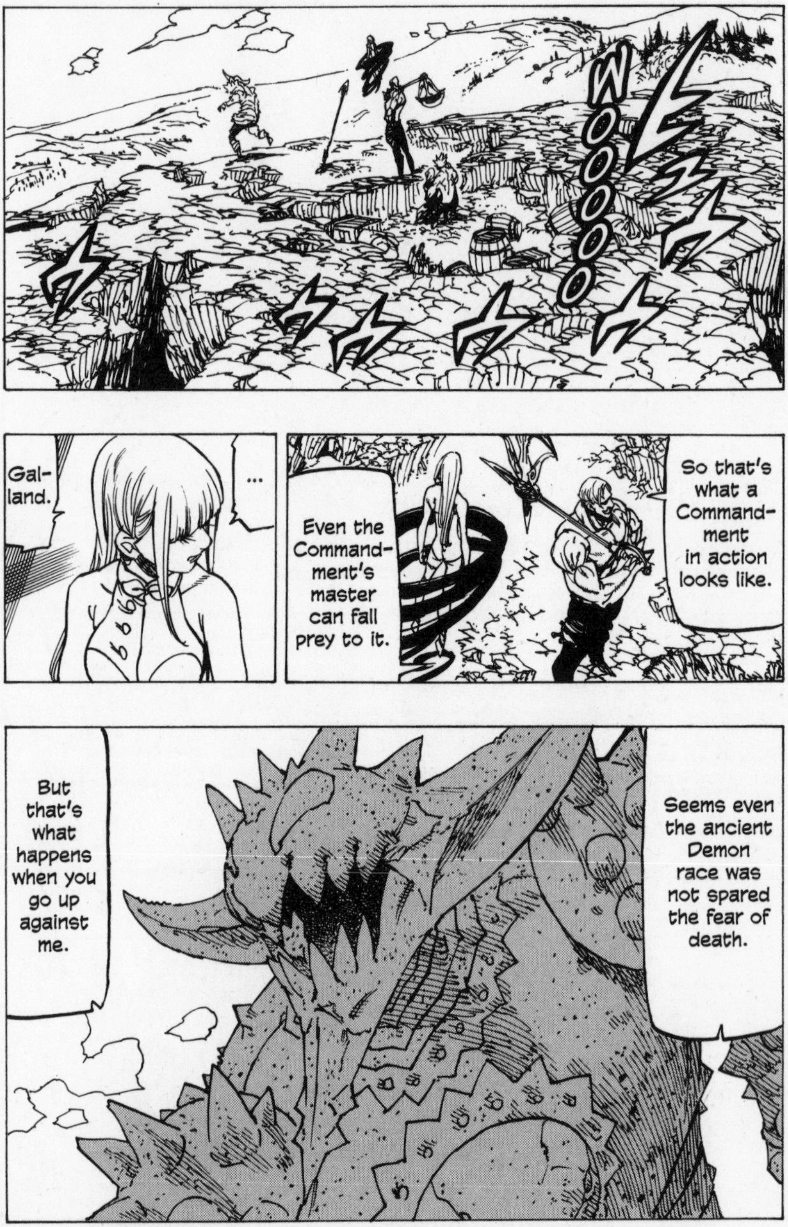
WOOOOOO
So that's what a Commandment in action looks like.
Even the Commandment's master can fall prey to it.
...
Galland.
Seems even the ancient Demon race was not spared the fear of death.
But that's what happens when you go up against me.

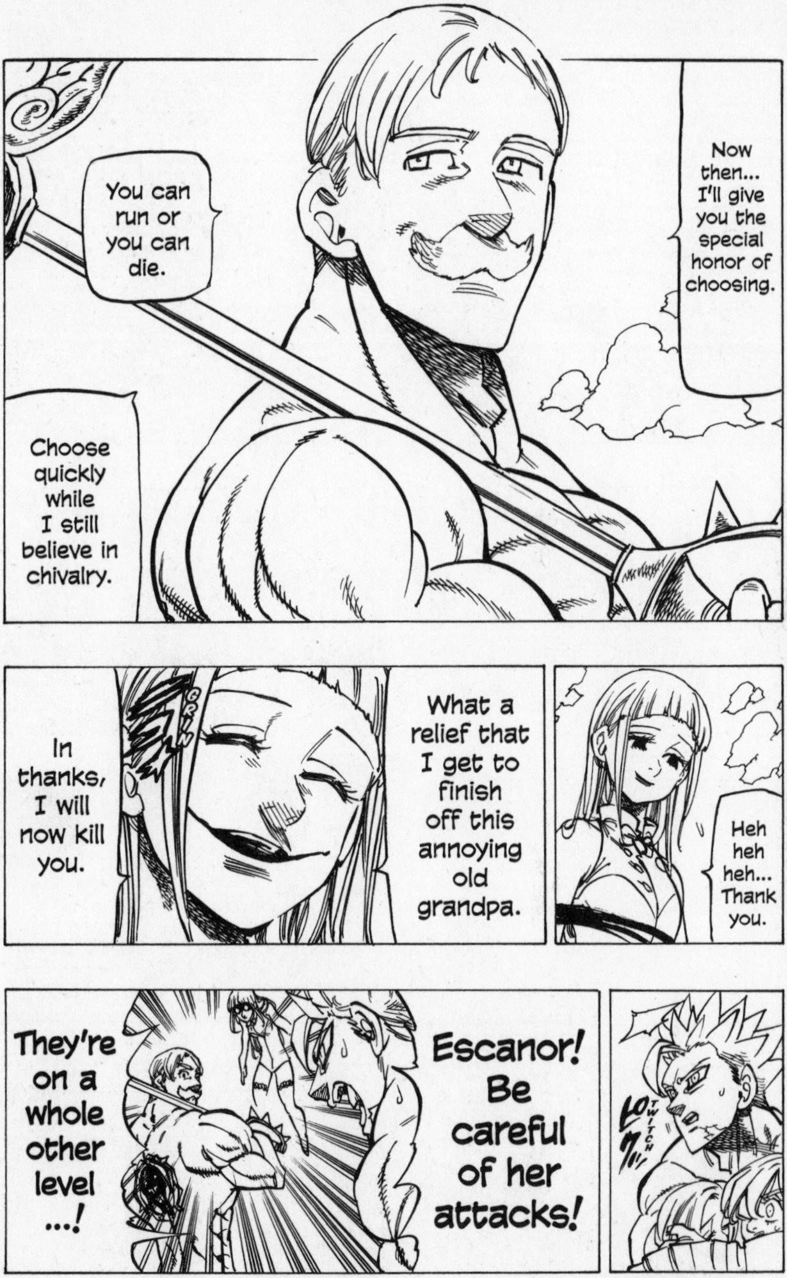
Now then... I'll give you the special honor of choosing.
You can run or you can die.
Choose quickly while I still believe in chivalry.
Heh heh heh... Thank you.
What a relief that I get to finish off this annoying old grandpa.
GRIN
In thanks, I will now kill you.
TWITCH
Escanor! Be careful of her attacks!
They're on a whole other level ...!

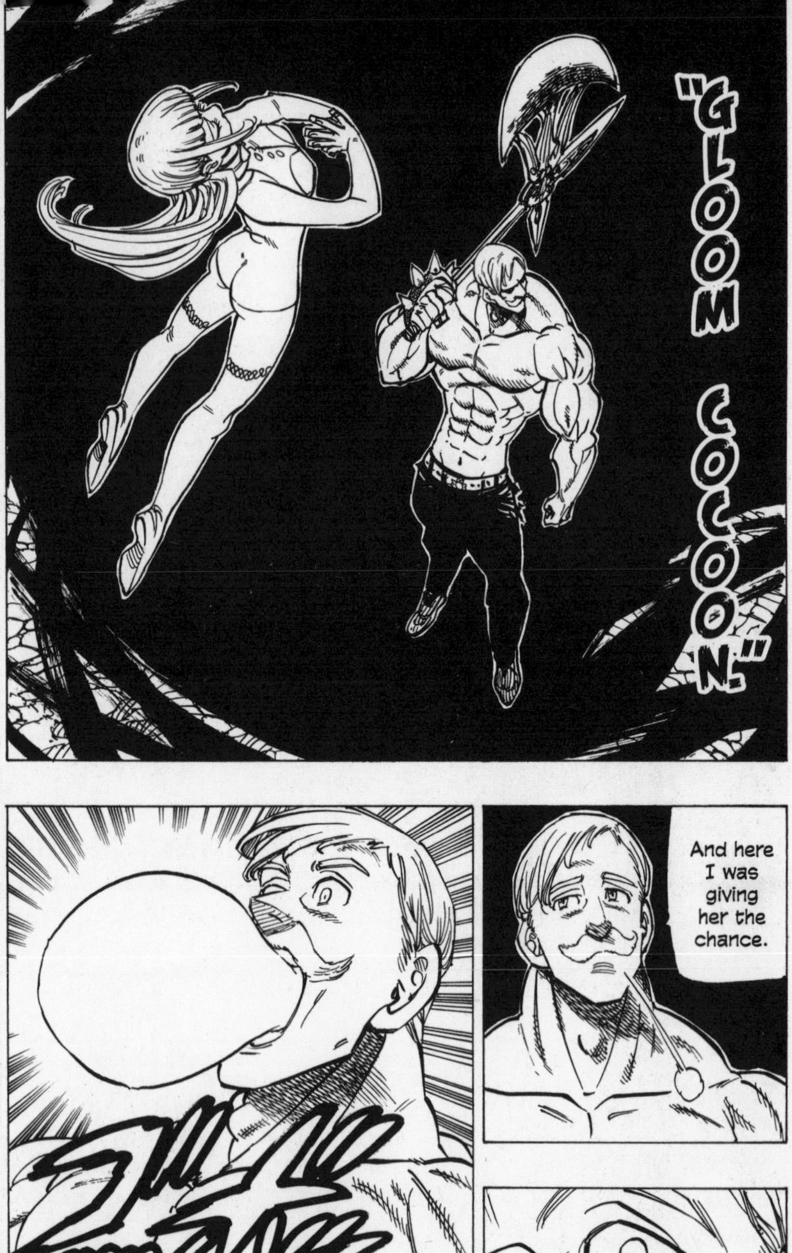
"GLOOM COCOON."
And here I was giving her the chance.
?
BLORP

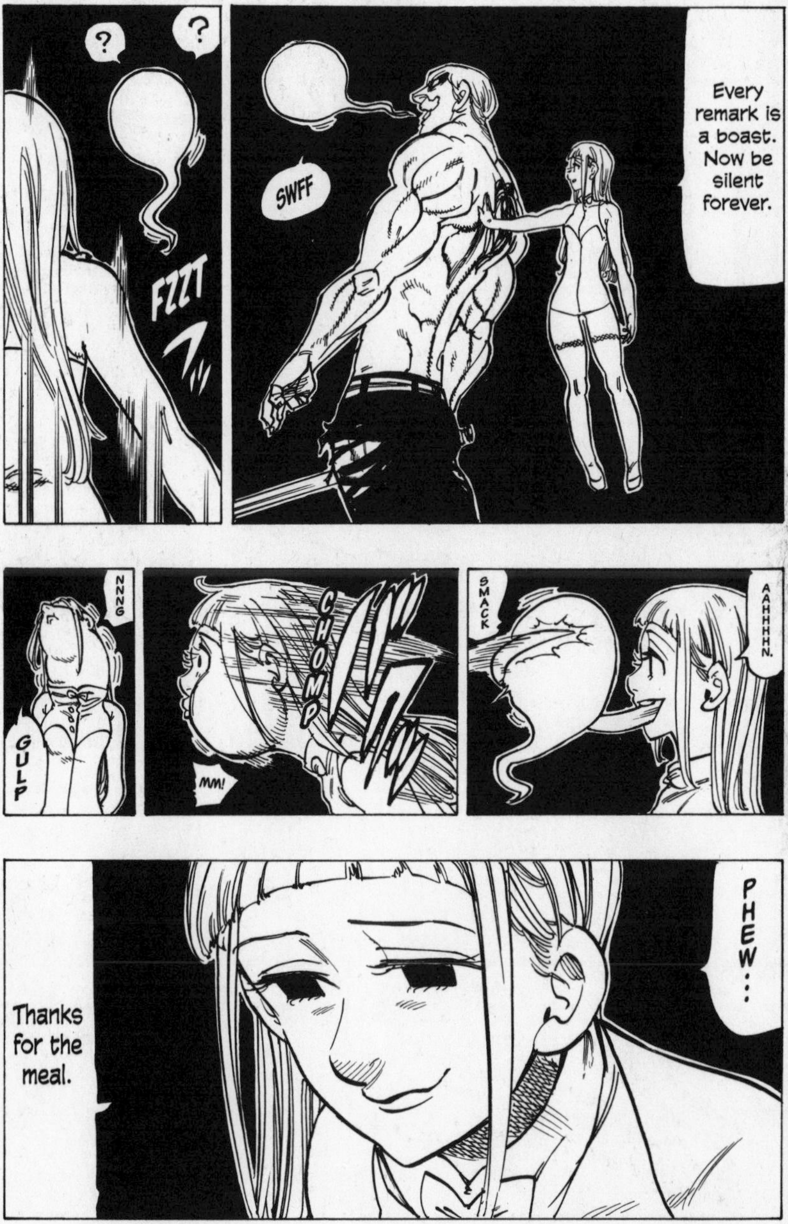
Every remark is a boast. Now be silent forever.
SWFF
?
?
FZZT
AAHHHHN.
SMACK
CHOMP
MM!
NNG
GULP
PHEW...
Thanks for the meal.

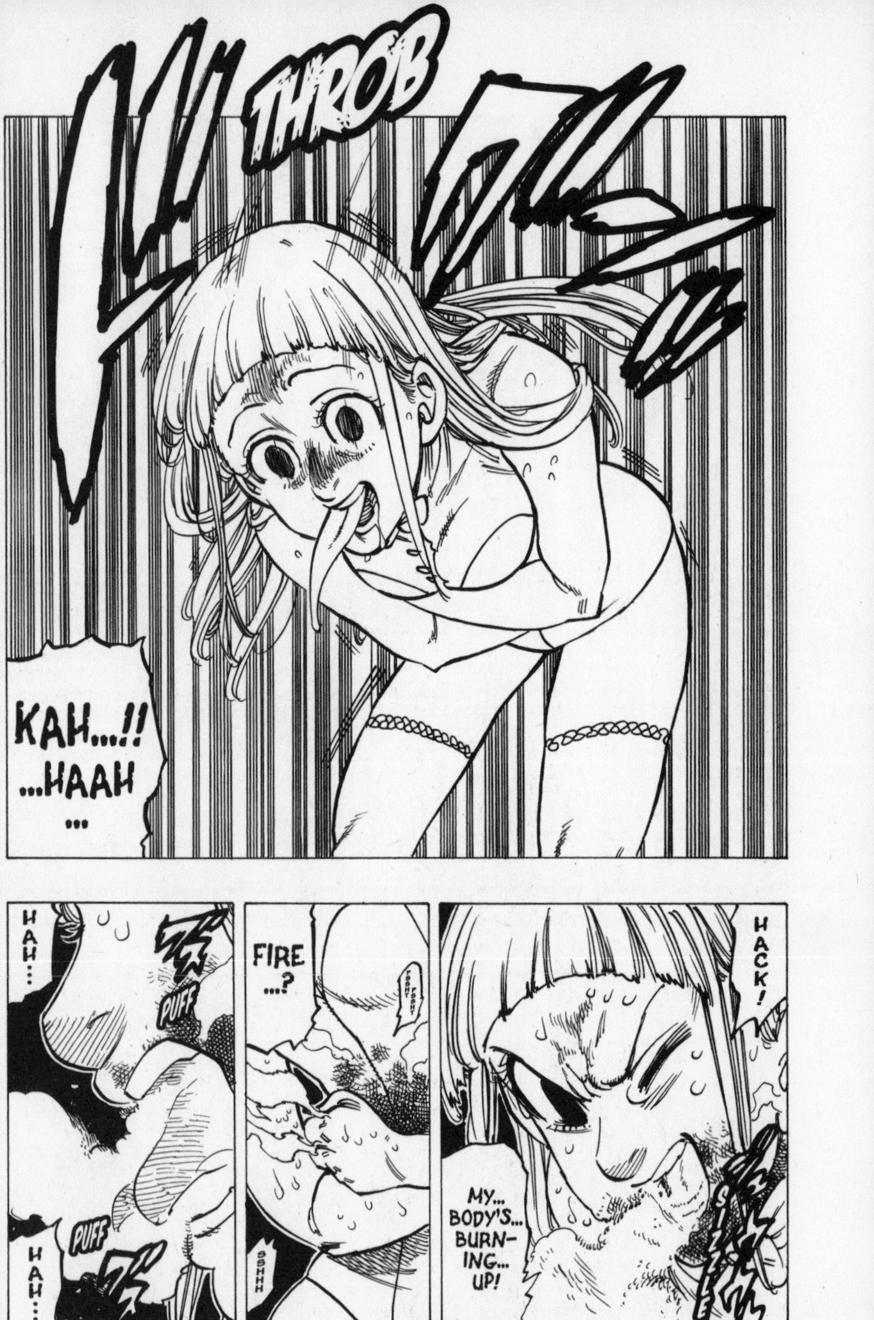
THROB
KAH...!! ...HAAH ...
HACK!
MY... BODY'S... BURN-ING... UP!
SIZZLE
FIRE ...?
FSSHT FSSHT
SSHH
HAH...
PUFF
PUFF
HAH...

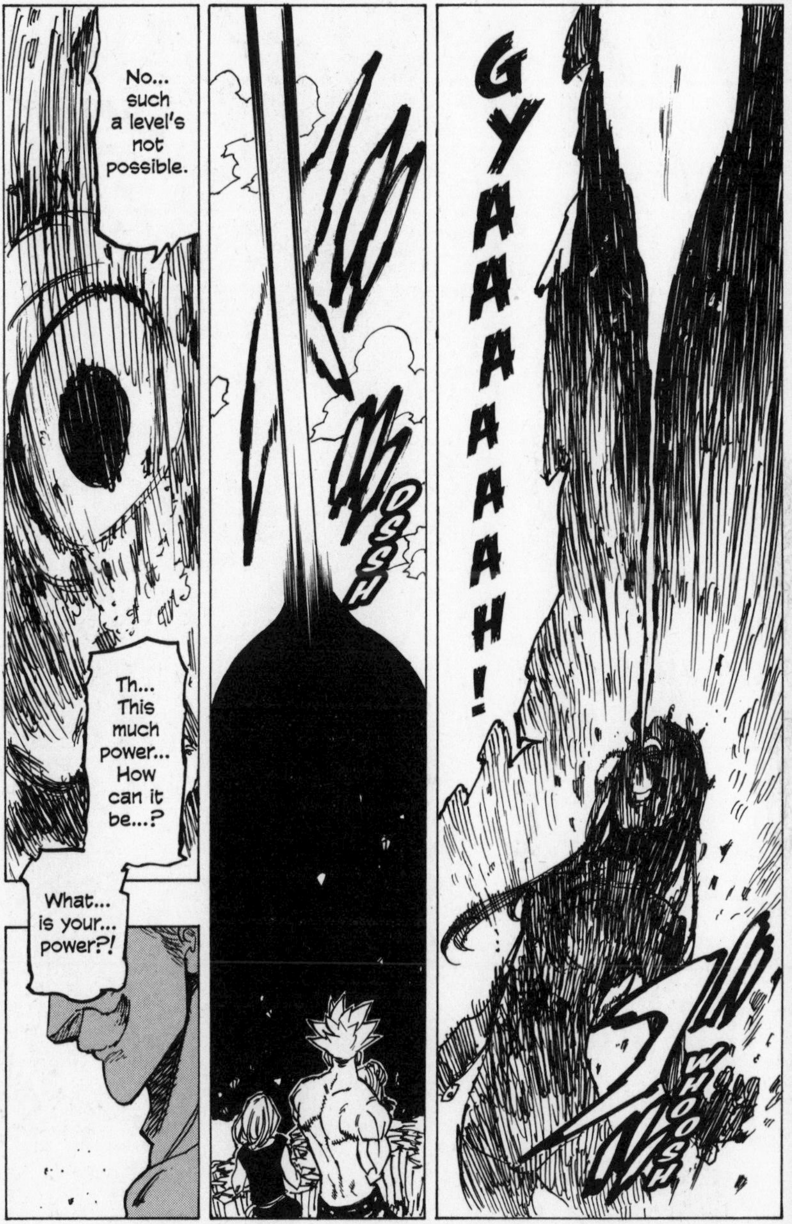
GYAAAAAAH!
WHOOSH
DOSSH
No... such a level's not possible.
Th... This much power... How can it be...?
What... is your... power?!

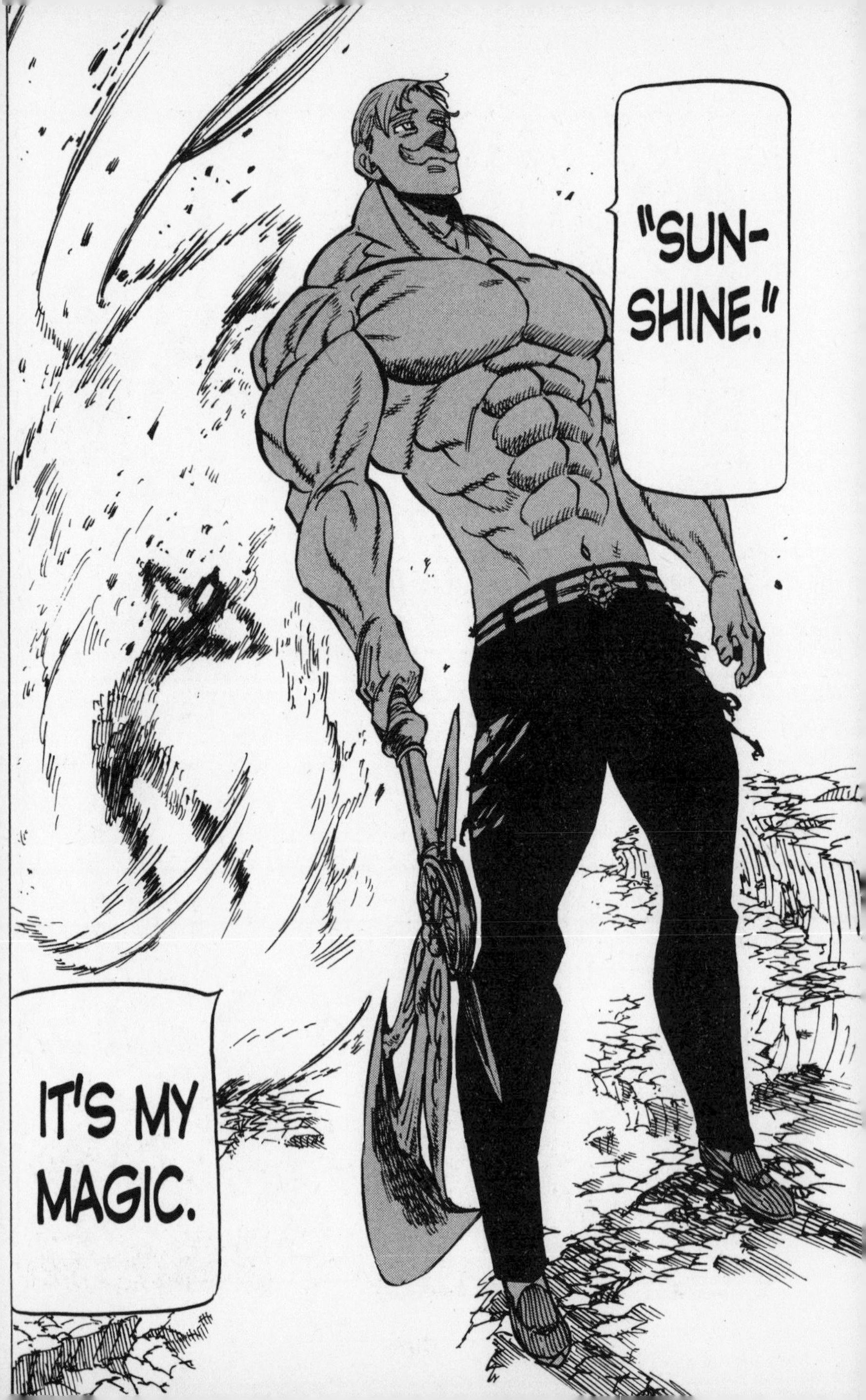
"SUN-SHINE."
IT'S MY MAGIC.

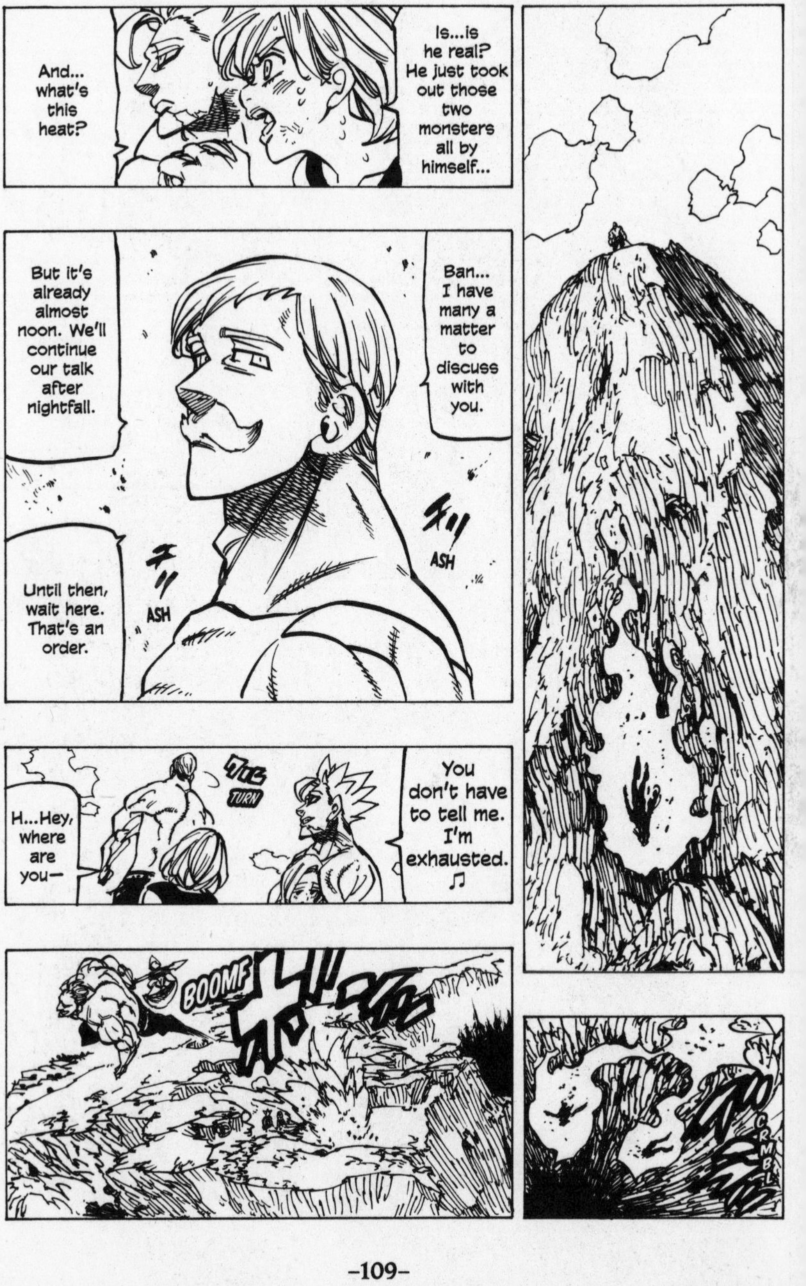
Is...is he real? He just took out those two monsters all by himself...
And... what's this heat?
Ban... I have many a matter to discuss with you.
But it's already almost noon. We'll continue our talk after nightfall.
ASH
ASH
Until then, wait here. That's an order.
You don't have to tell me. I'm exhausted. ♫
TURN
H...Hey, where are you—
CRMBL
BOOMF

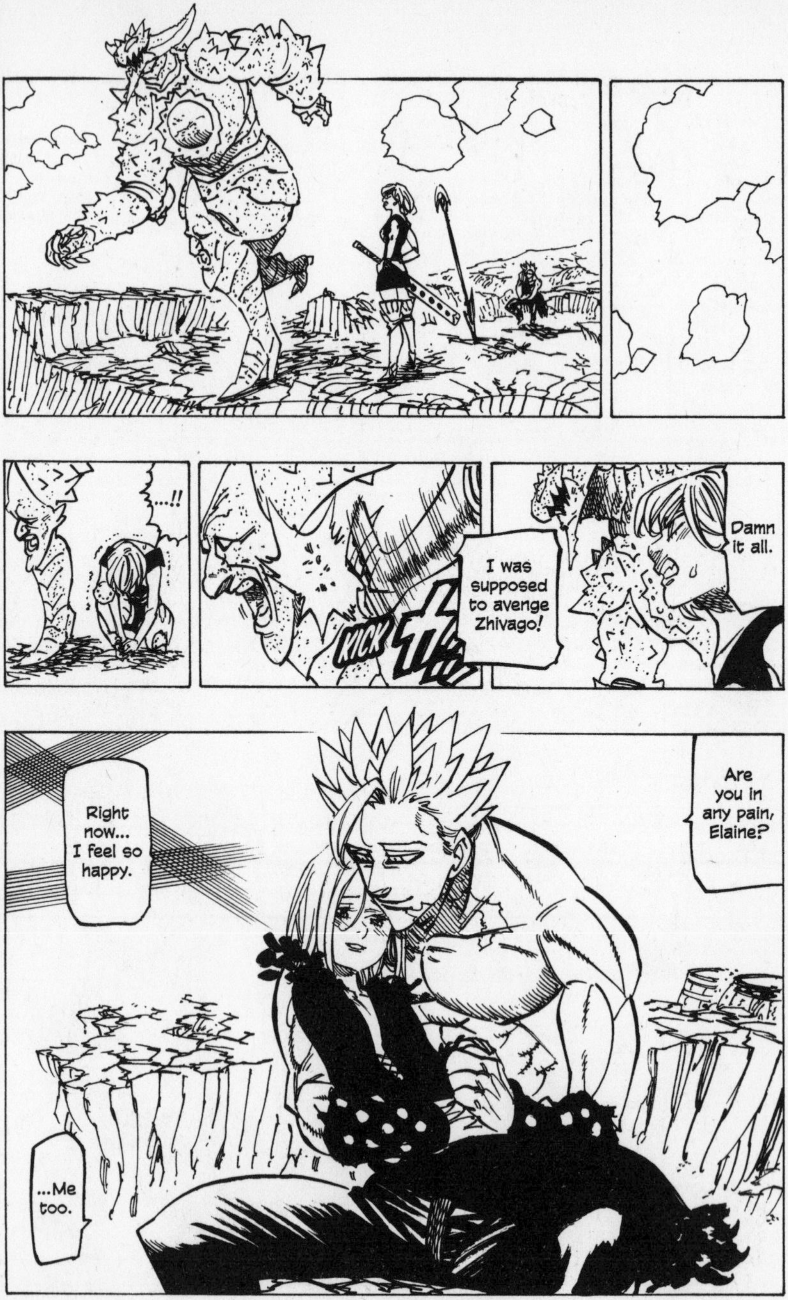
Damn it all.
I was supposed to avenge Zhivago!
KICK
...!!
Are you in any pain, Elaine?
Right now... I feel so happy.
...Me too.

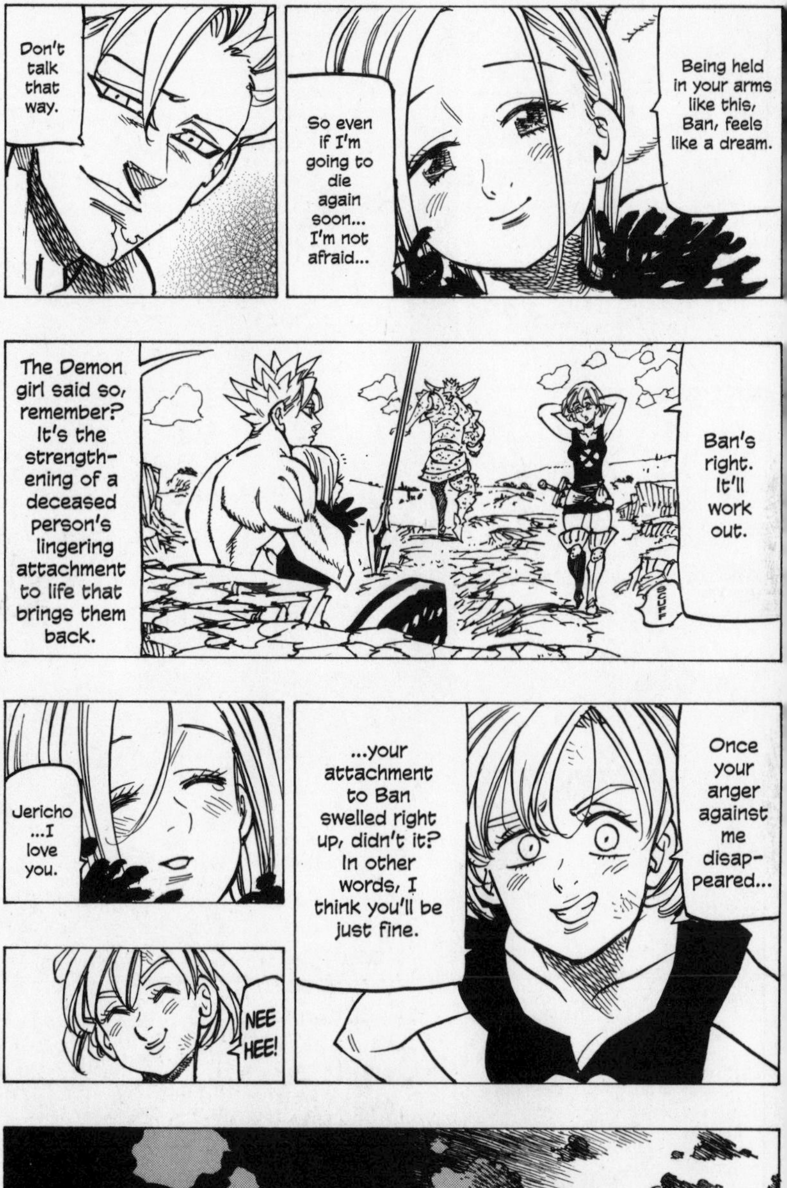
Being held in your arms like this, Ban, feels like a dream.
So even if I'm going to die again soon... I'm not afraid...
Don't talk that way.
Ban's right. It'll work out.
SCUFF
The Demon girl said so, remember? It's the strength-ening of a deceased person's lingering attachment to life that brings them back.
Once your anger against me disap-peared...
...your attachment to Ban swelled right up, didn't it? In other words, I think you'll be just fine.
Jericho ...I love you.
NEE HEE!

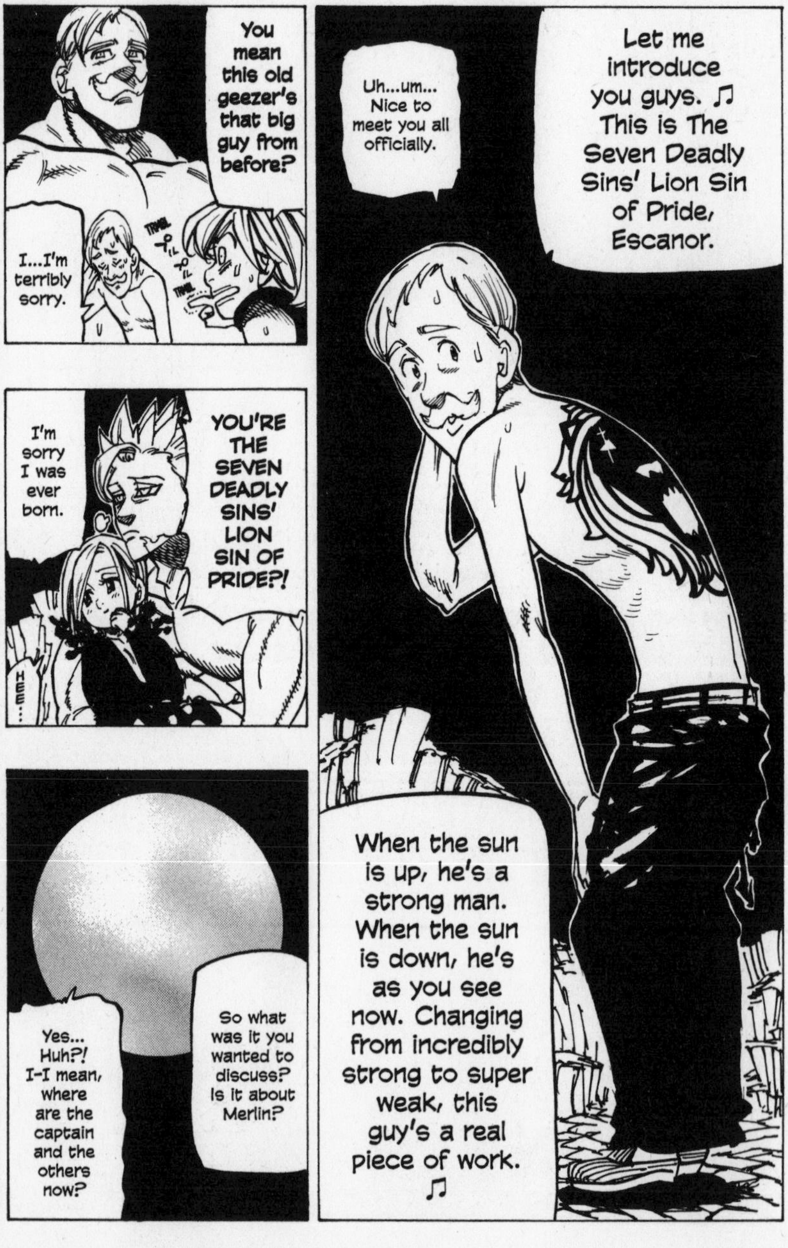
Let me introduce you guys. ♫ This is The Seven Deadly Sins' Lion Sin of Pride, Escanor.
Uh...um... Nice to meet you all officially.
When the sun is up, he's a strong man. When the sun is down, he's as you see now. Changing from incredibly strong to super weak, this guy's a real piece of work. ♫
You mean this old geezer's that big guy from before?
I...I'm terribly sorry.
YOU'RE THE SEVEN DEADLY SINS' LION SIN OF PRIDE?!
I'm sorry I was ever born.
HEE...
So what was it you wanted to discuss? Is it about Merlin?
Yes... Huh?! I-I mean, where are the captain and the others now?

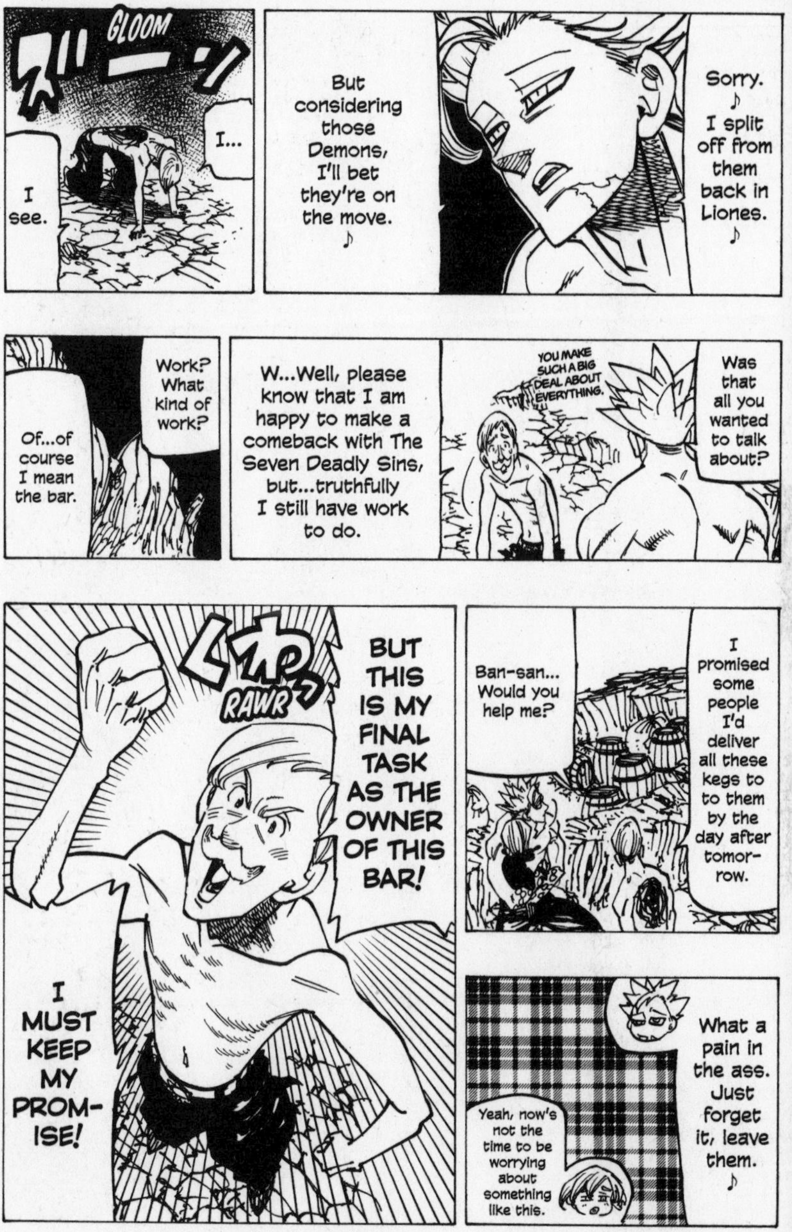

Sorry. ♪ I split off from them back in Liones. ♪
But considering those Demons, I'll bet they're on the move. ♪
GLOOM
I...
I see.
Was that all you wanted to talk about?
YOU MAKE SUCH A BIG DEAL ABOUT EVERYTHING.
W...Well, please know that I am happy to make a comeback with The Seven Deadly Sins, but...truthfully I still have work to do.
Work? What kind of work?
Of...of course I mean the bar.
I promised some people I'd deliver all these kegs to them by the day after tomor-row.
Ban-san... Would you help me?
What a pain in the ass. Just forget it, leave them. ♪
Yeah, now's not the time to be worrying about something like this.
RAWR
BUT THIS IS MY FINAL TASK AS THE OWNER OF THIS BAR!
I MUST KEEP MY PROM-ISE!

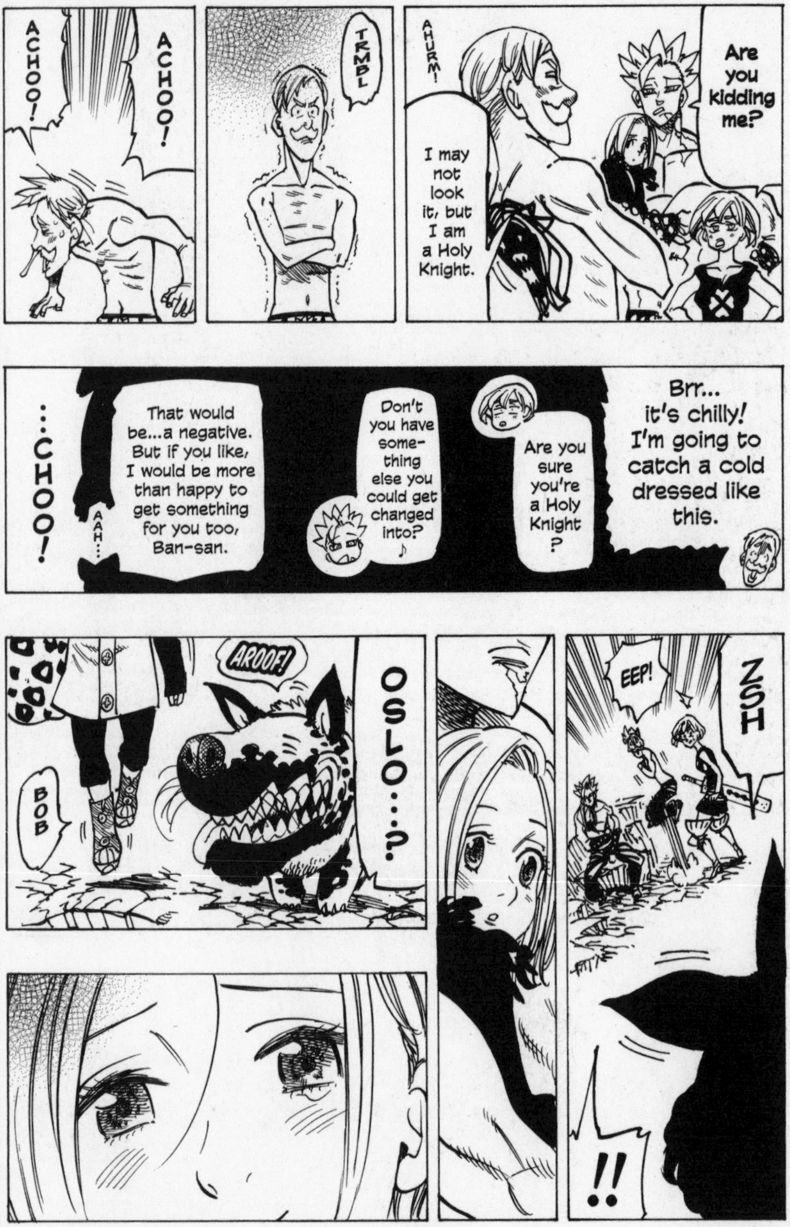
Are you kidding me?
AHURM!
I may not look it, but I am a Holy Knight.
TRMBL
ACHOO!
ACHOO!
Brr... it's chilly! I'm going to catch a cold dressed like this.
Are you sure you're a Holy Knight?
Don't you have something else you could get changed into? ♪
That would be...a negative. But if you like, I would be more than happy to get something for you too, Ban-san.
AAH...
...CHOO!
ZSH
EEP!
!!
OSLO...?
AROOF!
BOB

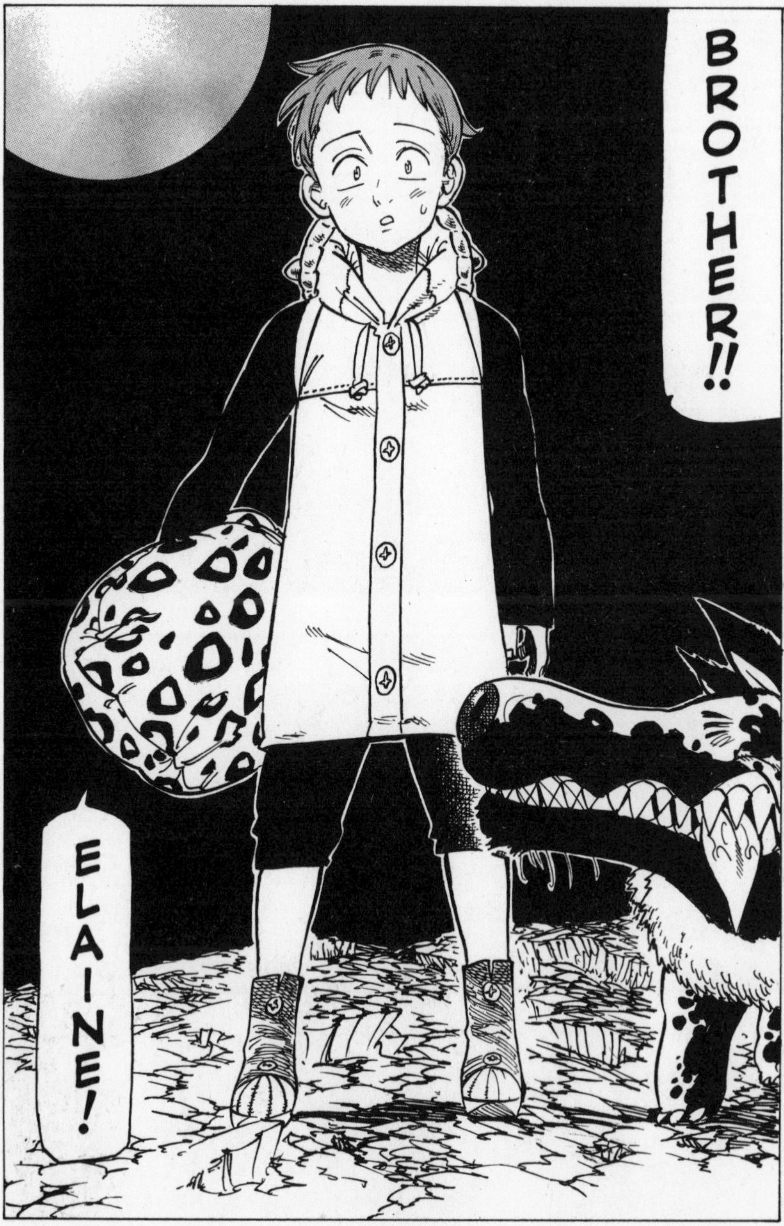
BROTHER!!
ELAINE!

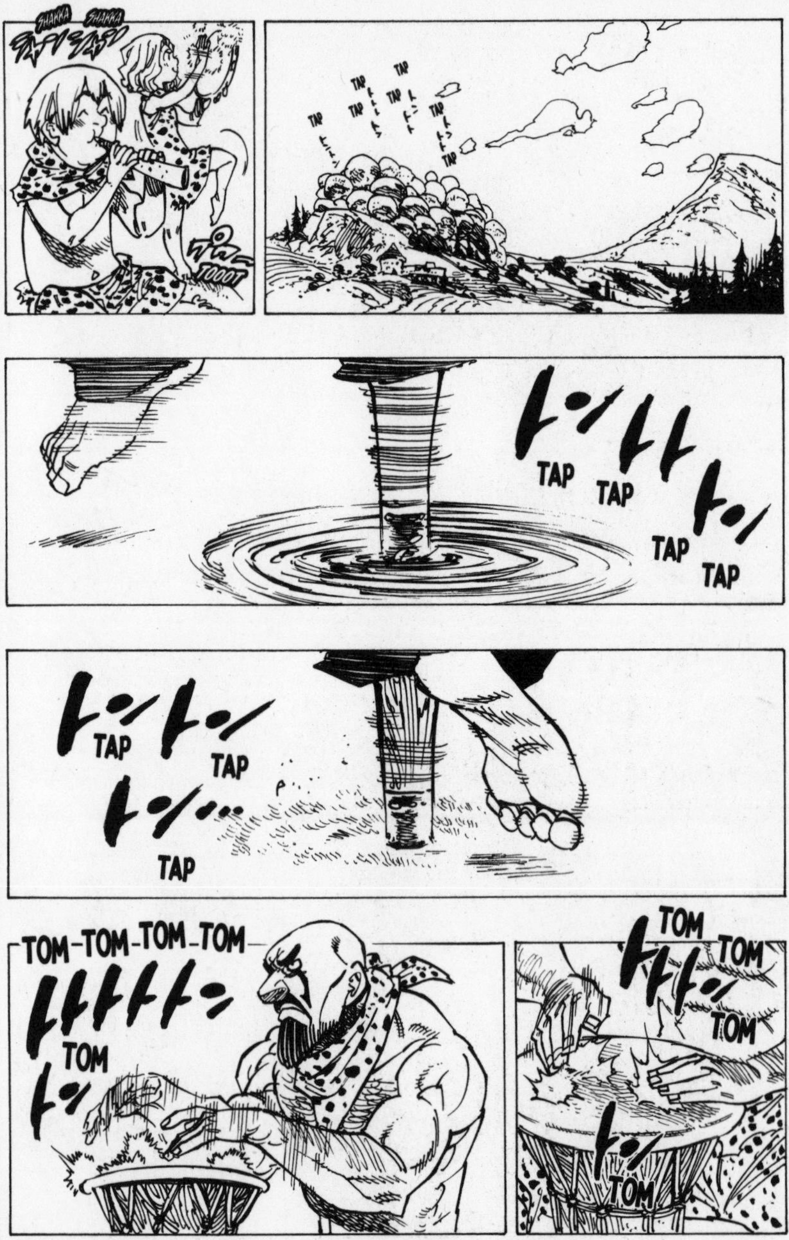
TAP
TAP
TAP
TAP
TAP
TAP
SHAKKA SHAKKA
TOOOT
TAP
TAP
TAP
TAP
TAP
TAP
TAP
TOM
TOM
TOM
TOM
TOM-TOM-TOM-TOM
TOM

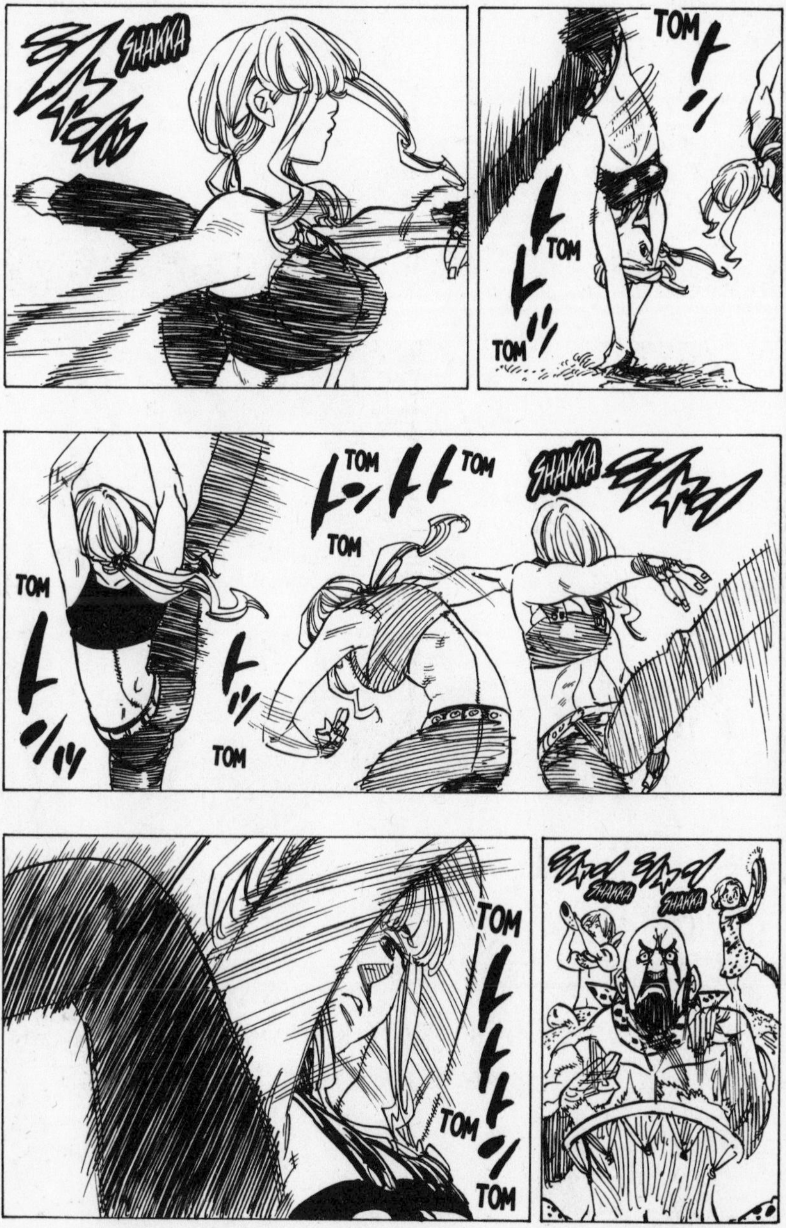
TOM
TOM
TOM
SHAKKA
SHAKKA
TOM
TOM
TOM
TOM
TOM
SHAKKA
SHAKKA
TOM
TOM
TOM

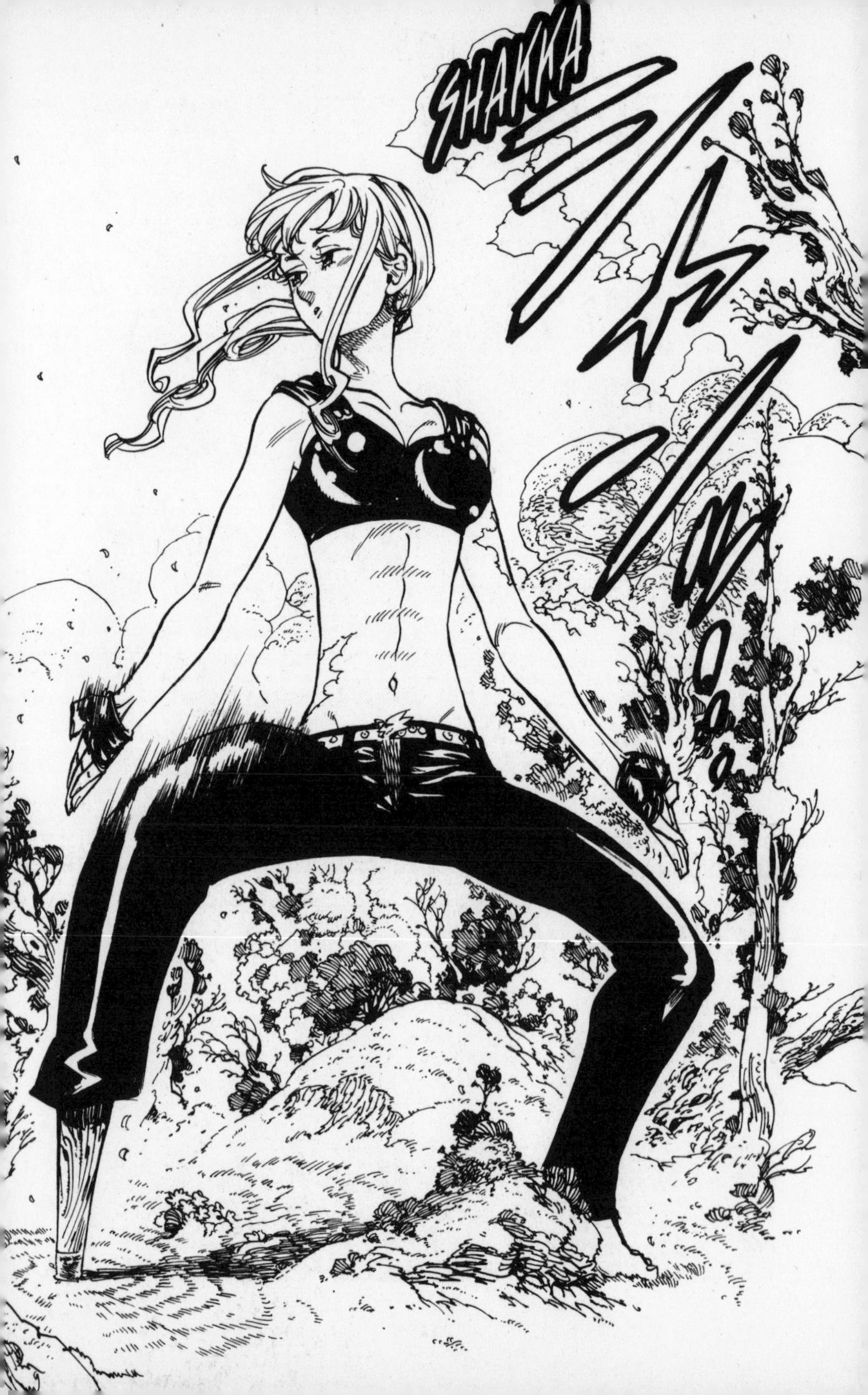
SHAKKA

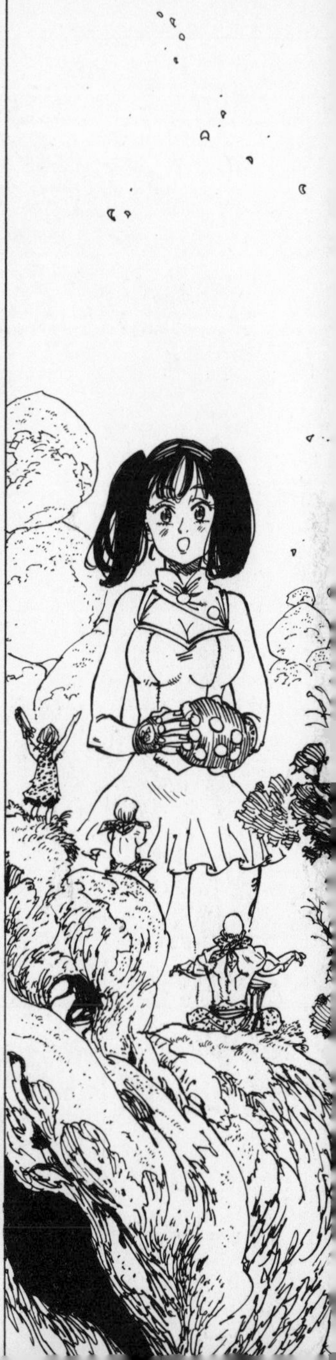

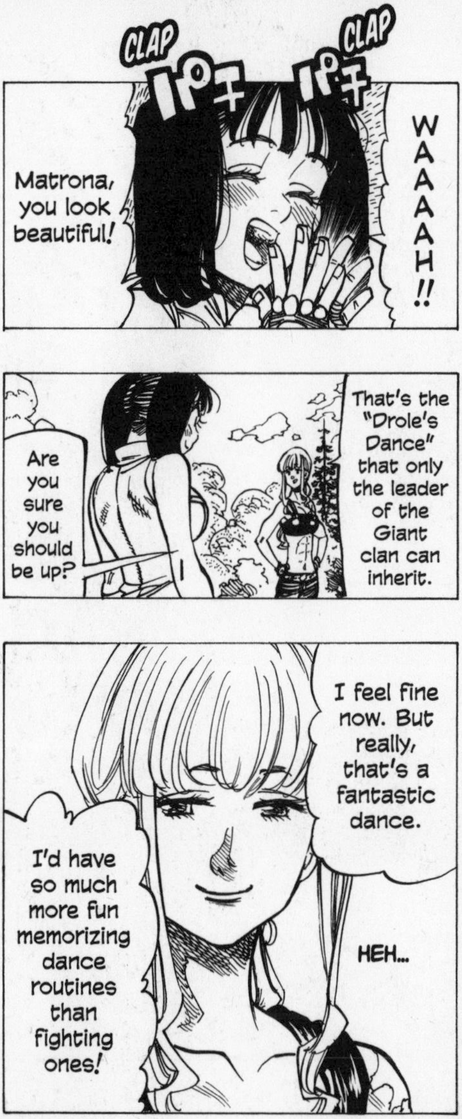
CLAP
パチ
CLAP
パチ
WAAAAAH!!
Matrona, you look beautiful!
That's the "Drole's Dance" that only the leader of the Giant clan can inherit.
Are you sure you should be up?
I feel fine now. But really, that's a fantastic dance.
HEH...
I'd have so much more fun memorizing dance routines than fighting ones!
Very well. Then you are no longer a warrior.

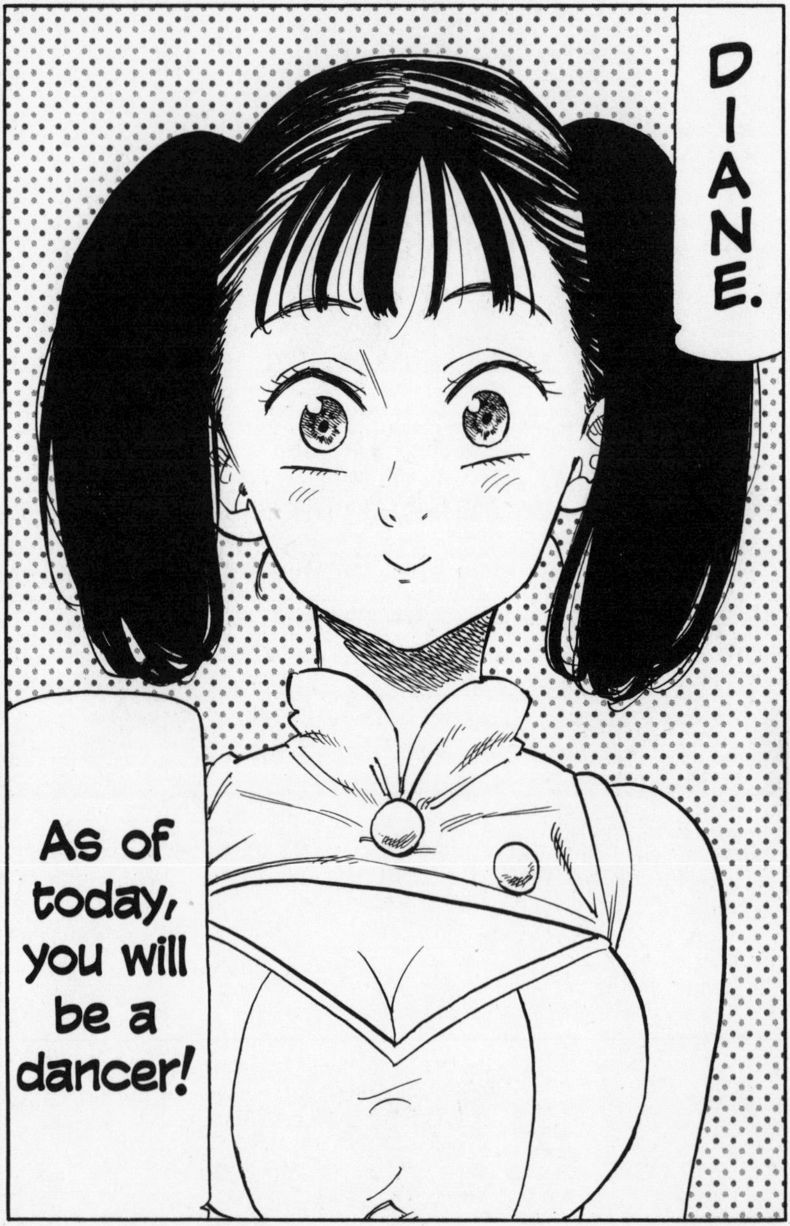
DIANE.
As of today, you will be a dancer!

Chapter 151 - The Stage Awaits Us

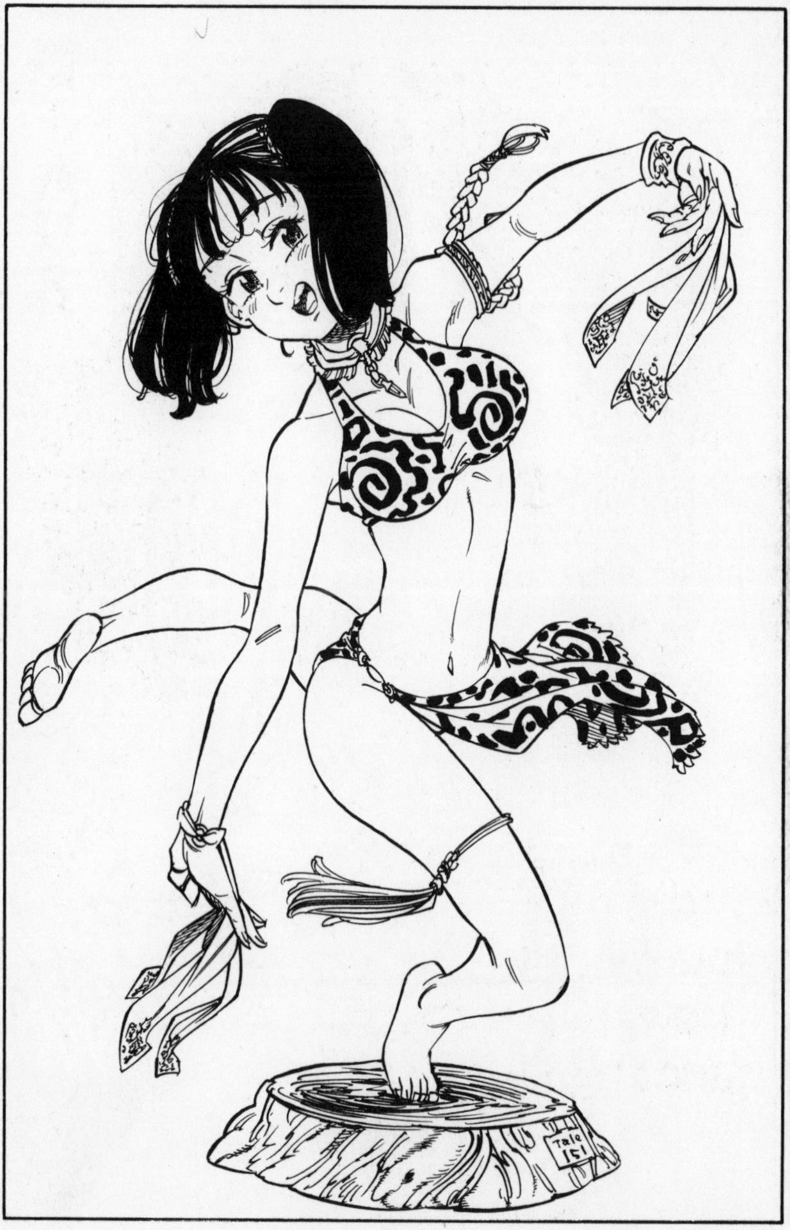
Tale 151

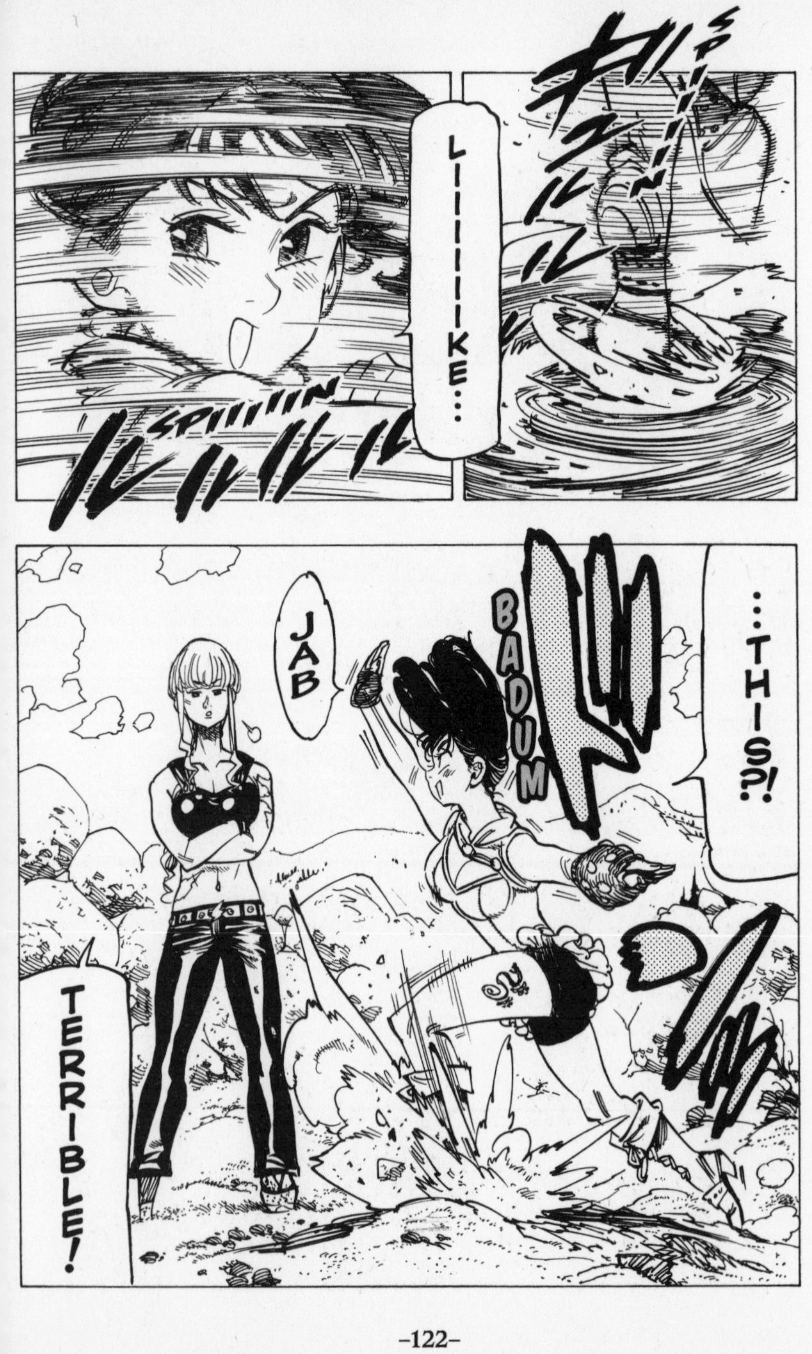
SPIIIIIIN
LIIIIIIIKE...
SPIIIIIIN
...THIS?!
BADUM
JAB
TERRIBLE!

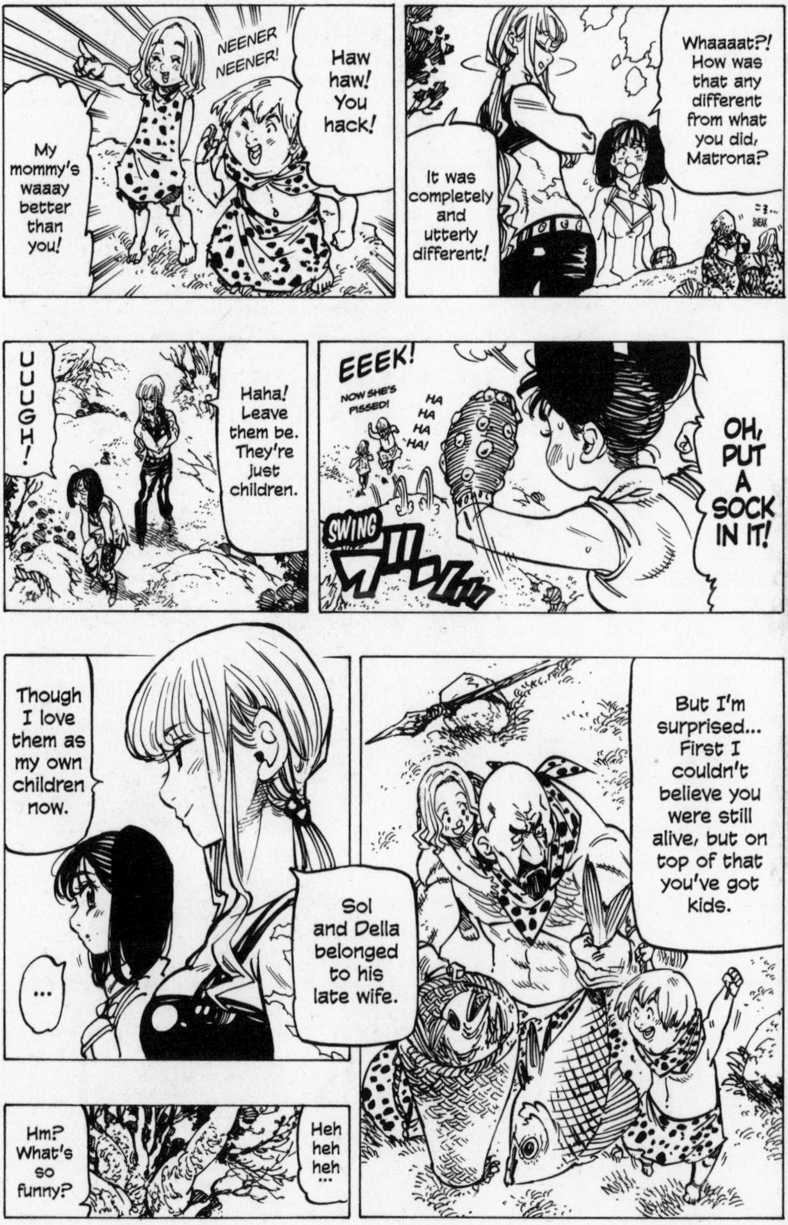

Whaaaat?! How was that any different from what you did, Matrona?
It was completely and utterly different!
SNEAK
Haw haw! You hack!
NEENER NEENER!
My mommy's waaay better than you!
OH, PUT A SOCK IN IT!
EEEK!
NOW SHE'S PISSED!
HA HA HA HA!
SWING
Haha! Leave them be. They're just children.
UUUGH!
But I'm surprised... First I couldn't believe you were still alive, but on top of that you've got kids.
Sol and Della belonged to his late wife.
Though I love them as my own children now.
...
Heh heh heh...
Hm? What's so funny?

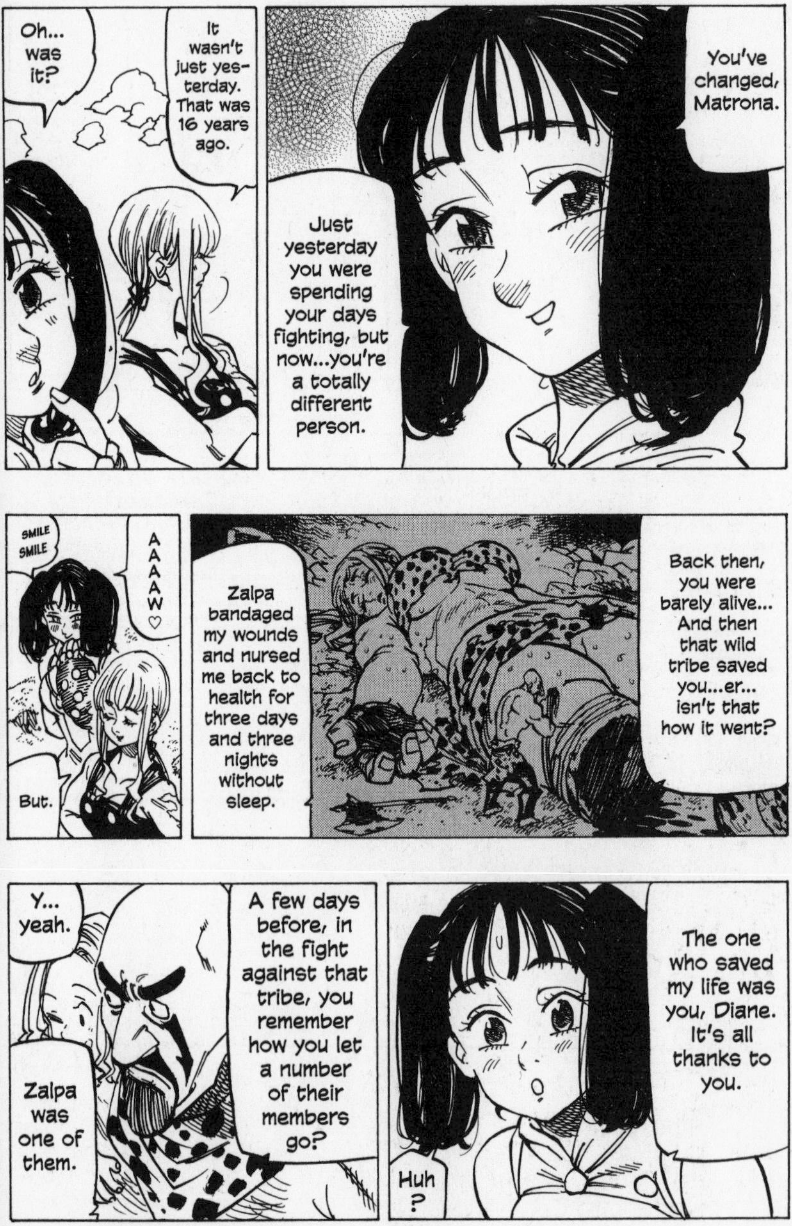
You've changed, Matrona.
Just yesterday you were spending your days fighting, but now...you're a totally different person.
It wasn't just yesterday. That was 16 years ago.
Oh... was it?
Back then, you were barely alive... And then that wild tribe saved you...er... isn't that how it went?
Zalpa bandaged my wounds and nursed me back to health for three days and three nights without sleep.
AAAAW♡
SMILE SMILE
But.
The one who saved my life was you, Diane. It's all thanks to you.
Huh?
A few days before, in the fight against that tribe, you remember how you let a number of their members go?
Y... yeah.
Zalpa was one of them.

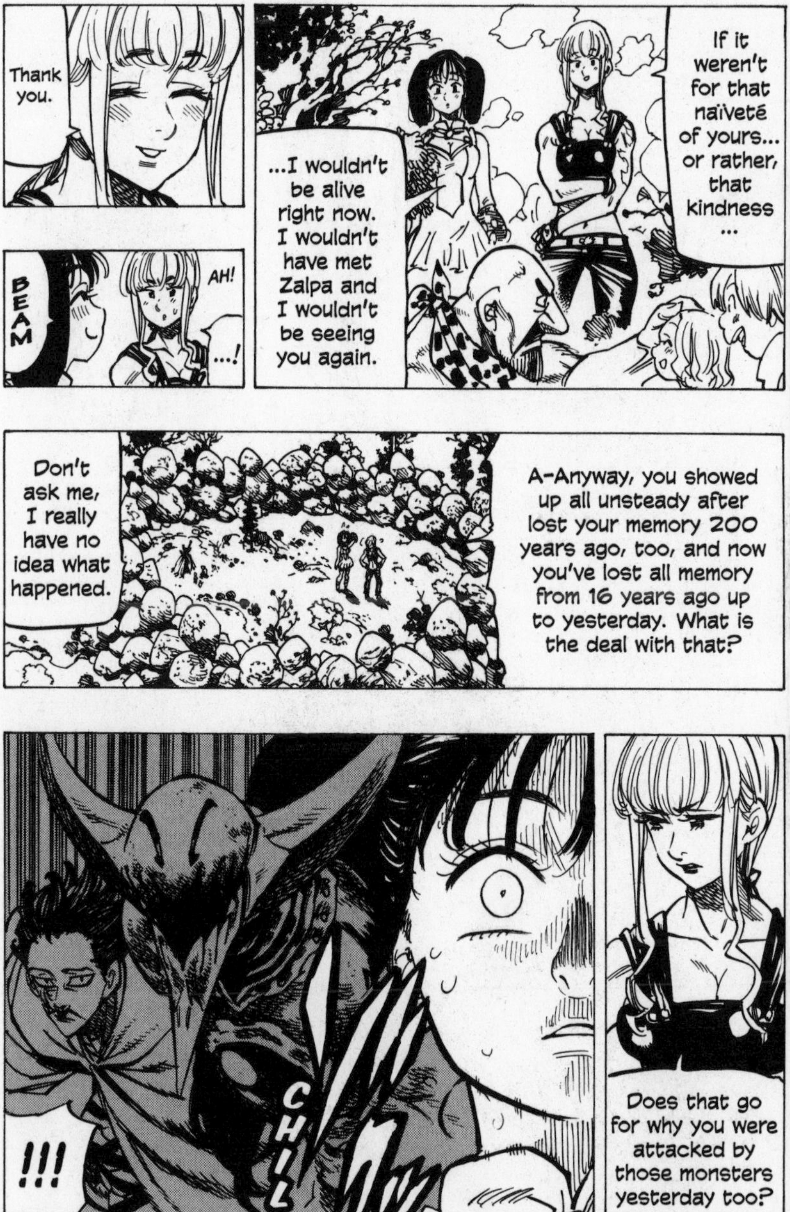
If it weren't for that naïveté of yours... or rather, that kindness ...
...I wouldn't be alive right now. I wouldn't have met Zalpa and I wouldn't be seeing you again.
Thank you.
AH!
BEAM
...!
A-Anyway, you showed up all unsteady after lost your memory 200 years ago, too, and now you've lost all memory from 16 years ago up to yesterday. What is the deal with that?
Don't ask me, I really have no idea what happened.
Does that go for why you were attacked by those monsters yesterday too?
CHILL
!!!

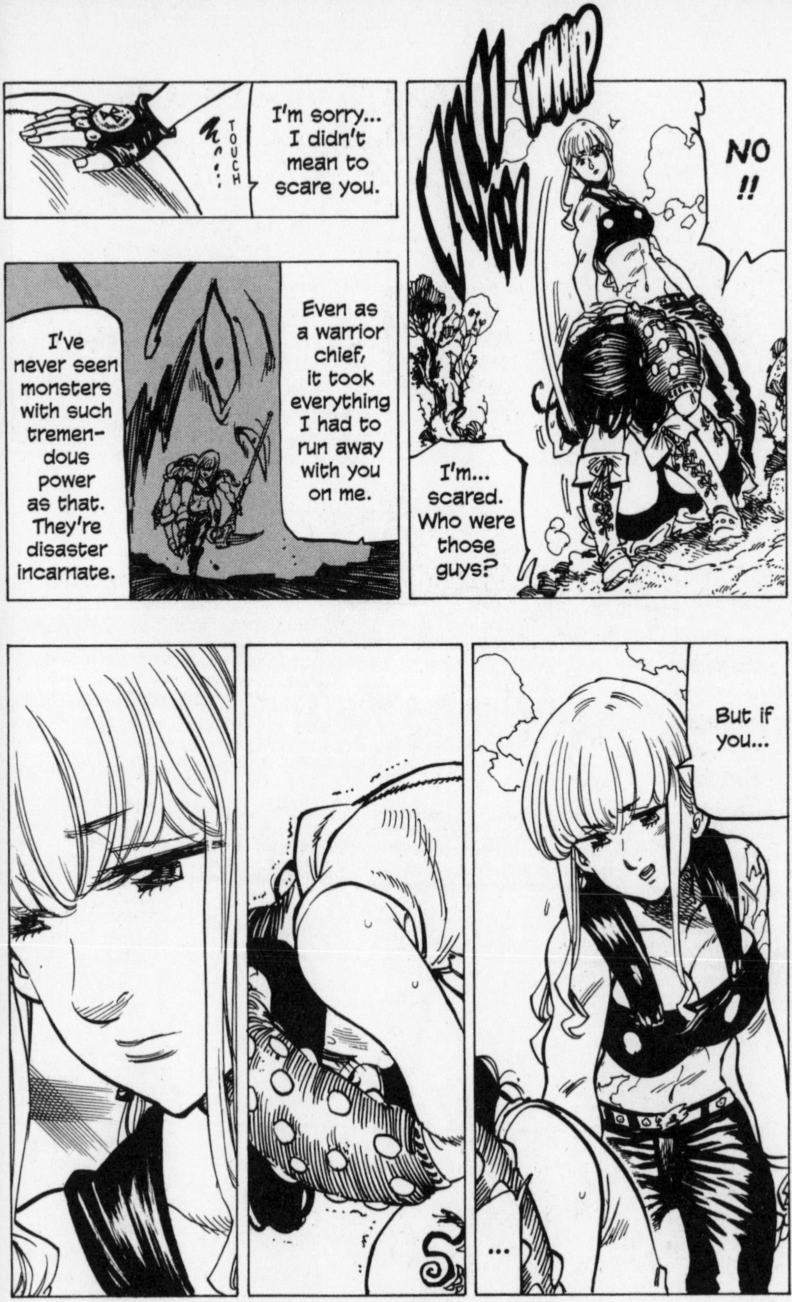
NO!!
WHIP
I'm... scared. Who were those guys?
I'm sorry... I didn't mean to scare you.
TOUCH
Even as a warrior chief, it took everything I had to run away with you on me.
I've never seen monsters with such tremendous power as that. They're disaster incarnate.
But if you...
...

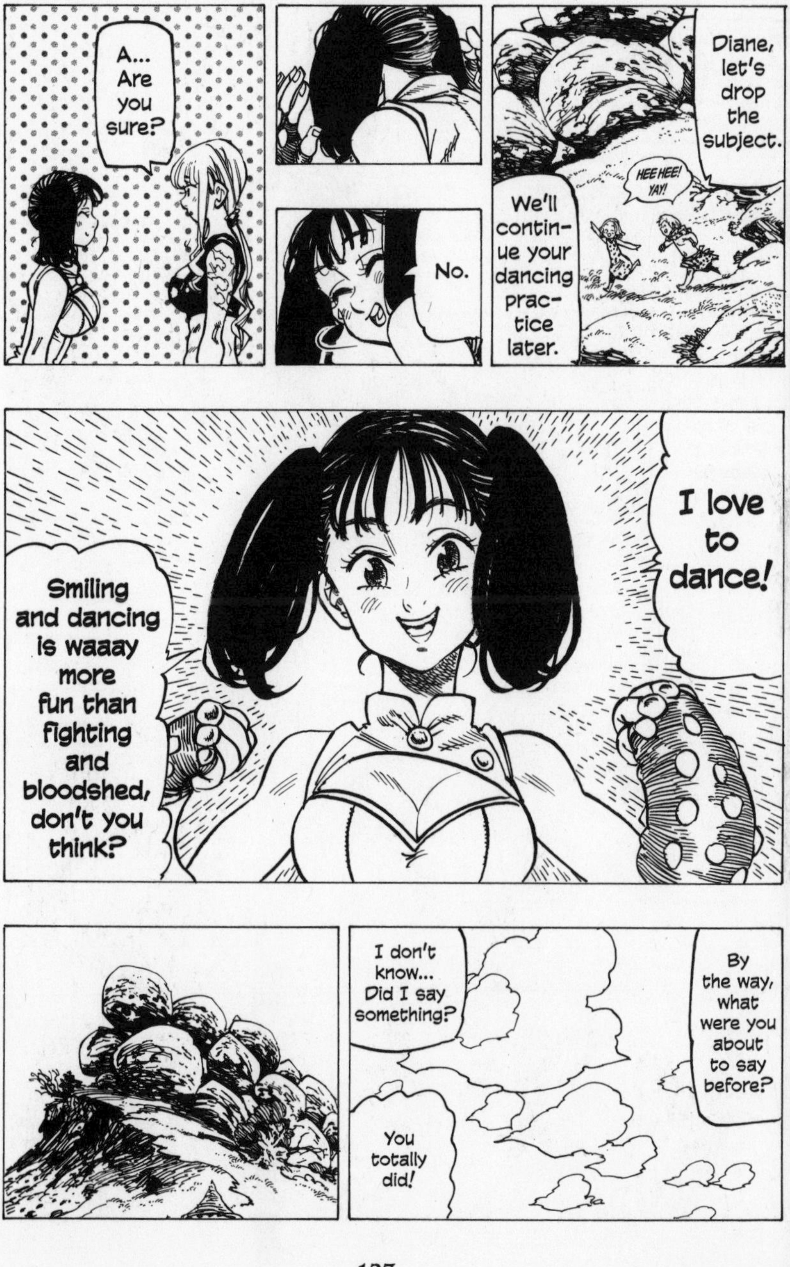
Diane, let's drop the subject.
HEE HEE! YAY!
We'll continue your dancing practice later.
No.
A... Are you sure?
I love to dance!
Smiling and dancing is waaay more fun than fighting and bloodshed, don't you think?
By the way, what were you about to say before?
I don't know... Did I say something?
You totally did!

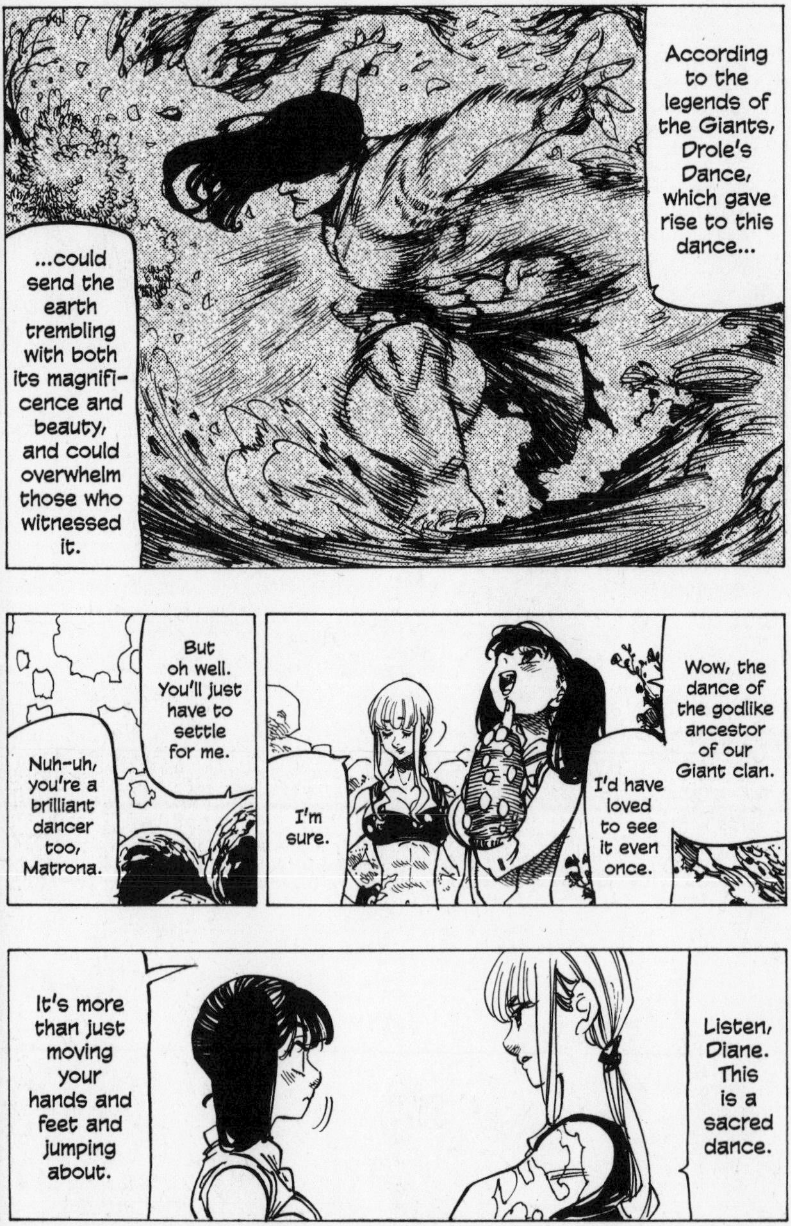
According to the legends of the Giants, Drole's Dance, which gave rise to this dance...
...could send the earth trembling with both its magnificence and beauty, and could overwhelm those who witnessed it.
Wow, the dance of the godlike ancestor of our Giant clan.
I'd have loved to see it even once.
I'm sure.
But oh well. You'll just have to settle for me.
Nuh-uh, you're a brilliant dancer too, Matrona.
Listen, Diane. This is a sacred dance.
It's more than just moving your hands and feet and jumping about.

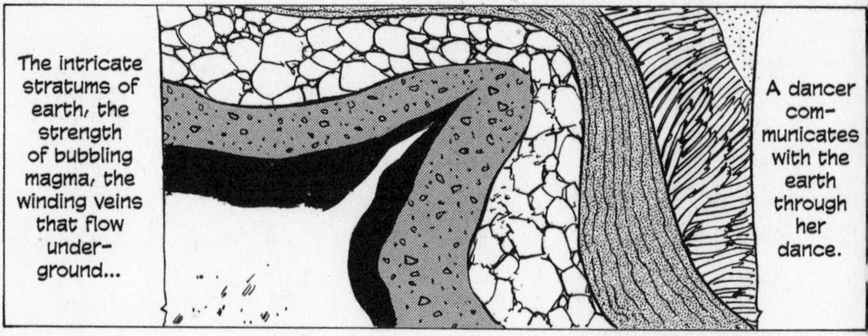
A dancer communicates with the earth through her dance.
The intricate stratums of earth, the strength of bubbling magma, the winding veins that flow underground...

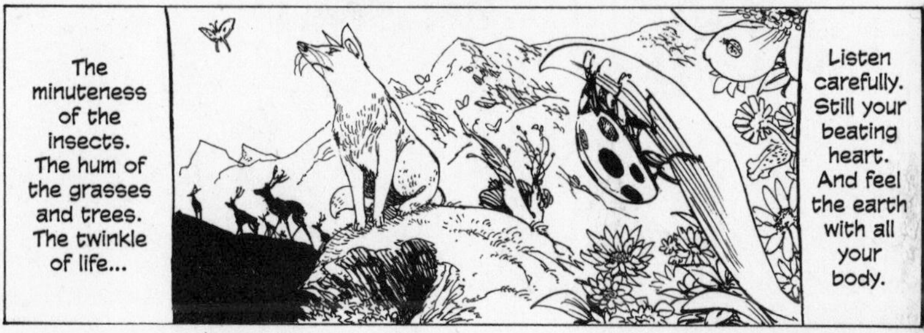
Listen carefully. Still your beating heart. And feel the earth with all your body.
The minuteness of the insects. The hum of the grasses and trees. The twinkle of life...

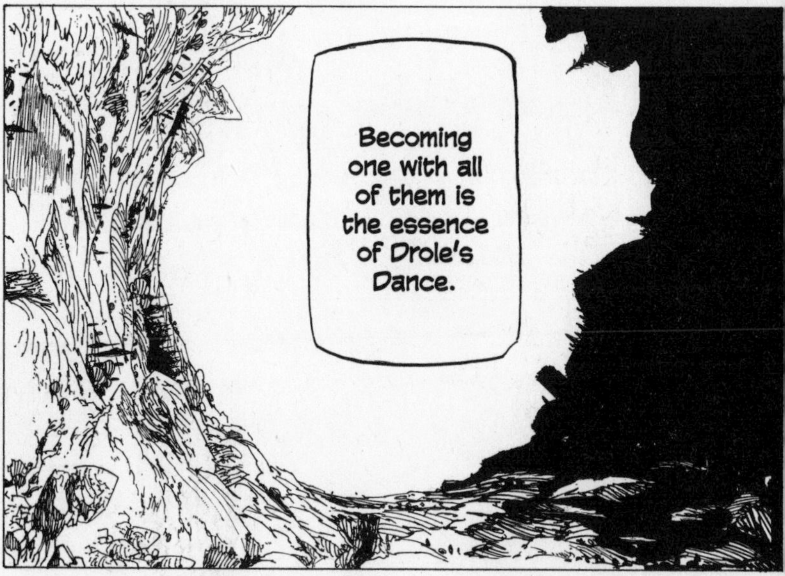
Becoming one with all of them is the essence of Drole's Dance.

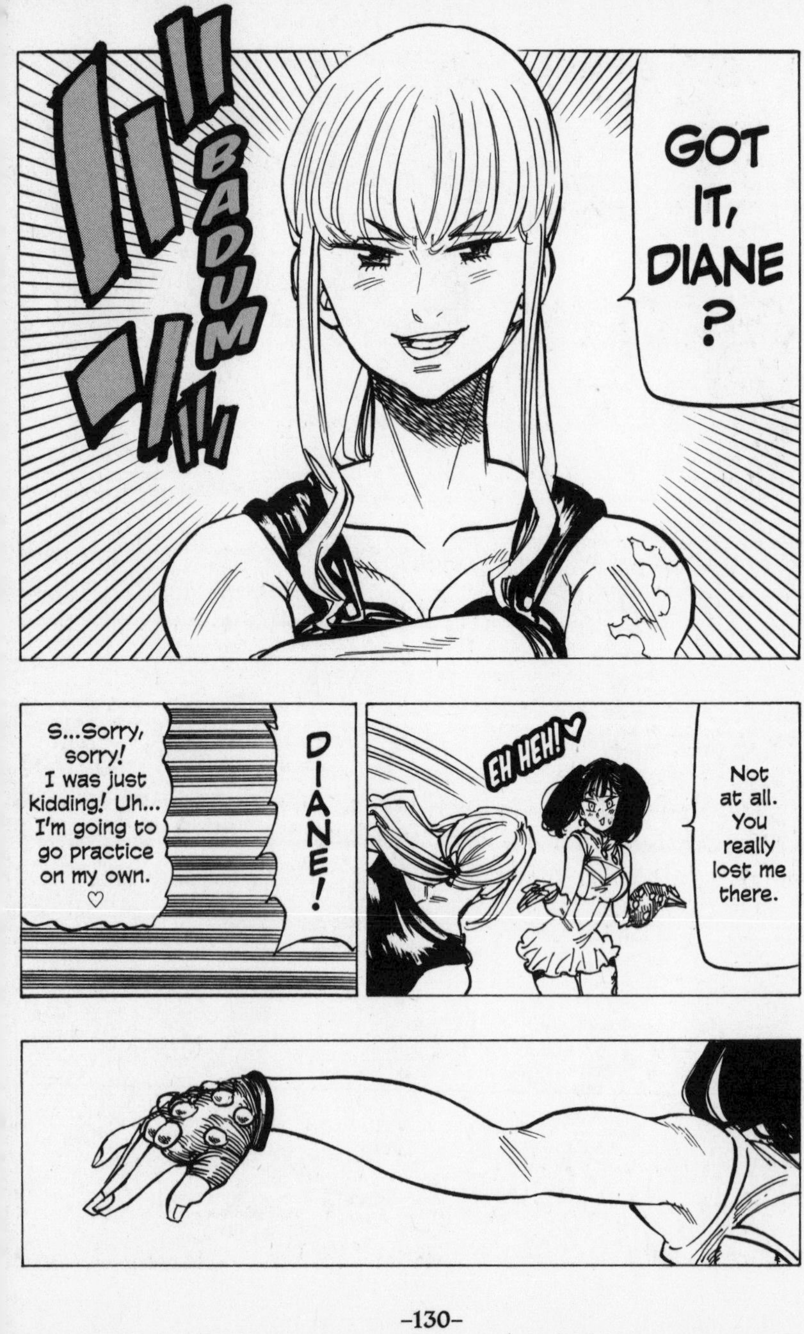
GOT IT, DIANE?
BADUM
Not at all. You really lost me there.
EH HEH!♡
DIANE!
S...Sorry, sorry! I was just kidding! Uh... I'm going to go practice on my own. ♡

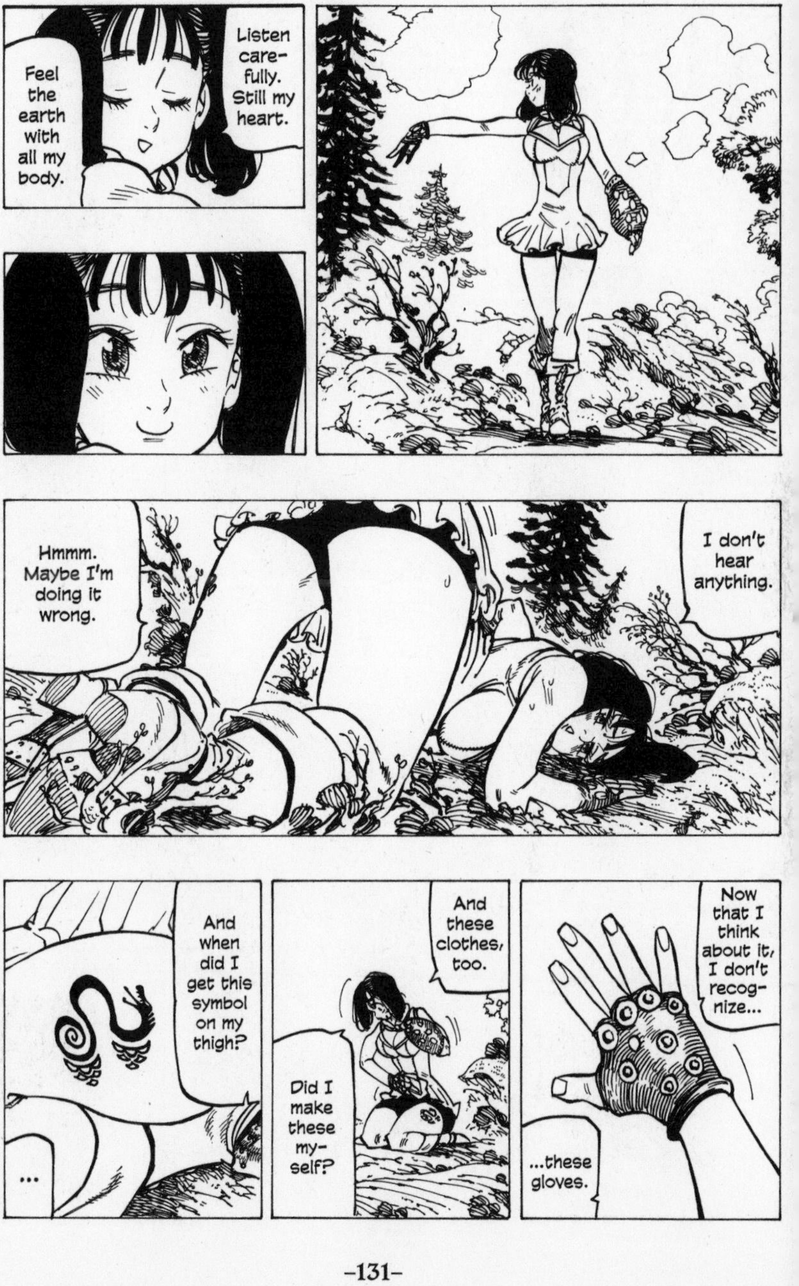
Listen care-fully. Still my heart.
Feel the earth with all my body.
I don't hear anything.
Hmmm. Maybe I'm doing it wrong.
Now that I think about it, I don't recog-nize...
...these gloves.
And these clothes, too.
Did I make these my-self?
And when did I get this symbol on my thigh?
...

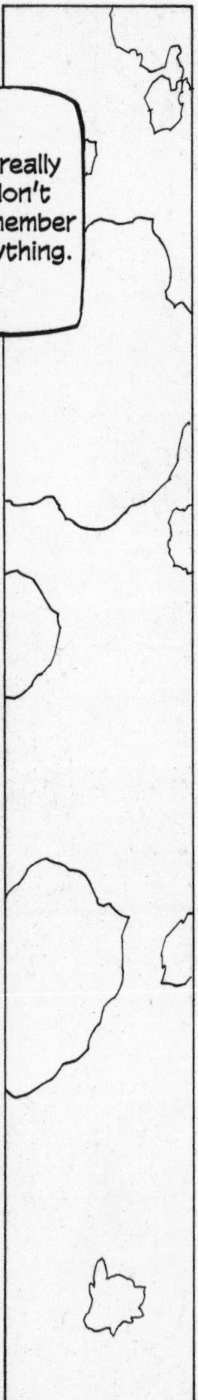

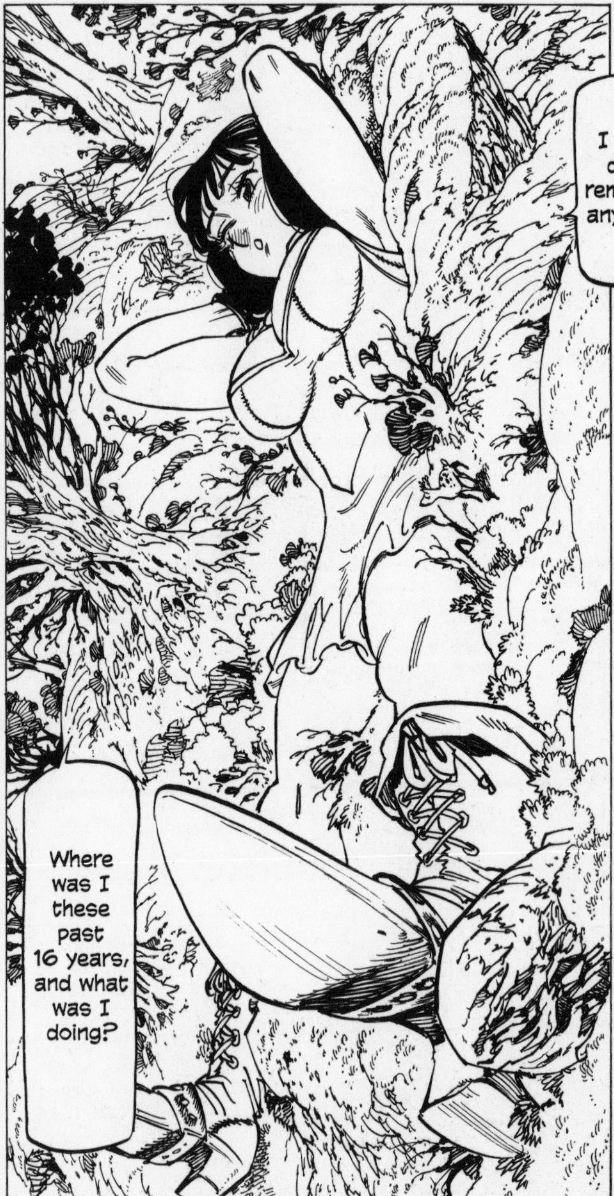
I really don't remember anything.
Where was I these past 16 years, and what was I doing?

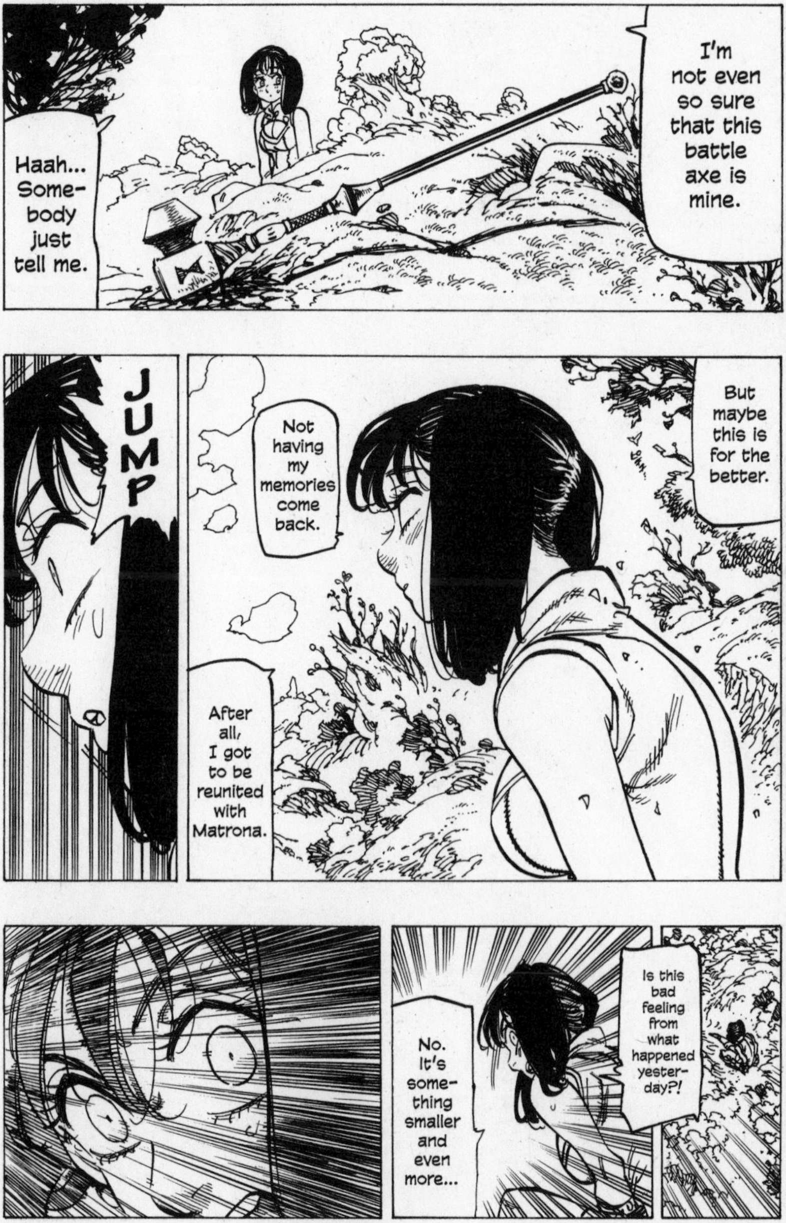
I'm not even so sure that this battle axe is mine.
Haah... Some-body just tell me.
But maybe this is for the better.
Not having my memories come back.
After all, I got to be reunited with Matrona.
JUMP
Is this bad feeling from what happened yester-day?!
No. It's some-thing smaller and even more...

FLAP

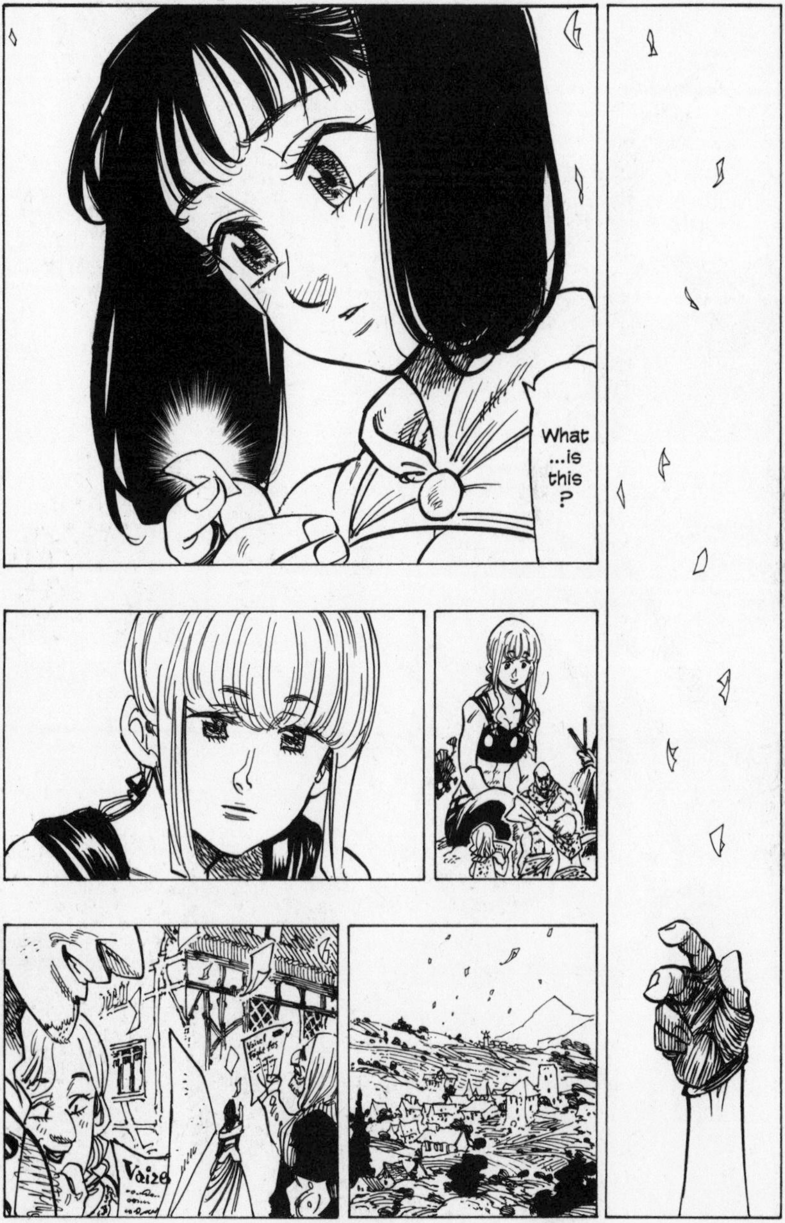
What ...is this ?
Vaize

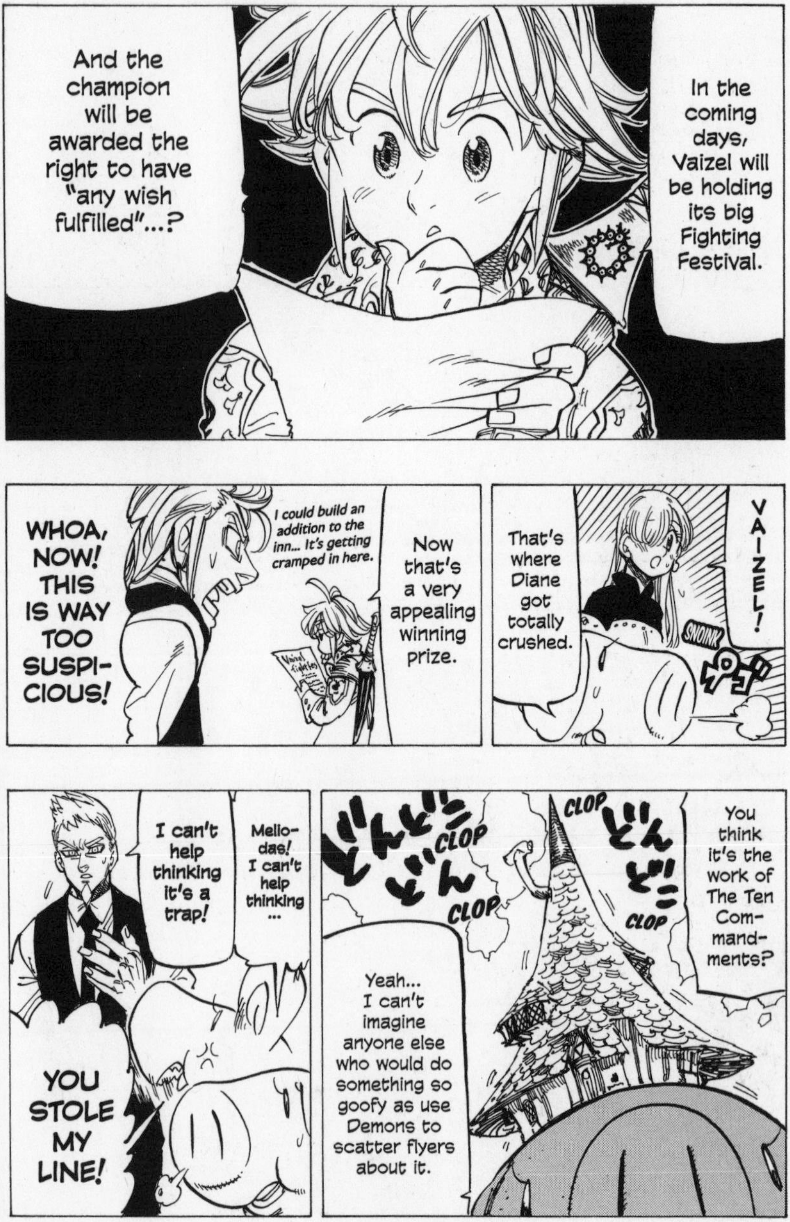
In the coming days, Vaizel will be holding its big Fighting Festival.
And the champion will be awarded the right to have "any wish fulfilled"...?
VAIZEL!
That's where Diane got totally crushed.
SNOINK
Now that's a very appealing winning prize.
I could build an addition to the inn... It's getting cramped in here.
WHOA, NOW! THIS IS WAY TOO SUSPICIOUS!
You think it's the work of The Ten Commandments?
CLOP
CLOP
CLOP
CLOP
Yeah... I can't imagine anyone else who would do something so goofy as use Demons to scatter flyers about it.
Meliodas! I can't help thinking ...
I can't help thinking it's a trap!
YOU STOLE MY LINE!

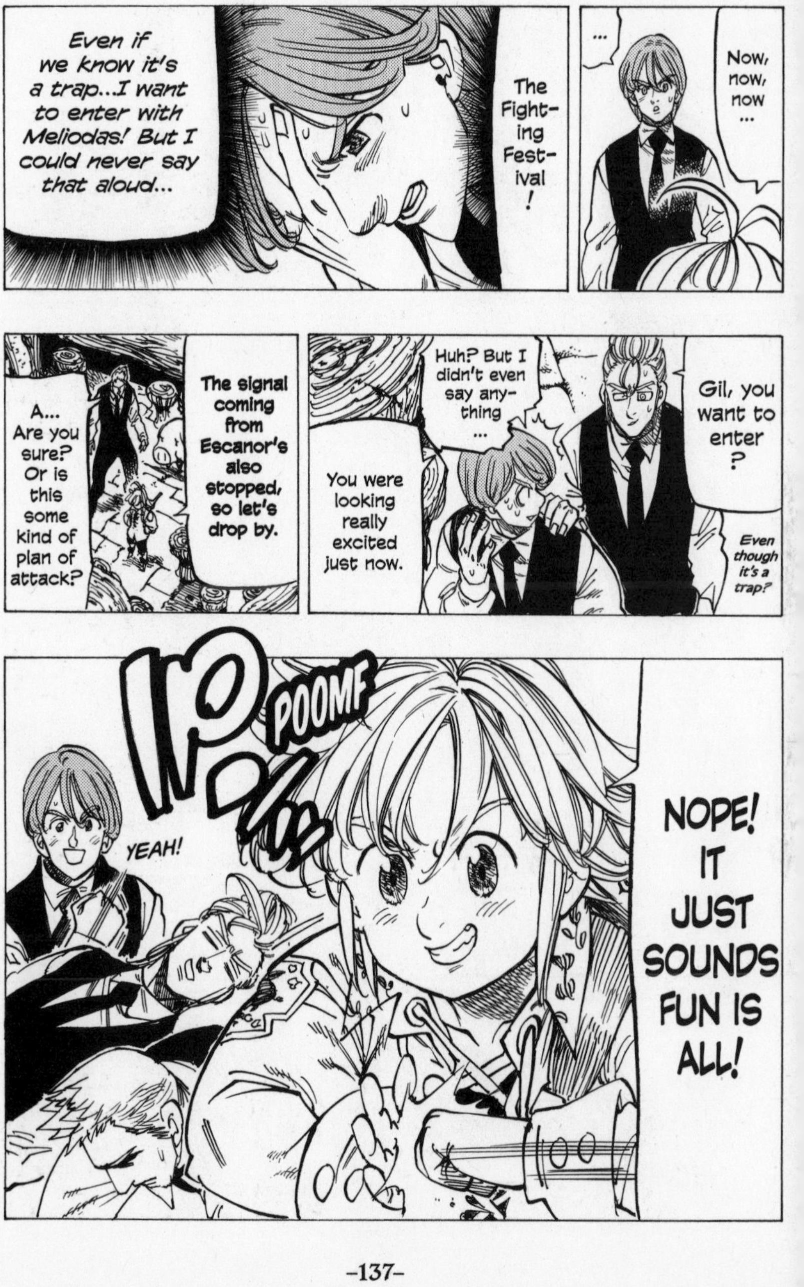

Now, now, now...
...
The Fighting-Festival!
Even if we know it's a trap...I want to enter with Meliodas! But I could never say that aloud...
Gil, you want to enter?
Huh? But I didn't even say anything...
Even though it's a trap?
You were looking really excited just now.
The signal coming from Escanor's also stopped, so let's drop by.
A... Are you sure? Or is this some kind of plan of attack?
NOPE! IT JUST SOUNDS FUN IS ALL!
POOMF
YEAH!

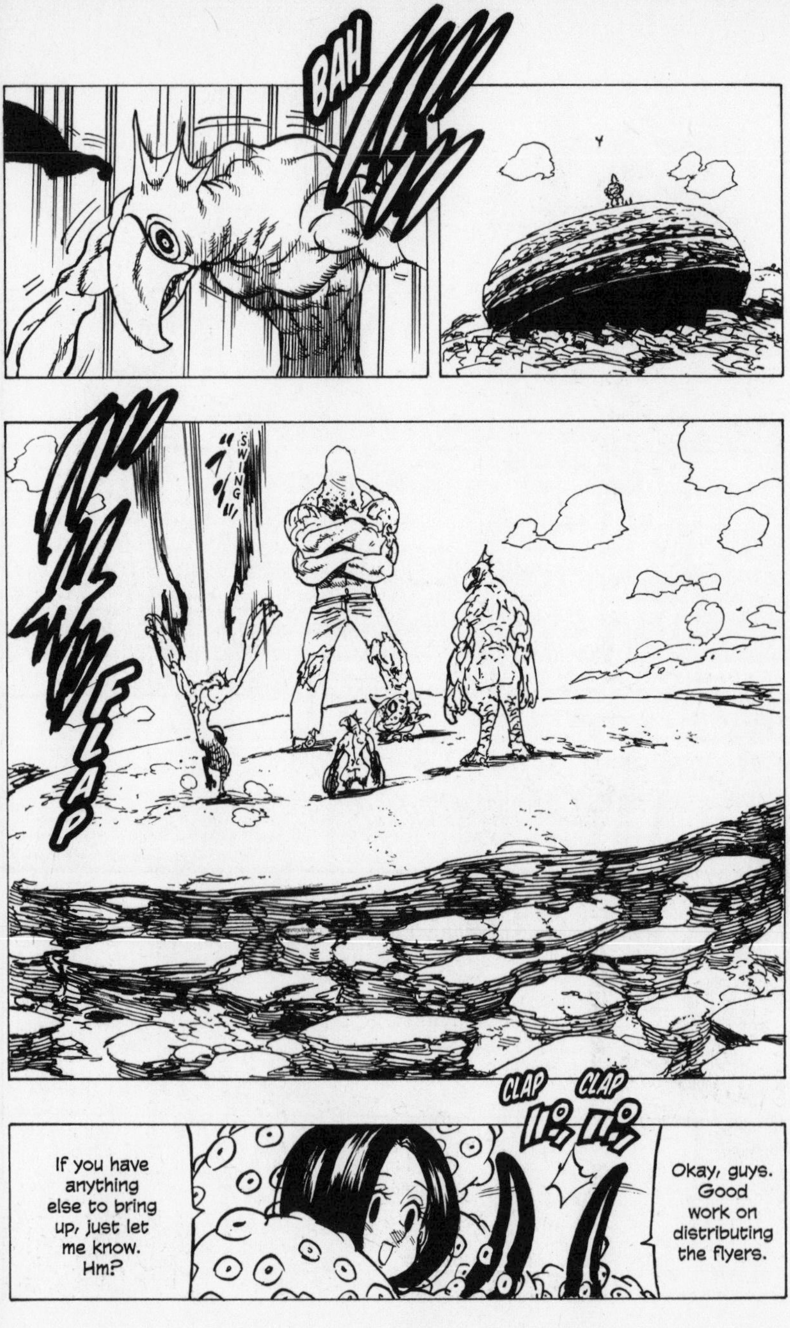
BAH
SWING
FLAP
CLAP CLAP
Okay, guys. Good work on distributing the flyers.
If you have anything else to bring up, just let me know. Hm?

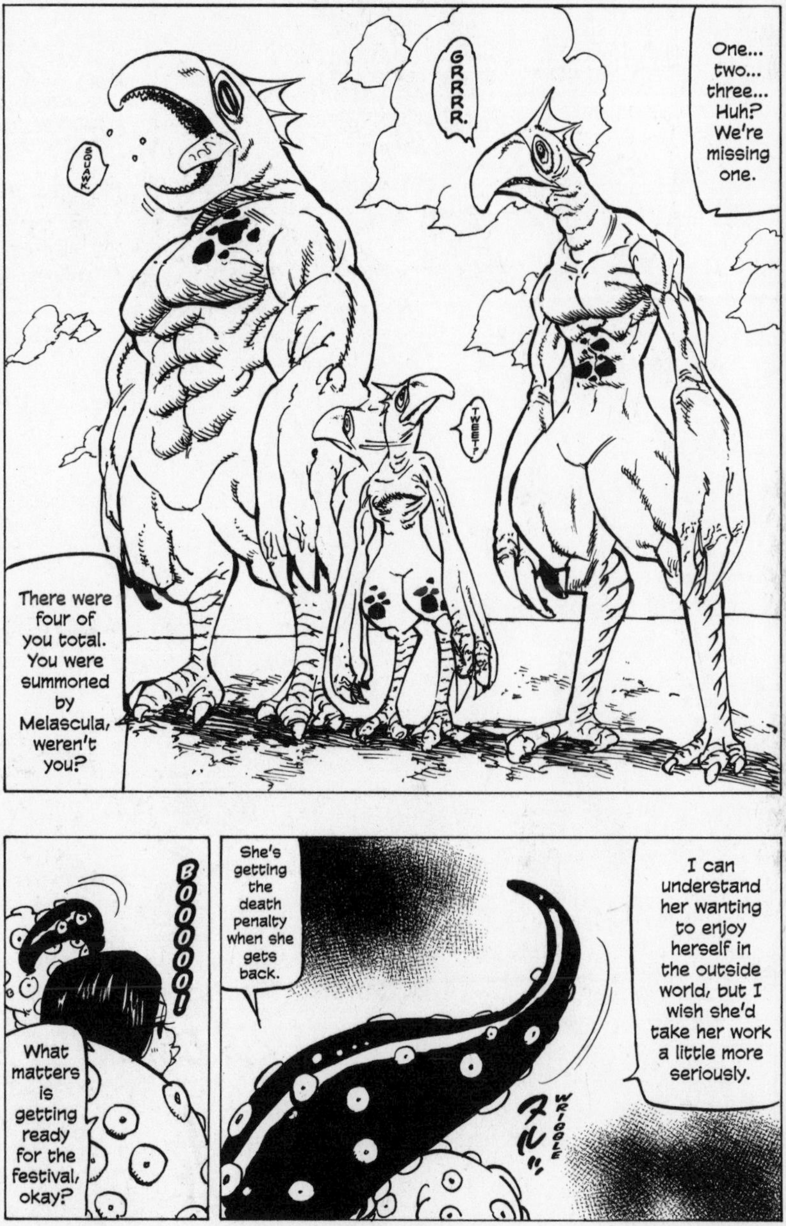
One... two... three... Huh? We're missing one.
GRRRR.
SQUAWK
TWEET?
There were four of you total. You were summoned by Melascula, weren't you?
I can understand her wanting to enjoy herself in the outside world, but I wish she'd take her work a little more seriously.
She's getting the death penalty when she gets back.
WRIGGLE
フル!!
BOOOOOO!
What matters is getting ready for the festival, okay?

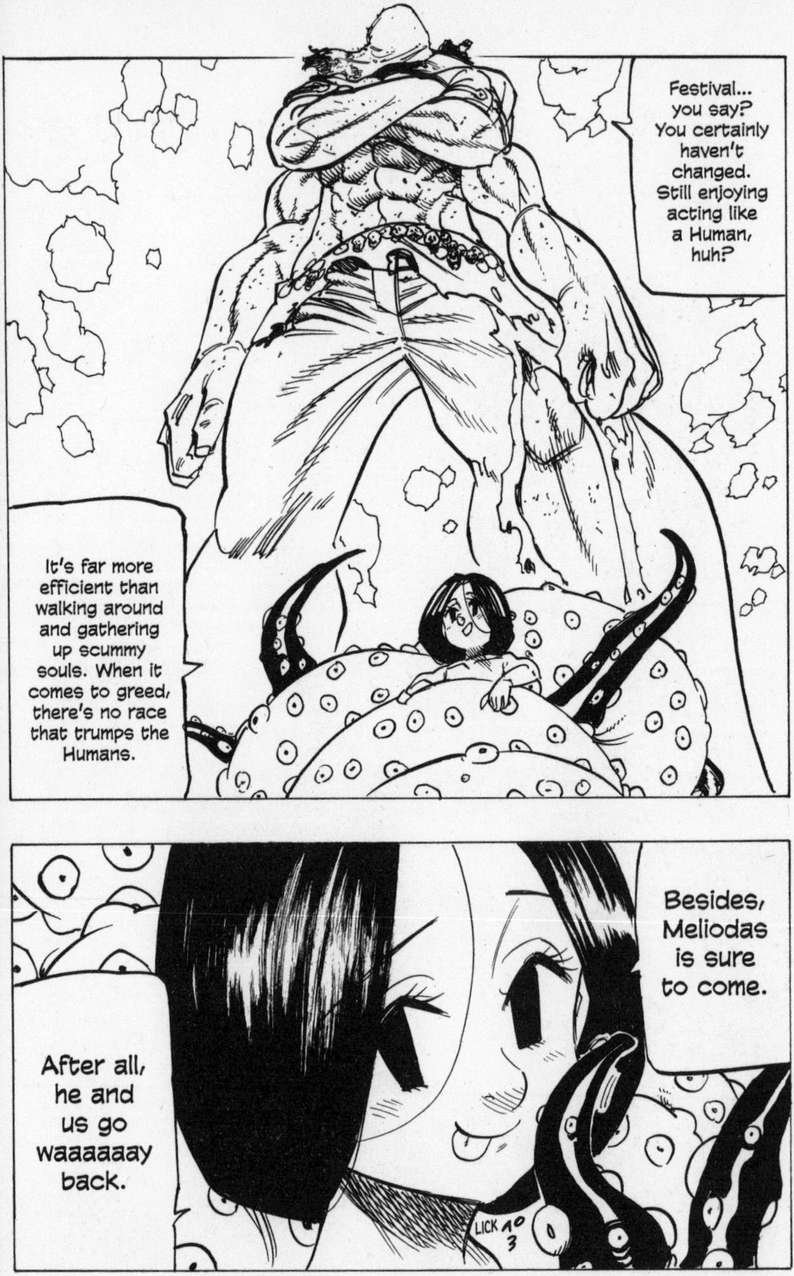
Festival... you say? You certainly haven't changed. Still enjoying acting like a Human, huh?
It's far more efficient than walking around and gathering up scummy souls. When it comes to greed, there's no race that trumps the Humans.
Besides, Meliodas is sure to come.
After all, he and us go waaaaaay back.
LICK

Chapter 152 - Attracted by the Candle's Light

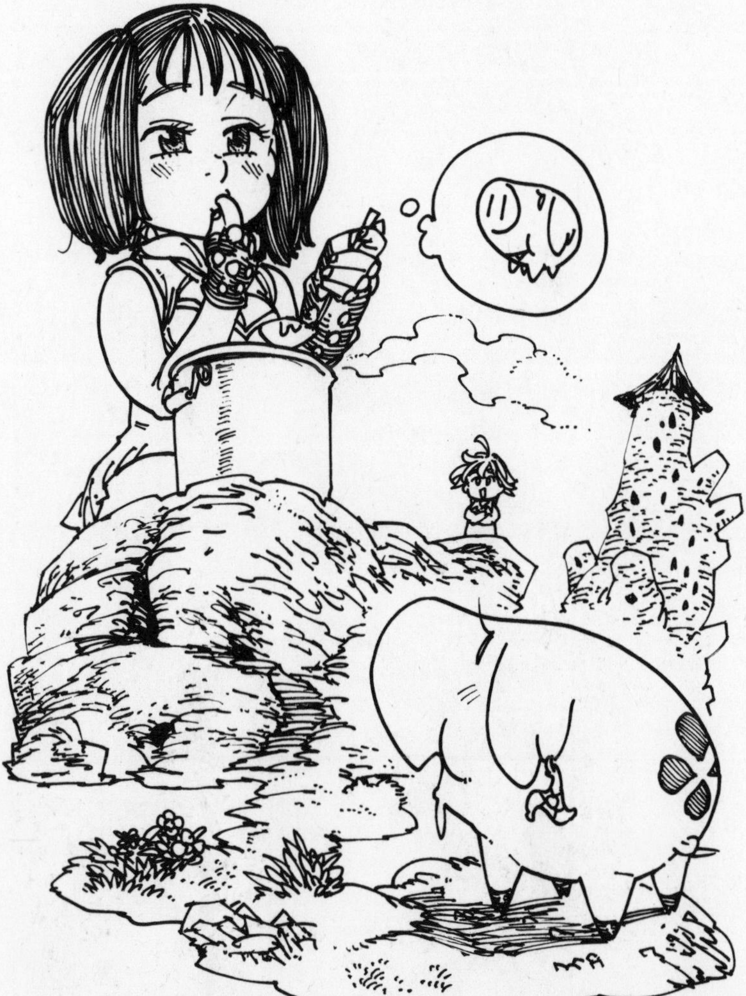

STAB
I did it!
Well done, Sol! You're great at this!
Della, you want to give it a try too?
Mm-mm.
I like being here with you like this best of all, mommy!
HEH HEH
You're hopelessly spoiled.

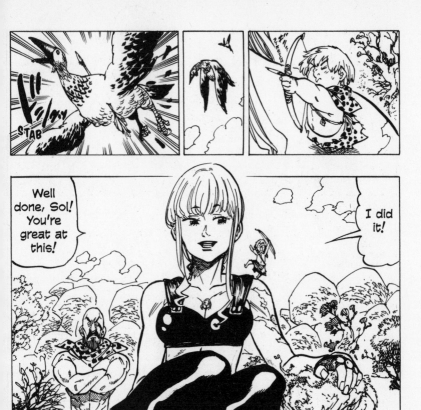

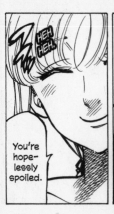

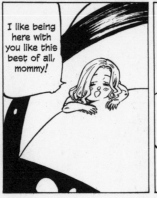

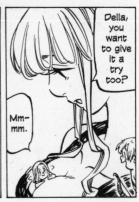

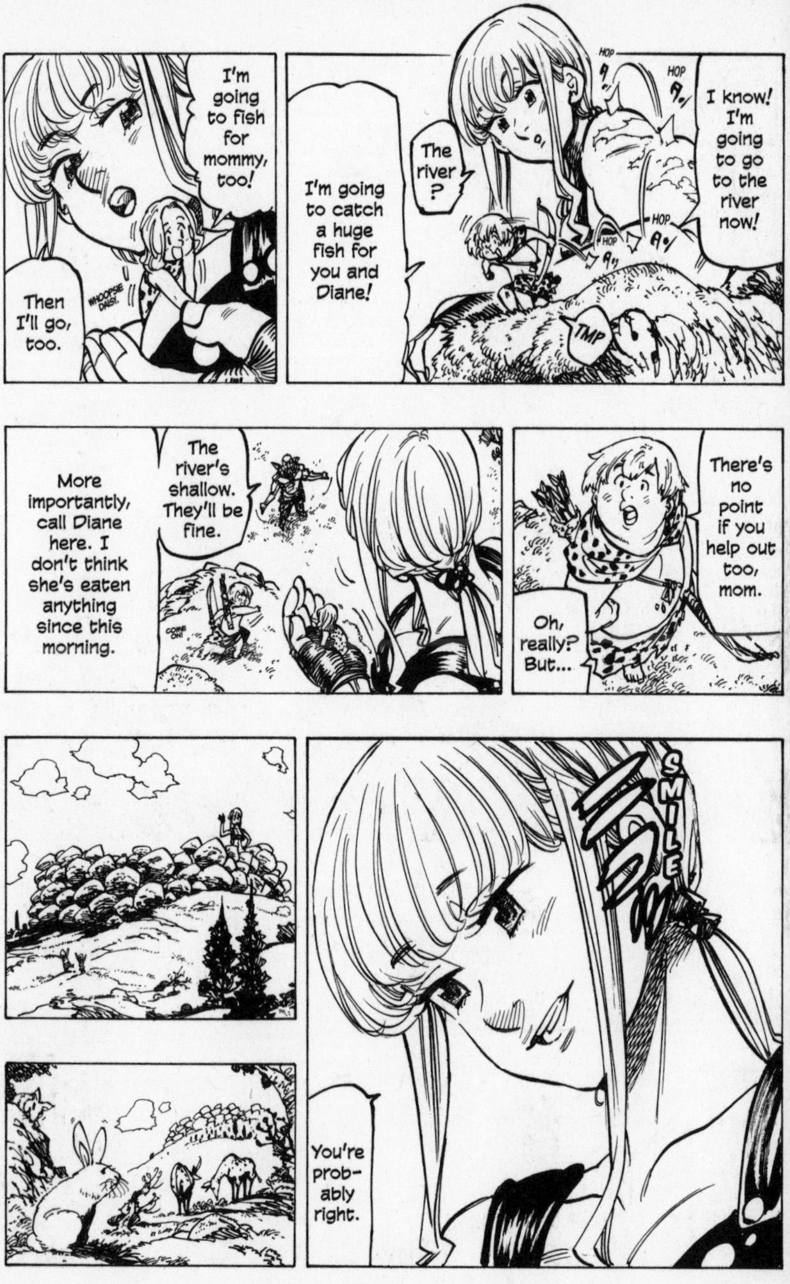

HOP
HOP
I know! I'm going to go to the river now!
HOP
HOP
The river?
I'm going to catch a huge fish for you and Diane!
TMP
I'm going to fish for mommy, too!
WHOOPSIE DAISY.
Then I'll go, too.
There's no point if you help out too, mom.
Oh, really? But...
The river's shallow. They'll be fine.
COME ON!
More importantly, call Diane here. I don't think she's eaten anything since this morning.
SMILE
You're prob-ably right.

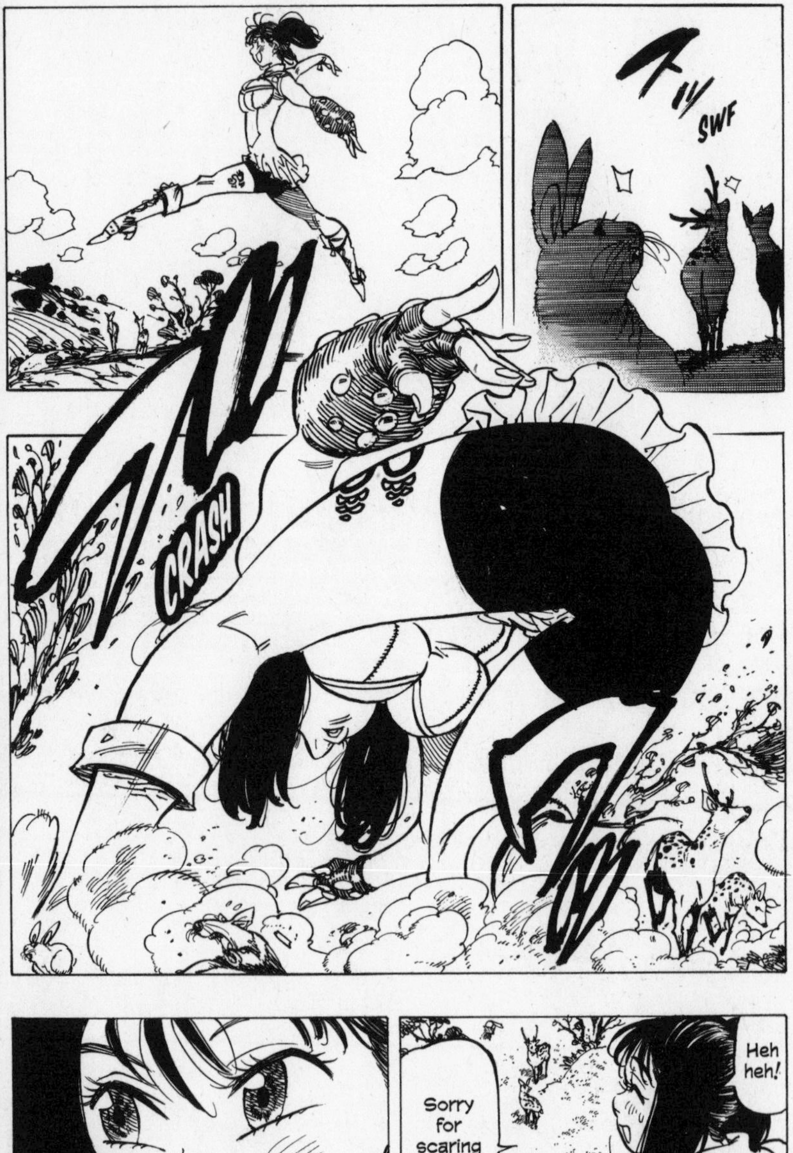
SWF
CRASH
Heh heh!
Sorry for scaring you.

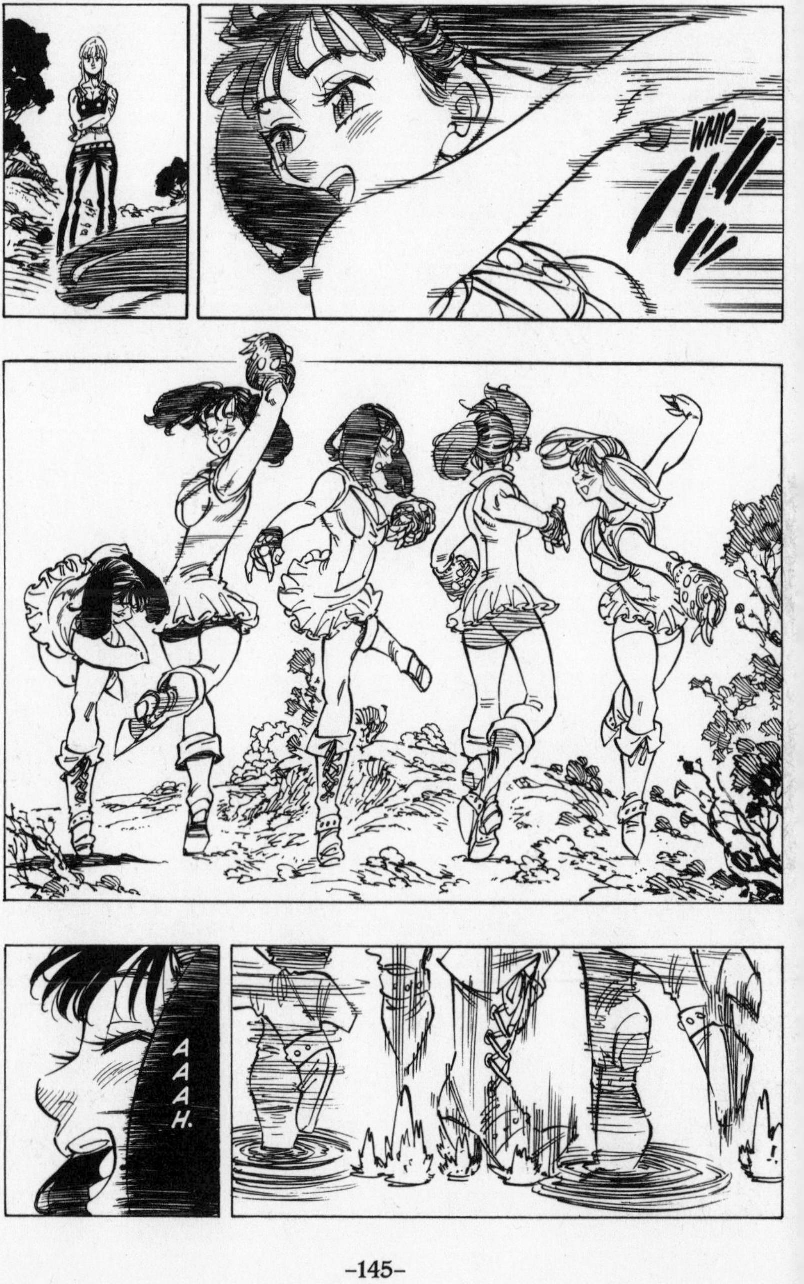
WHIP
!
AAAAH.

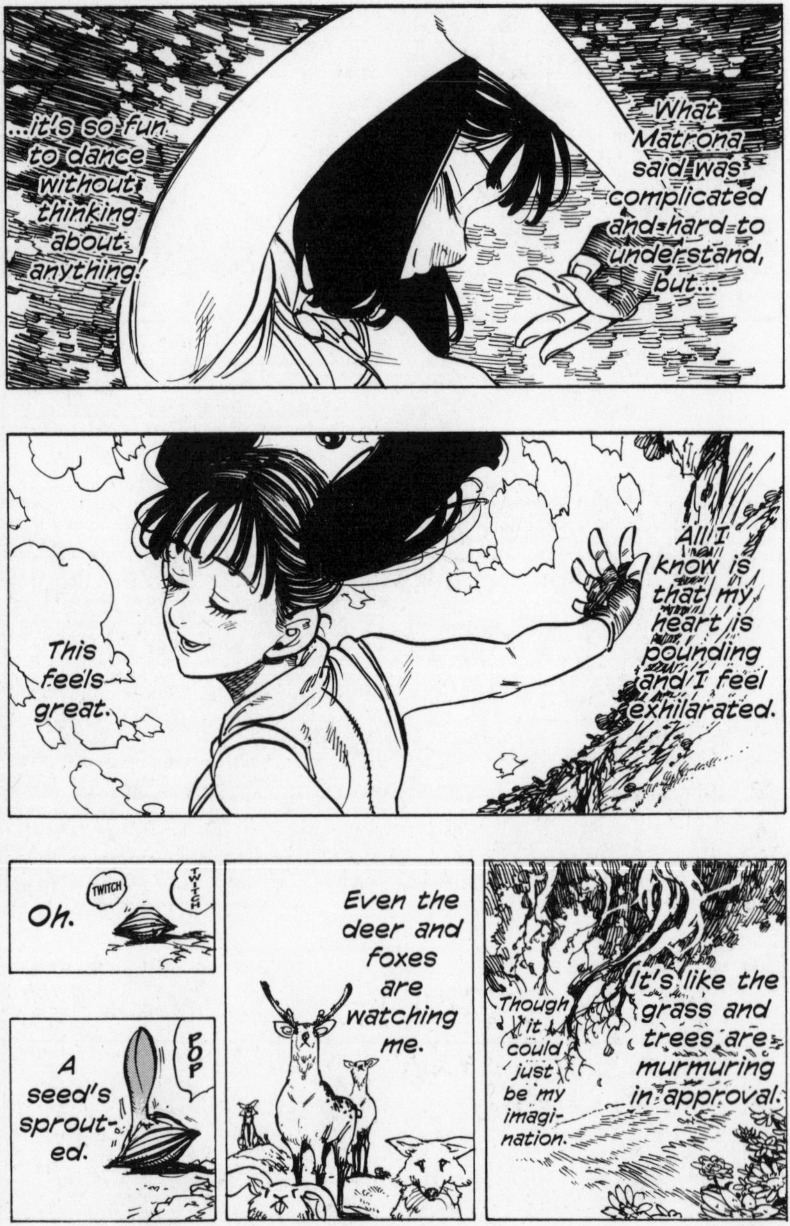
What Matrona said was complicated and hard to understand, but...
...it's so fun to dance without thinking about anything!
All I know is that my heart is pounding and I feel exhilarated.
This feels great.
It's like the grass and trees are murmuring in approval.
Though it could just be my imagination.
Even the deer and foxes are watching me.
TWITCH
TWITCH
Oh.
POP
A seed's sprout-ed.

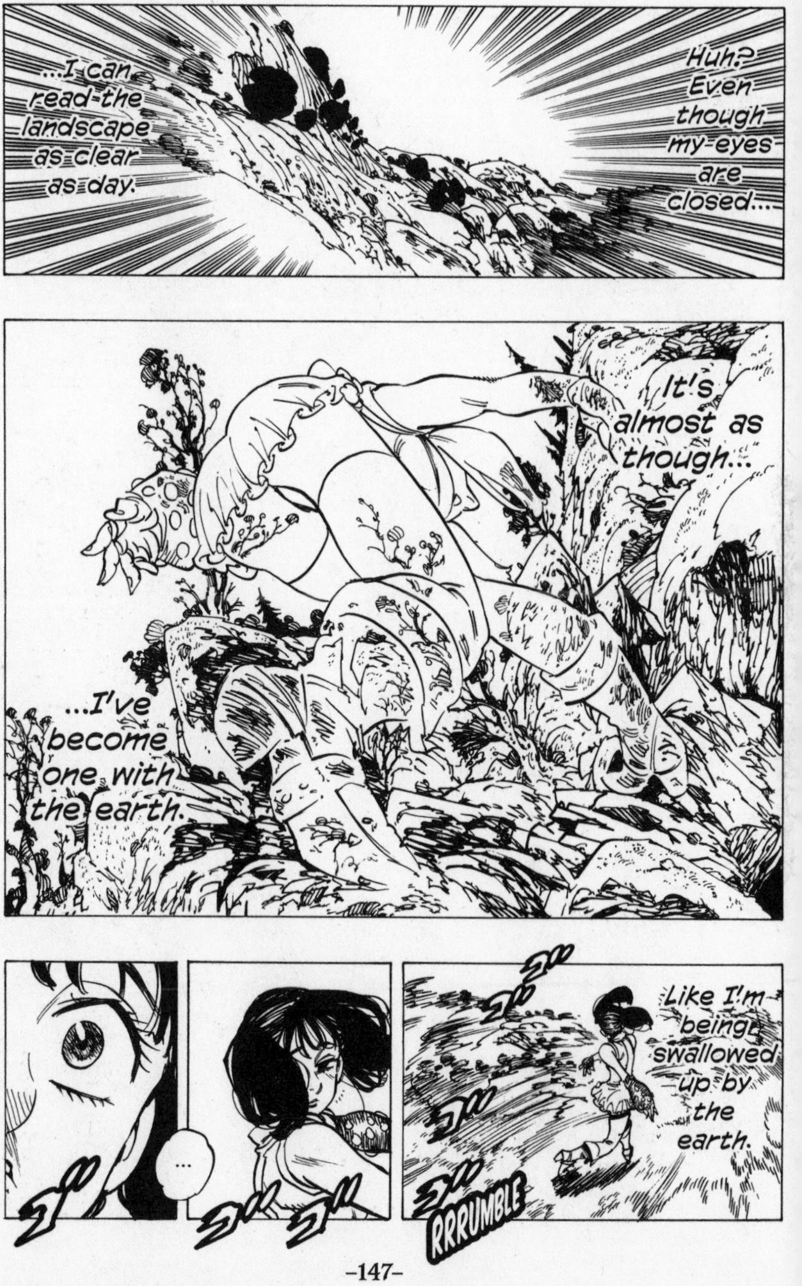
Huh? Even though my eyes are closed...
...I can read the landscape as clear as day.
It's almost as though...
...I've become one with the earth.
Like I'm being swallowed up by the earth.
RRRUMBLE
...

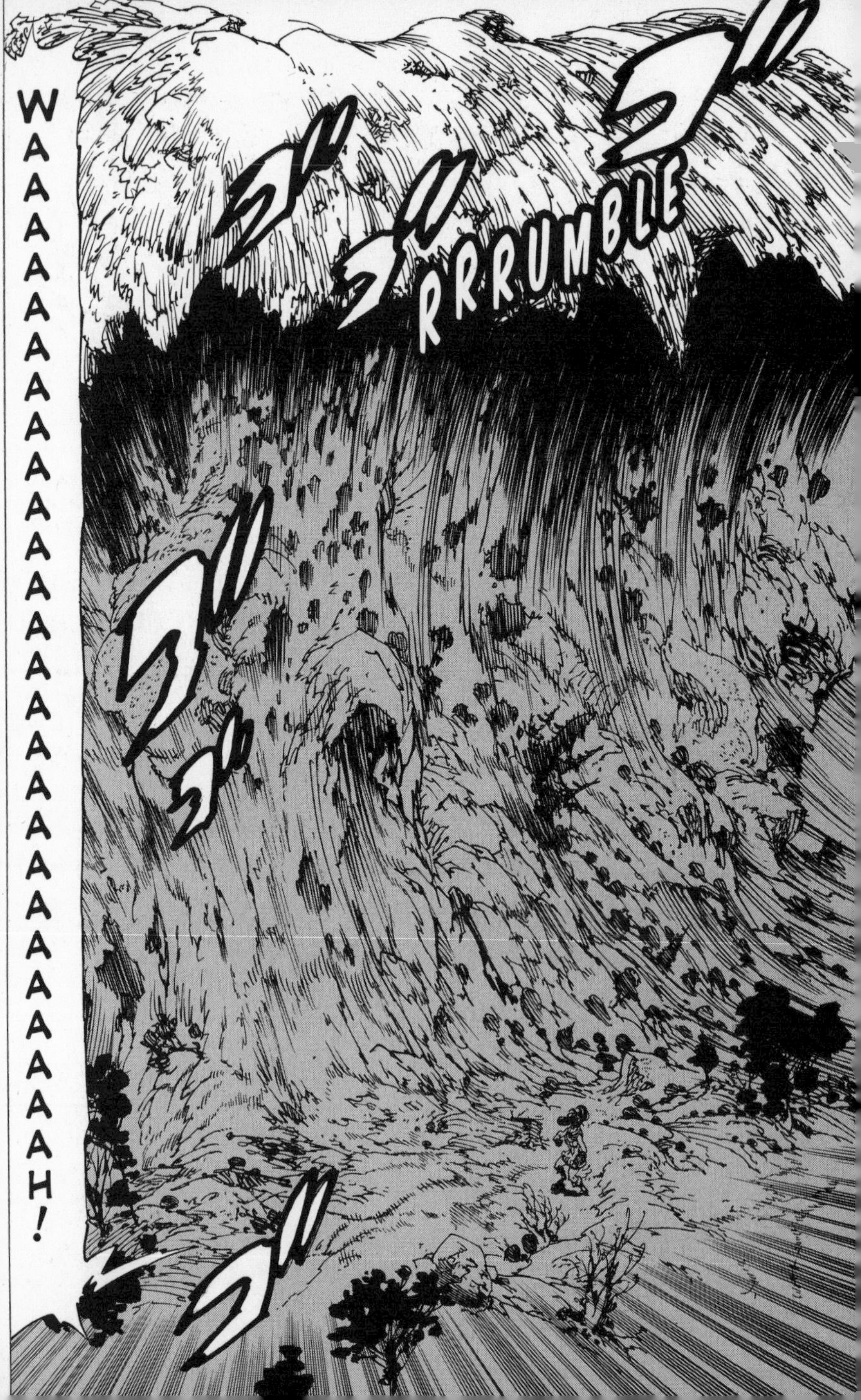
RRRUMBLE
WAAAAAAAAAAAAAAAAAAAAAAAAAAAAAAAAAAH!

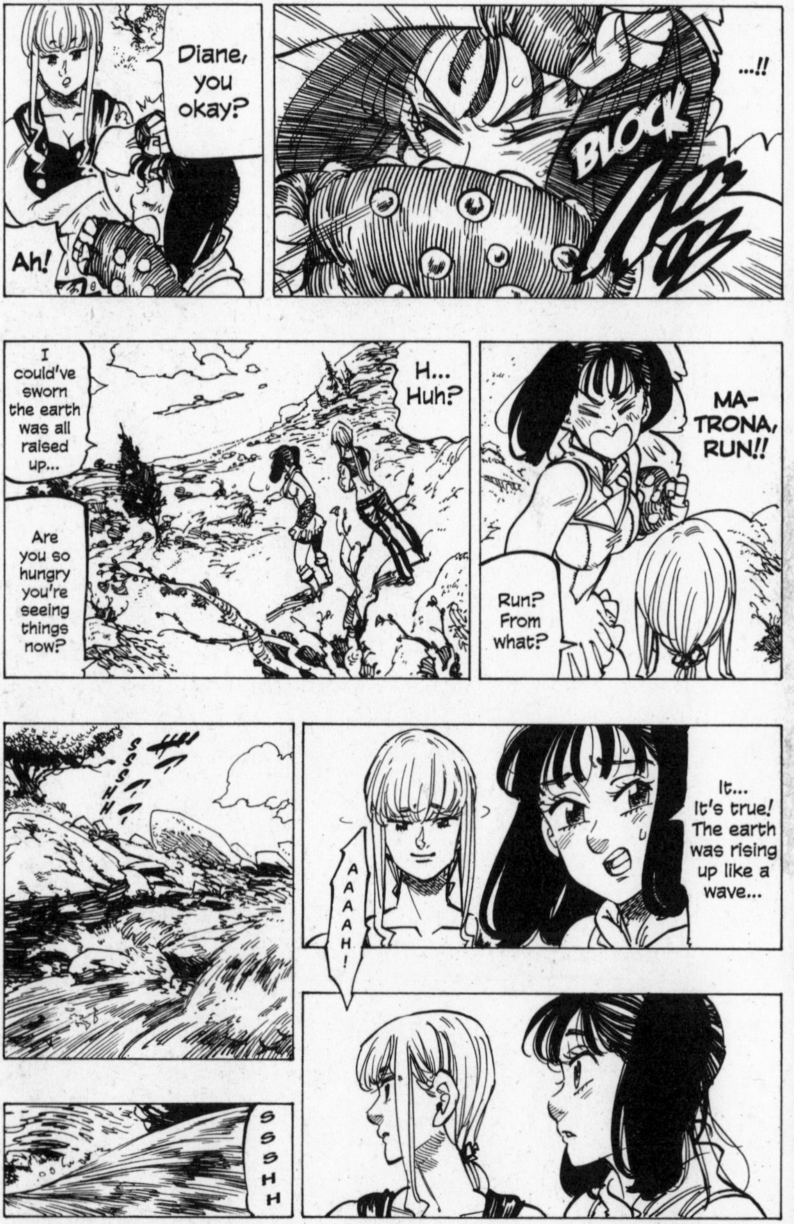

...!!
BLOCK
Diane, you okay?
Ah!
MA-TRONA, RUN!!
Run? From what?
H... Huh?
I could've sworn the earth was all raised up...
Are you so hungry you're seeing things now?
It... It's true! The earth was rising up like a wave...
AAAAH!
SSSHH
SSSHH

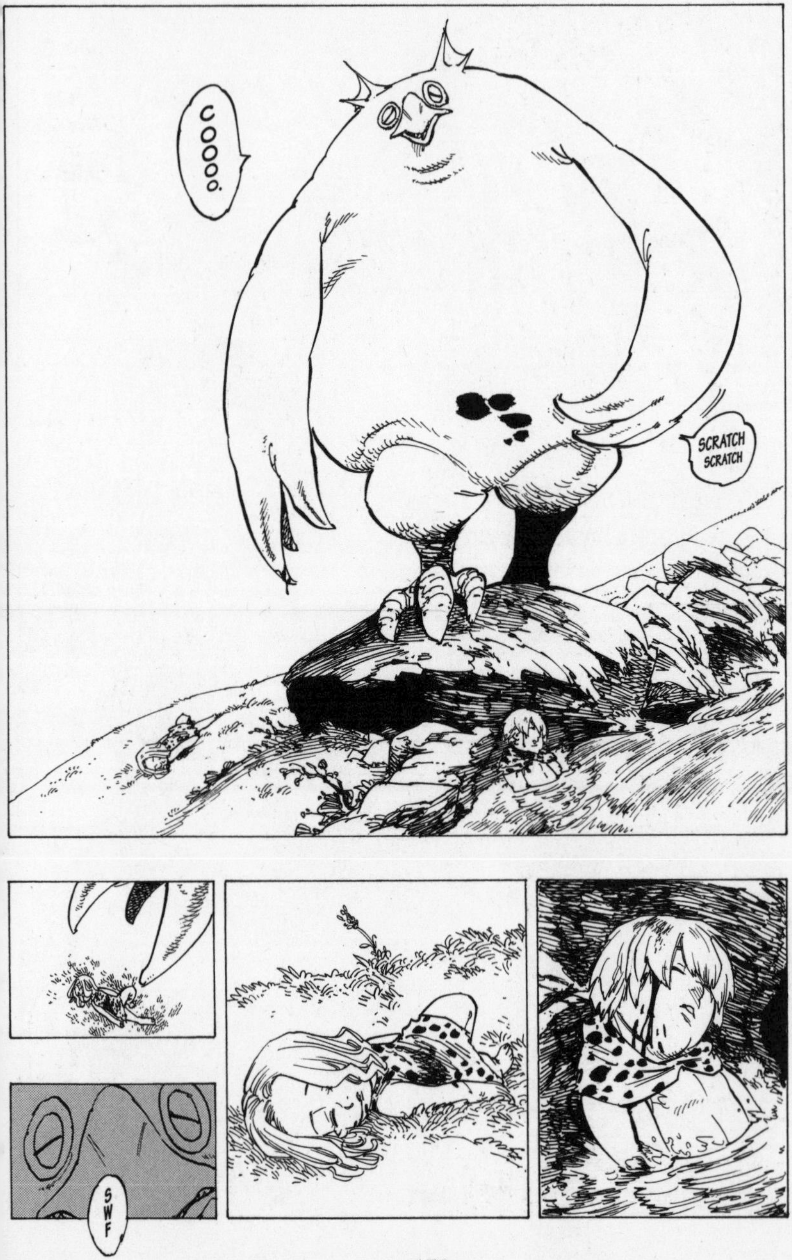
COOOO.
SCRATCH SCRATCH
SWF

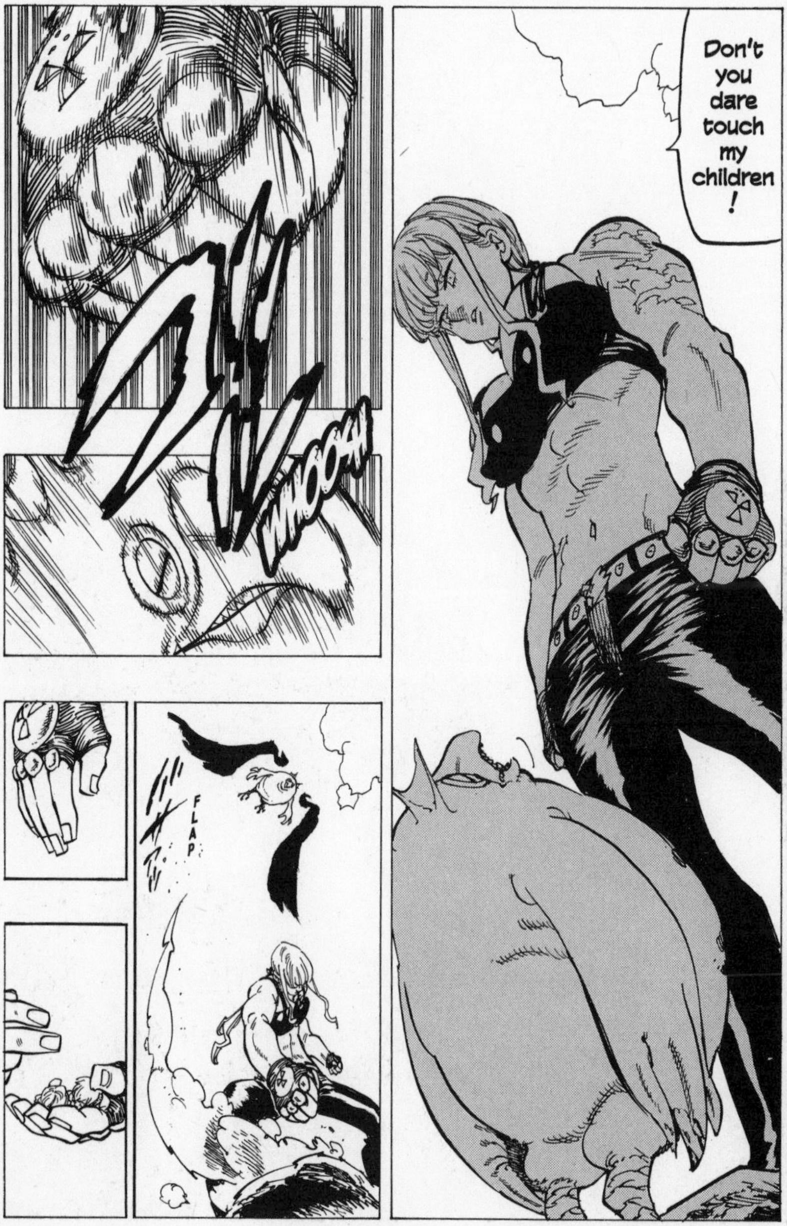
Don't you dare touch my children!
WHOOSH
FLAP

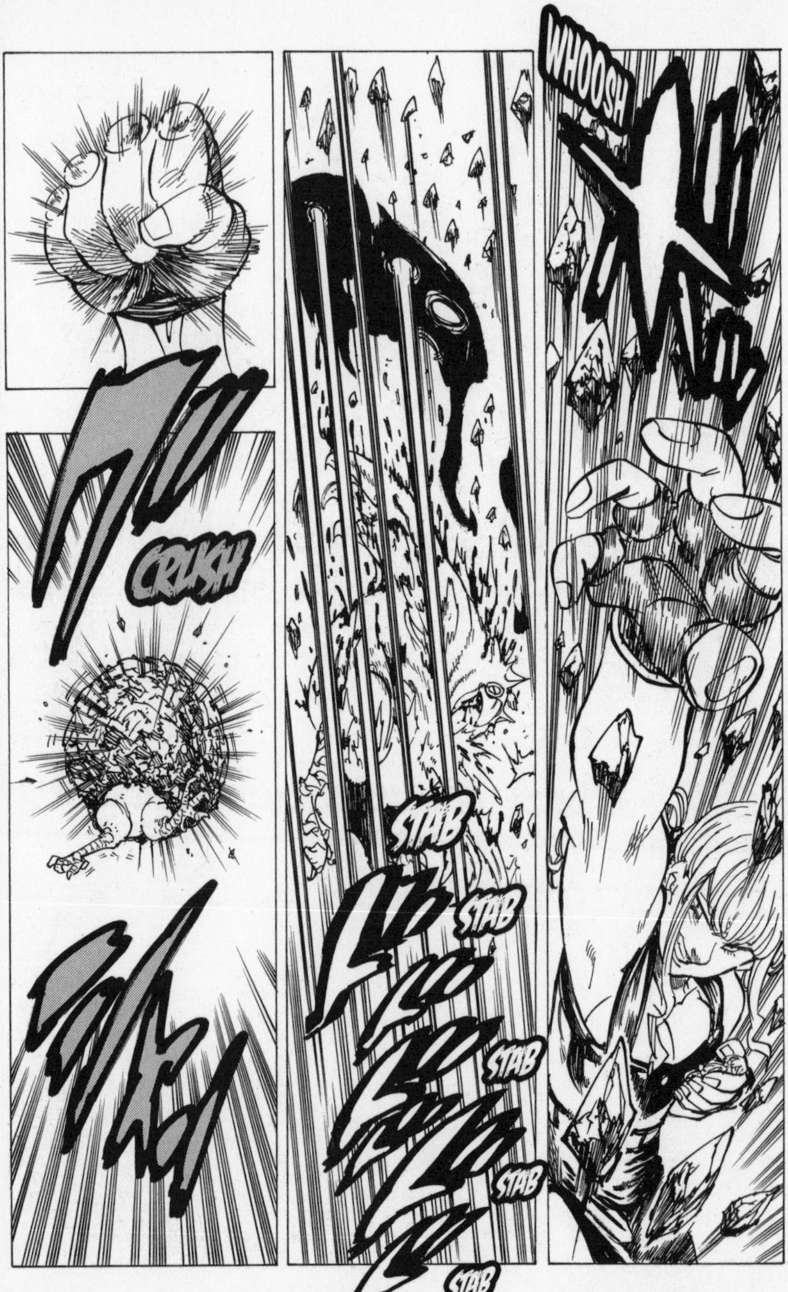
WHOOSH
STAB
STAB
STAB
STAB
STAB
CRUSH

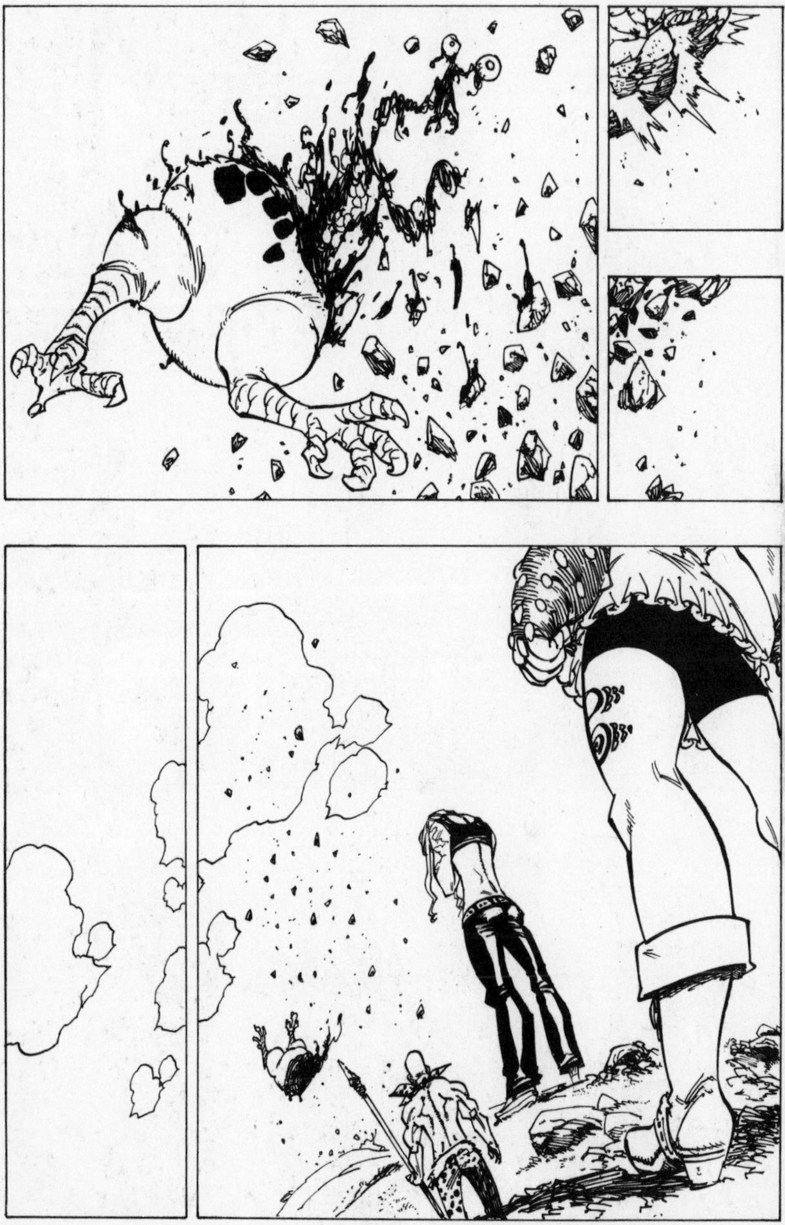

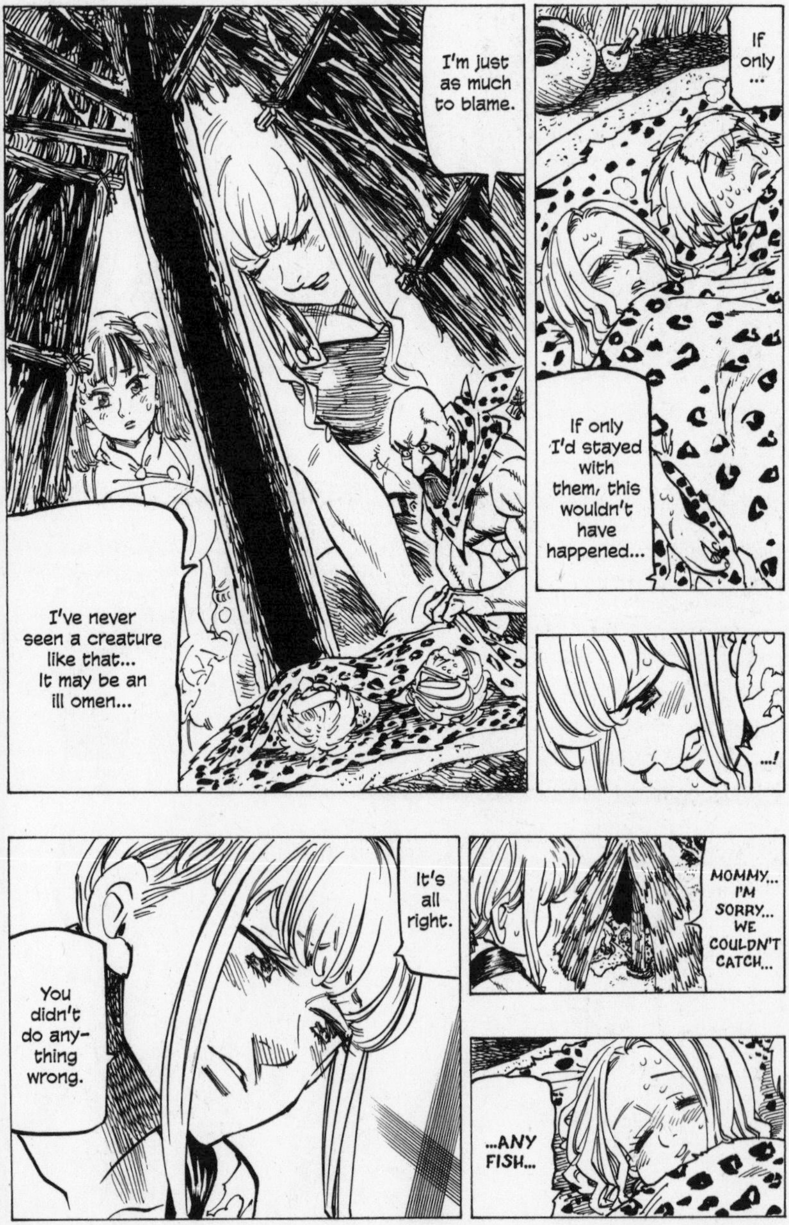
If only...
If only I'd stayed with them, this wouldn't have happened...
...!
I'm just as much to blame.
I've never seen a creature like that... It may be an ill omen...
MOMMY... I'M SORRY... WE COULDN'T CATCH...
...ANY FISH...
It's all right.
You didn't do any-thing wrong.

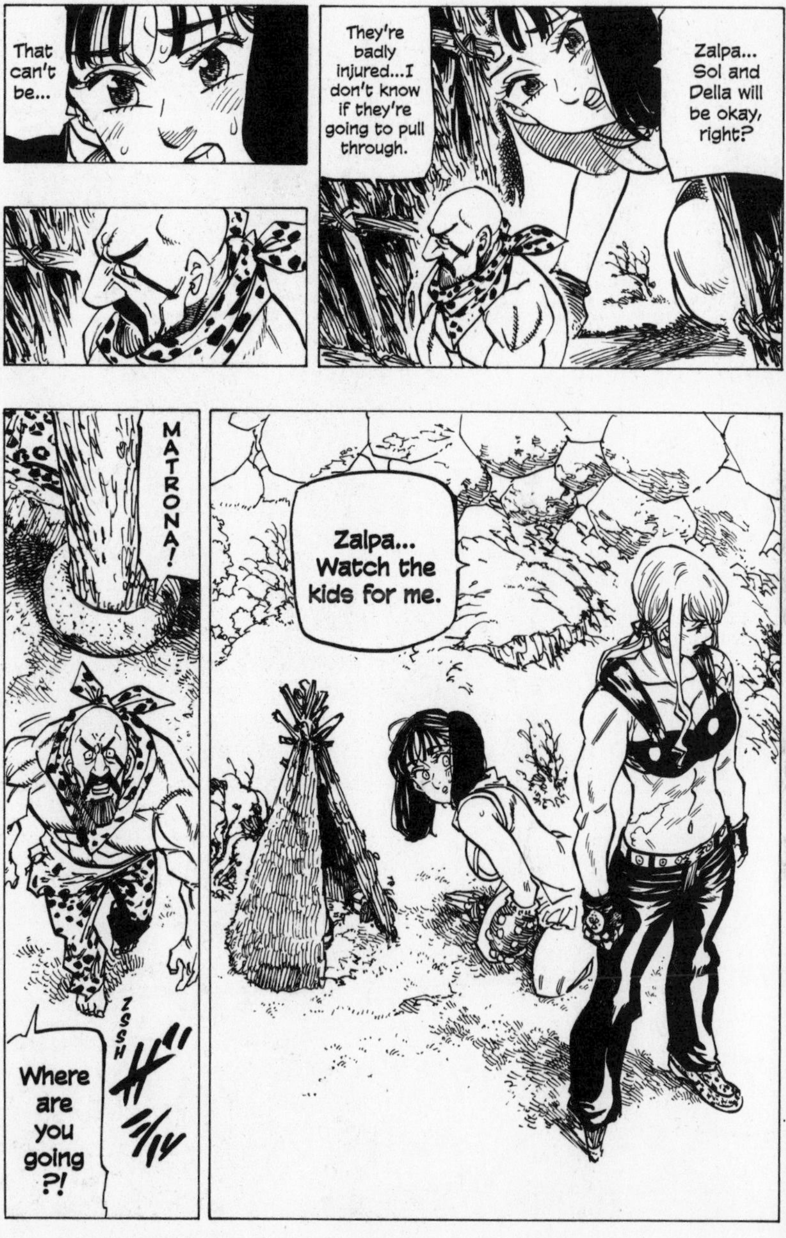

Zalpa... Sol and Della will be okay, right?
They're badly injured...I don't know if they're going to pull through.
That can't be...
Zalpa... Watch the kids for me.
MATRONA!
ZSSH
Where are you going?!

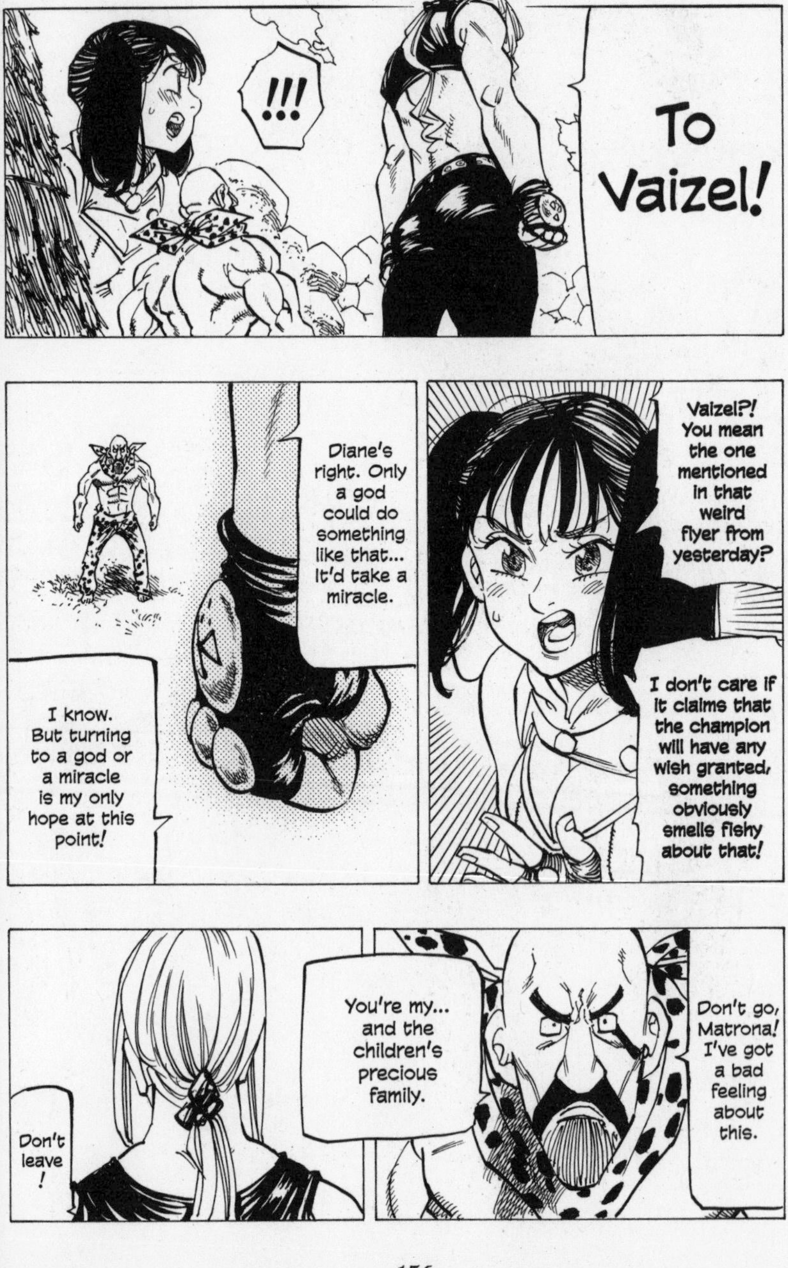
To Vaizel!
!!!
Vaizel?! You mean the one mentioned in that weird flyer from yesterday?
I don't care if it claims that the champion will have any wish granted, something obviously smells fishy about that!
Diane's right. Only a god could do something like that... It'd take a miracle.
I know. But turning to a god or a miracle is my only hope at this point!
Don't go, Matrona! I've got a bad feeling about this.
You're my... and the children's precious family.
Don't leave!

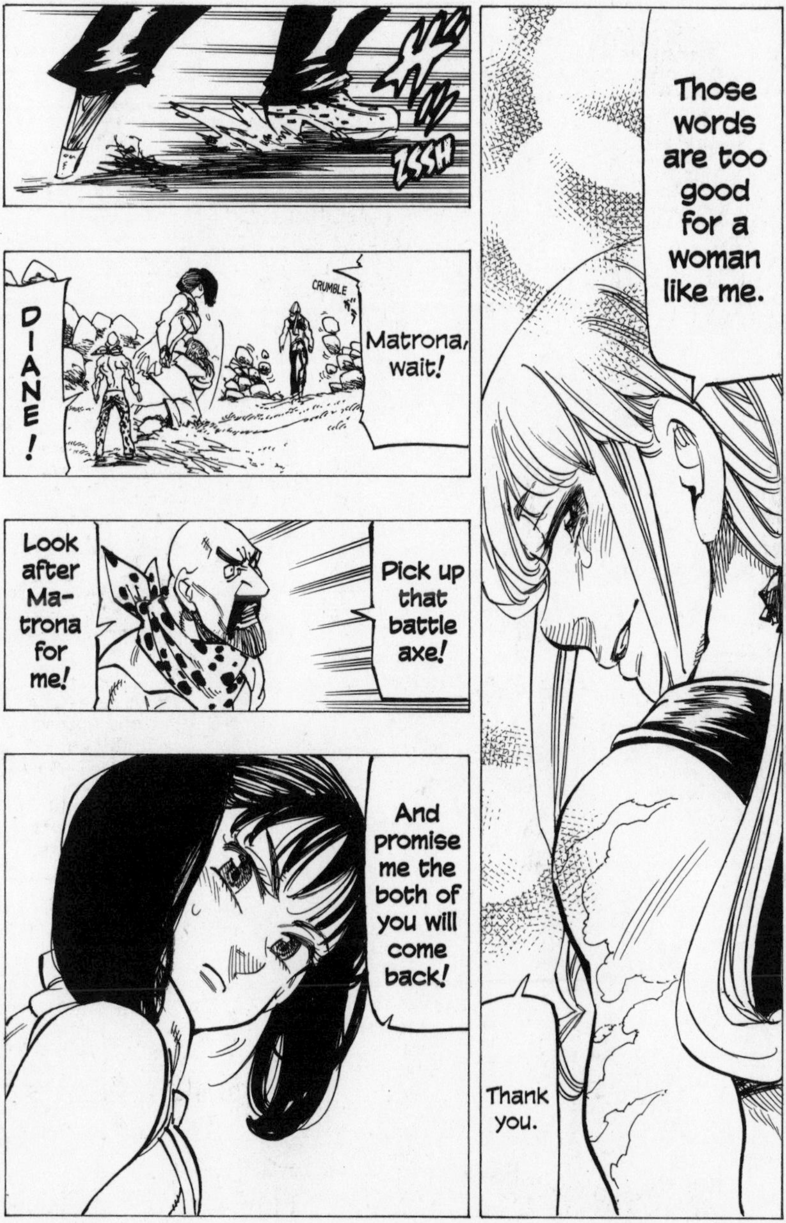

Those words are too good for a woman like me.
Thank you.
ZSSH
DIANE!
Matrona, wait!
CRUMBLE
Pick up that battle axe!
Look after Ma-trona for me!
And promise me the both of you will come back!

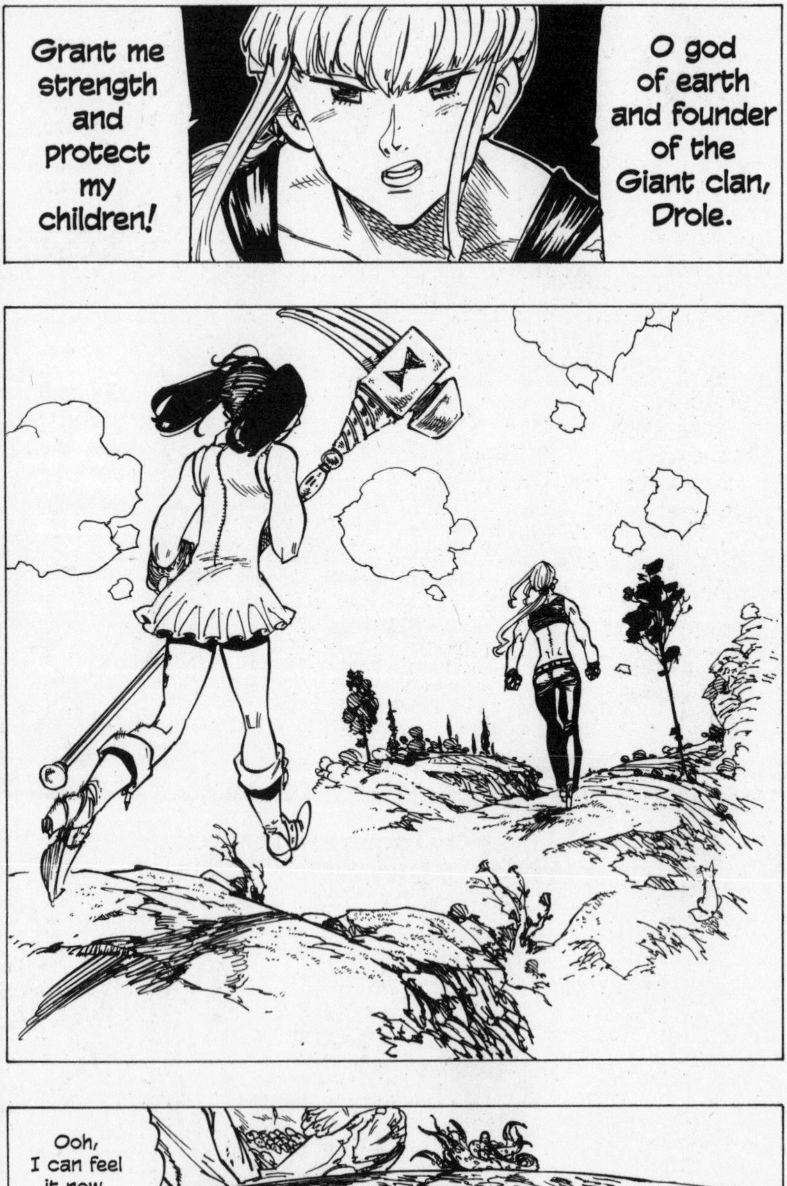
O god of earth and founder of the Giant clan, Drole.
Grant me strength and protect my children!
Ooh, I can feel it now.

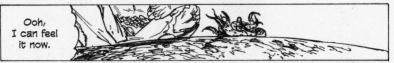

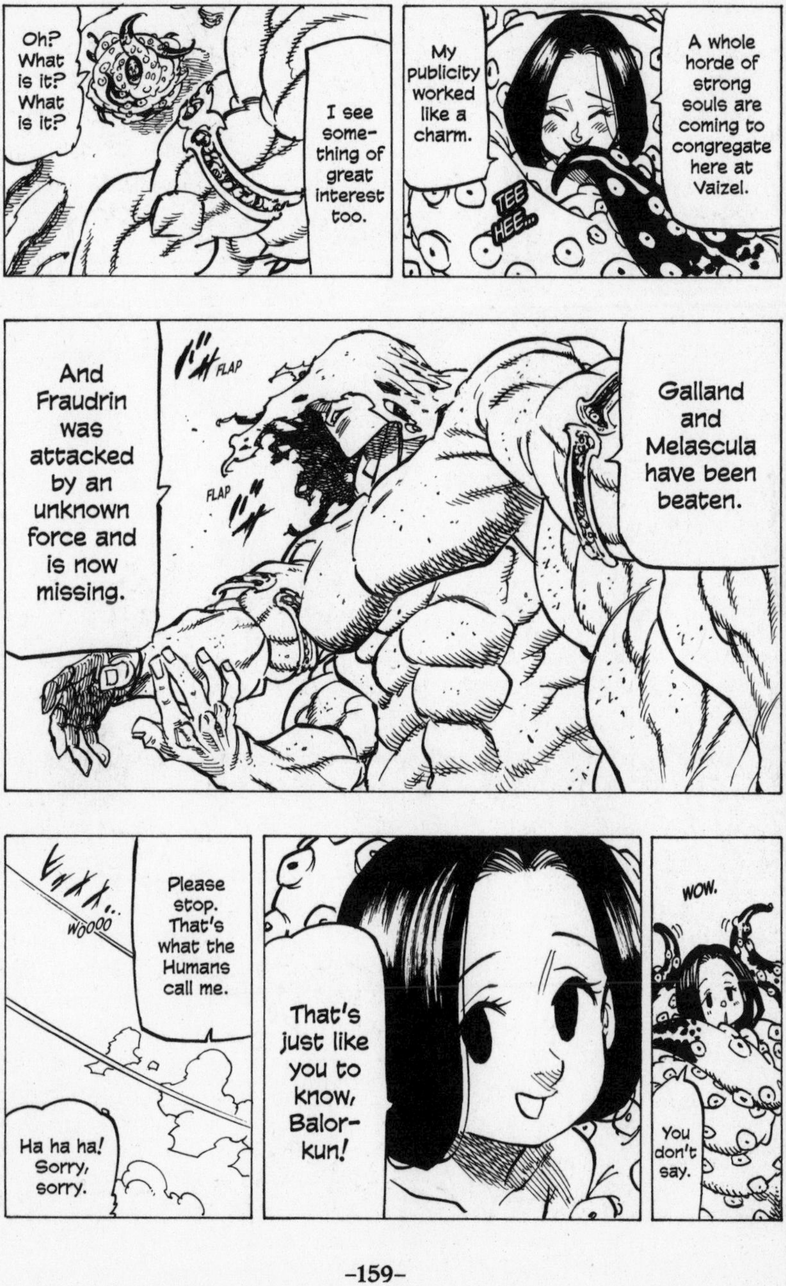
A whole horde of strong souls are coming to congregate here at Vaizel.
TEE HEE...
My publicity worked like a charm.
I see some-thing of great interest too.
Oh? What is it? What is it?
Galland and Melascula have been beaten.
FLAP
FLAP
And Fraudrin was attacked by an unknown force and is now missing.
WOW.
You don't say.
That's just like you to know, Balor-kun!
Please stop. That's what the Humans call me.
WOOOO
Ha ha ha! Sorry, sorry.

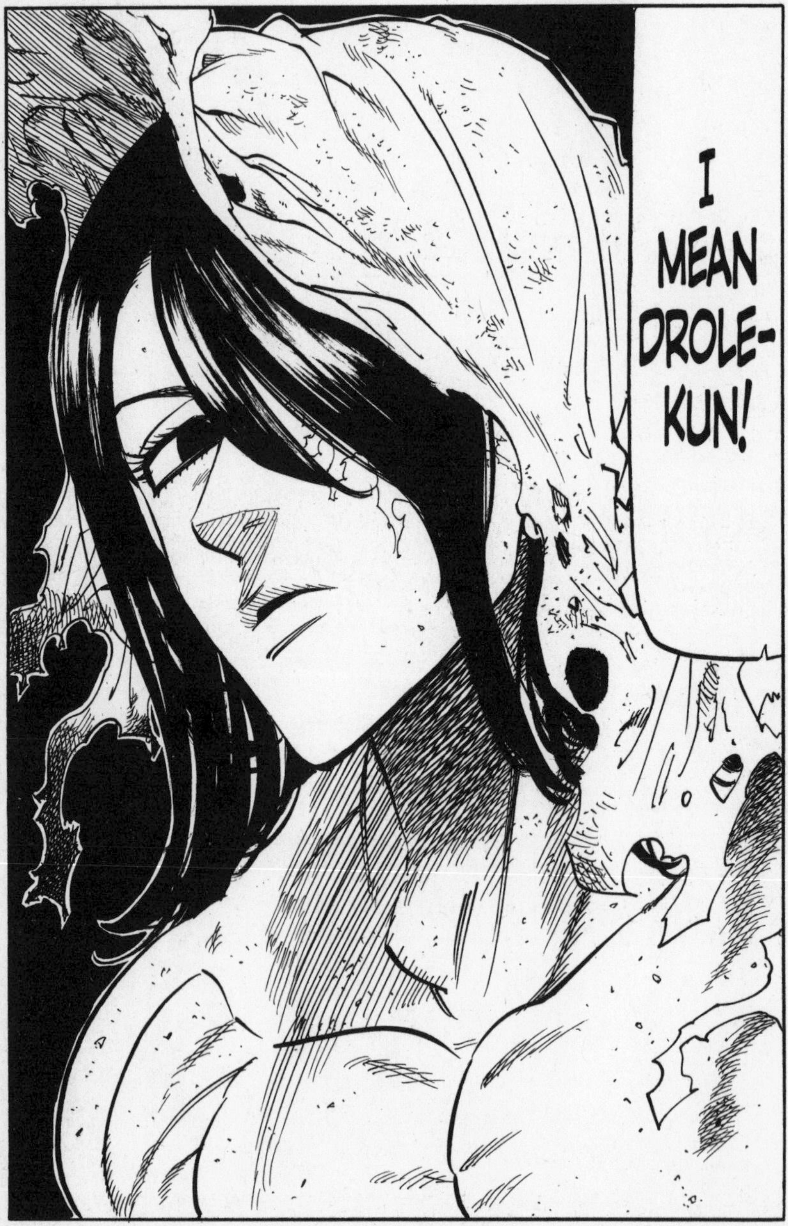
I MEAN DROLE-KUN!

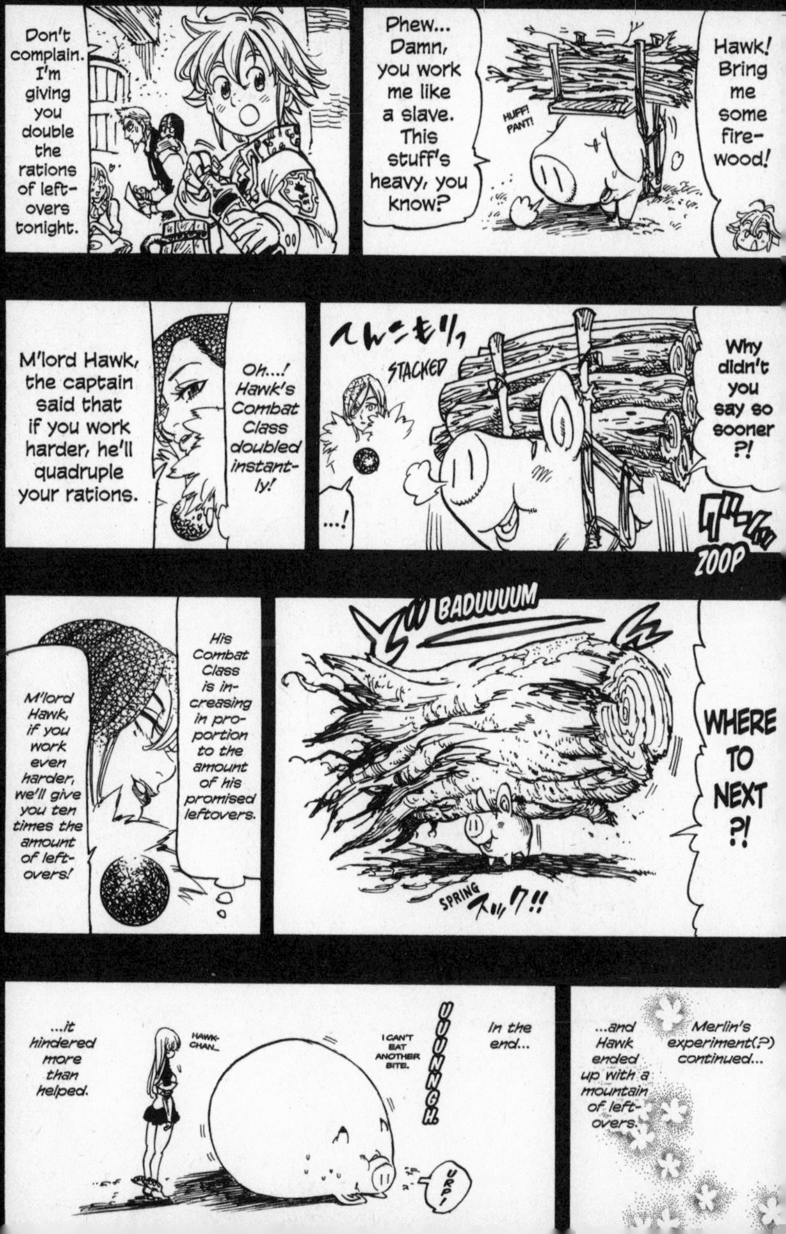
Hawk! Bring me some fire-wood!
Phew... Damn, you work me like a slave. This stuff's heavy, you know?
HUFF! PANT!
Don't complain. I'm giving you double the rations of left-overs tonight.
Why didn't you say so sooner?!
STACKED
...!
ZOOP
Oh...! Hawk's Combat Class doubled instantly!
M'lord Hawk, the captain said that if you work harder, he'll quadruple your rations.
BADUUUUM
WHERE TO NEXT?!
SPRING
His Combat Class is increasing in proportion to the amount of his promised leftovers.
M'lord Hawk, if you work even harder, we'll give you ten times the amount of left-overs!
In the end...
I CAN'T EAT ANOTHER BITE.
UUUNNGH.
URP!
HAWK-CHAN...
...it hindered more than helped.
...and Hawk ended up with a mountain of left-overs.
Merlin's experiment(?) continued...

Chapter 153 - A Bloodcurdling Confession

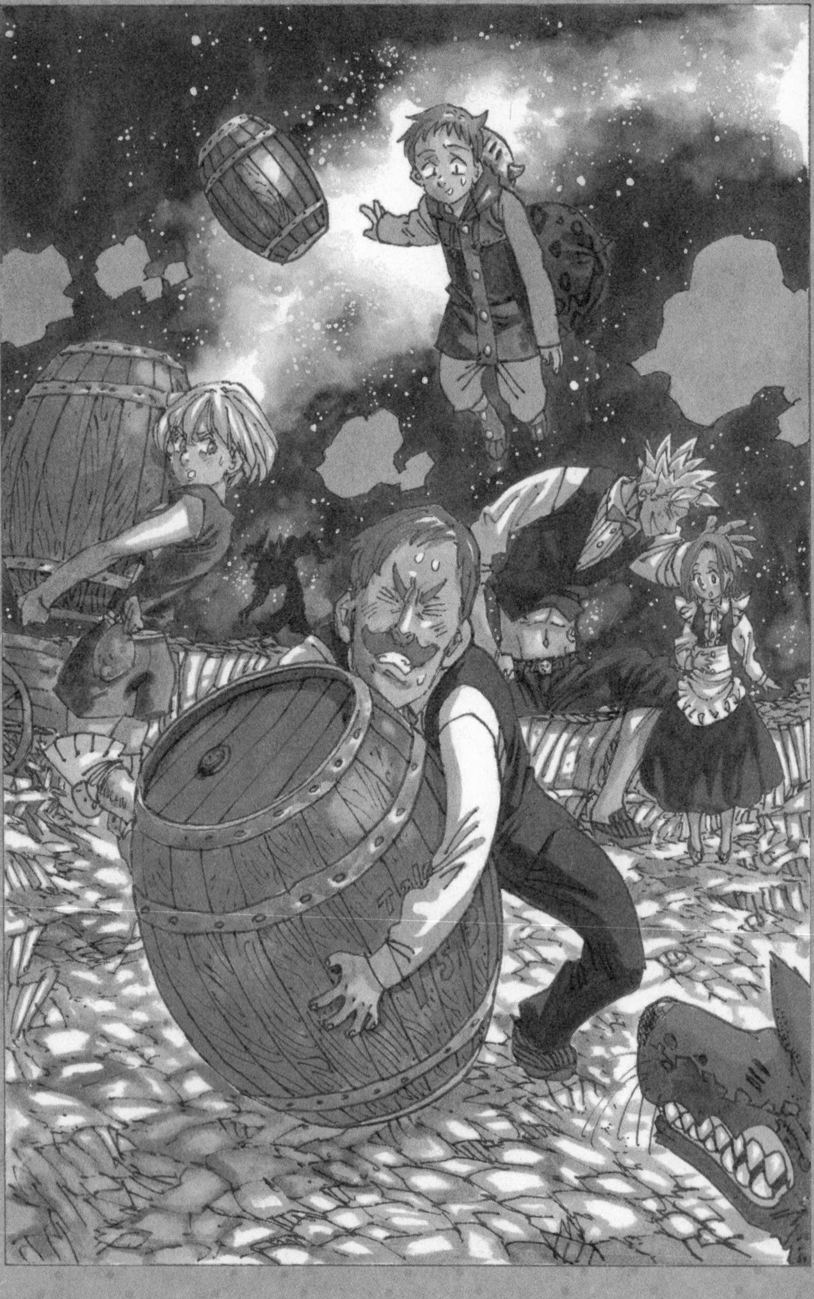

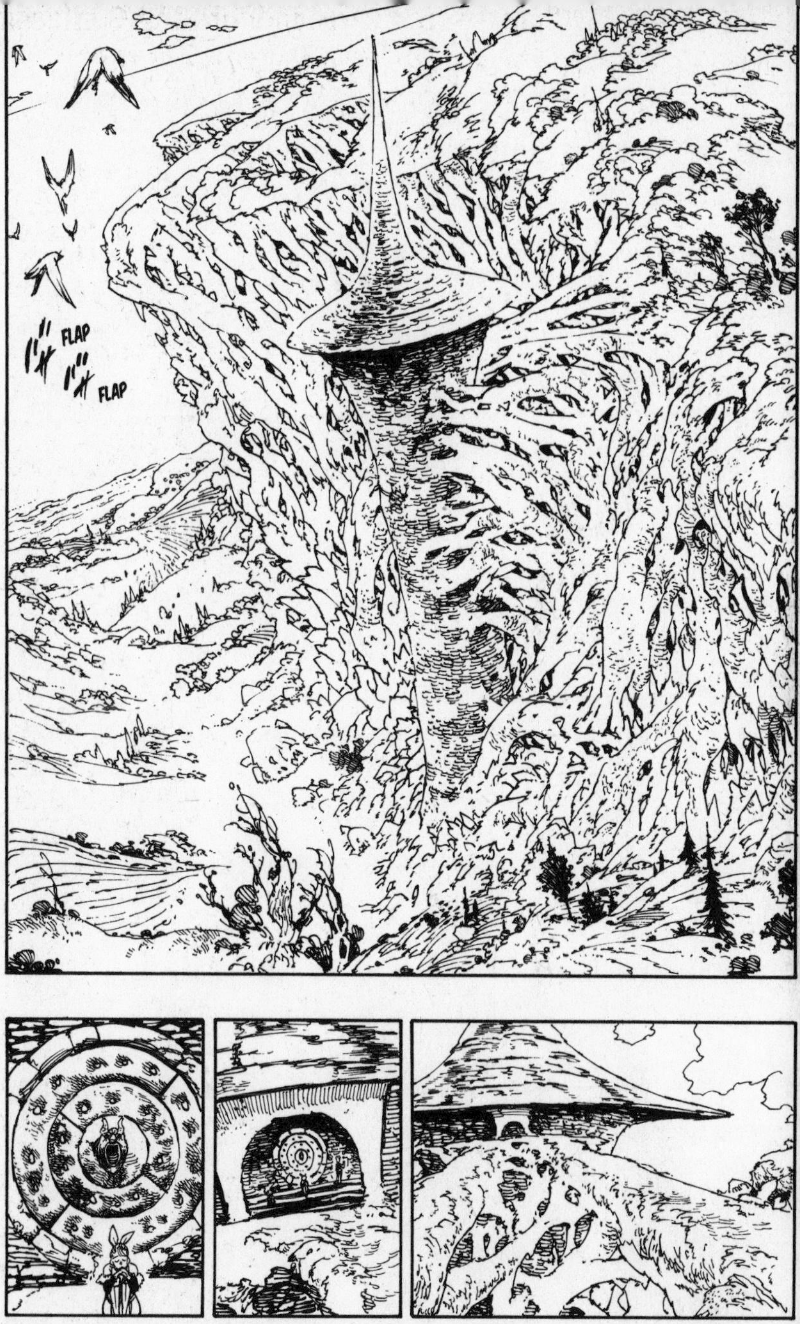
FLAP
FLAP

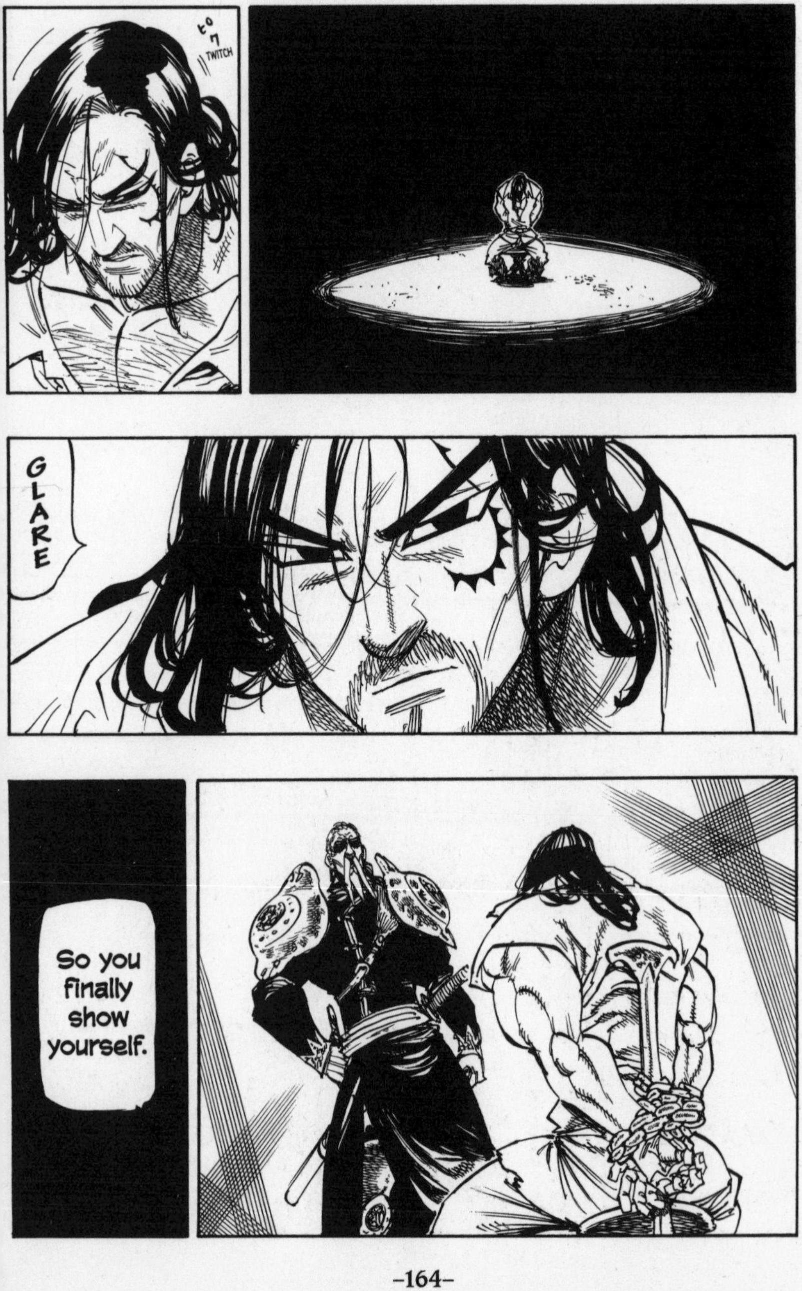
TWITCH
GLARE
So you finally show yourself.

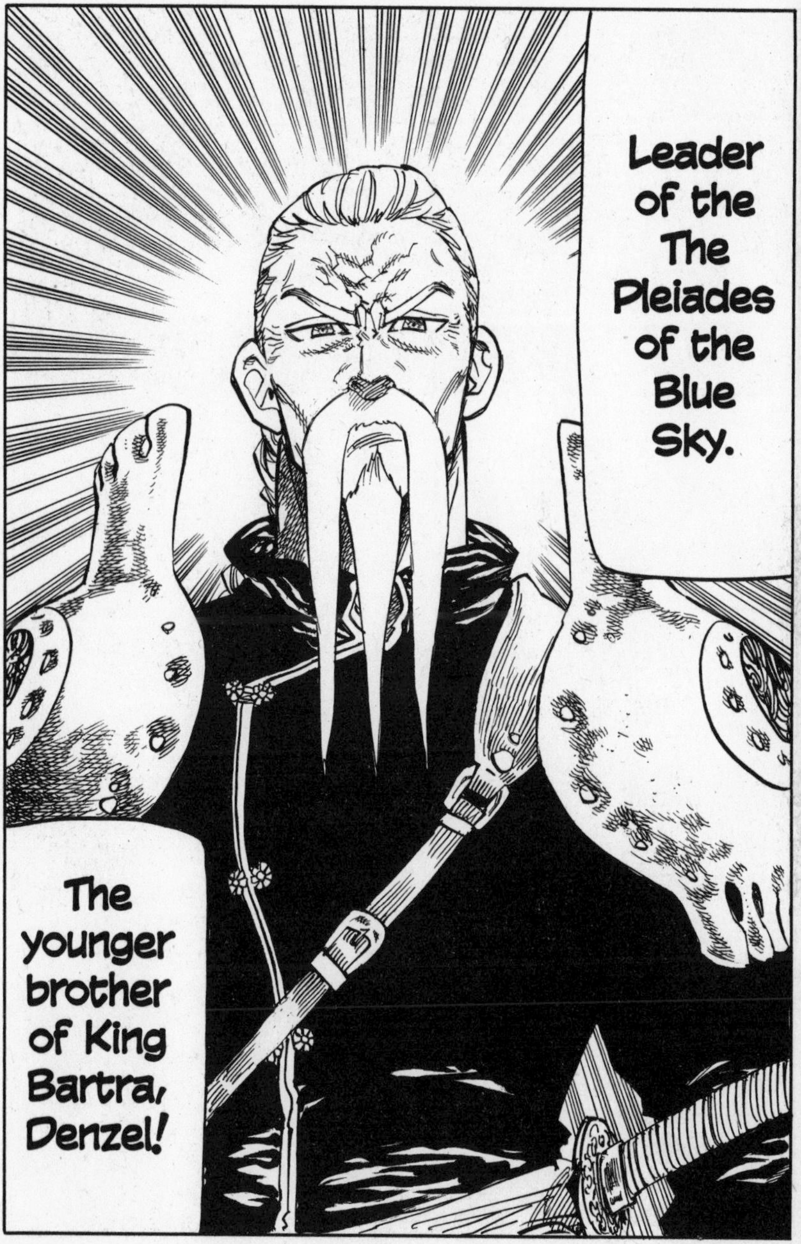
Leader of the The Pleiades of the Blue Sky.
The younger brother of King Bartra, Denzel!

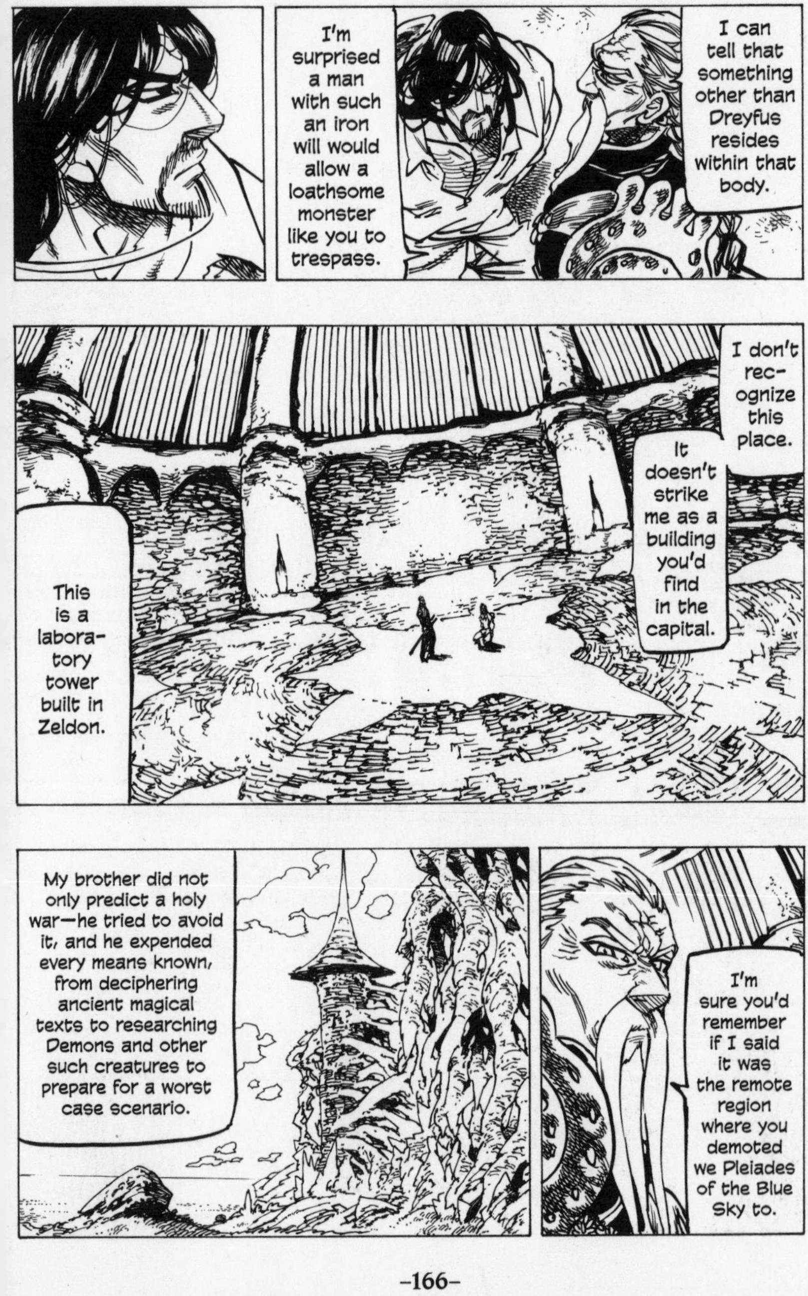
I can tell that something other than Dreyfus resides within that body.
I'm surprised a man with such an iron will would allow a loathsome monster like you to trespass.
I don't recognize this place.
It doesn't strike me as a building you'd find in the capital.
This is a laboratory tower built in Zeldon.
I'm sure you'd remember if I said it was the remote region where you demoted we Pleiades of the Blue Sky to.
My brother did not only predict a holy war—he tried to avoid it, and he expended every means known, from deciphering ancient magical texts to researching Demons and other such creatures to prepare for a worst case scenario.

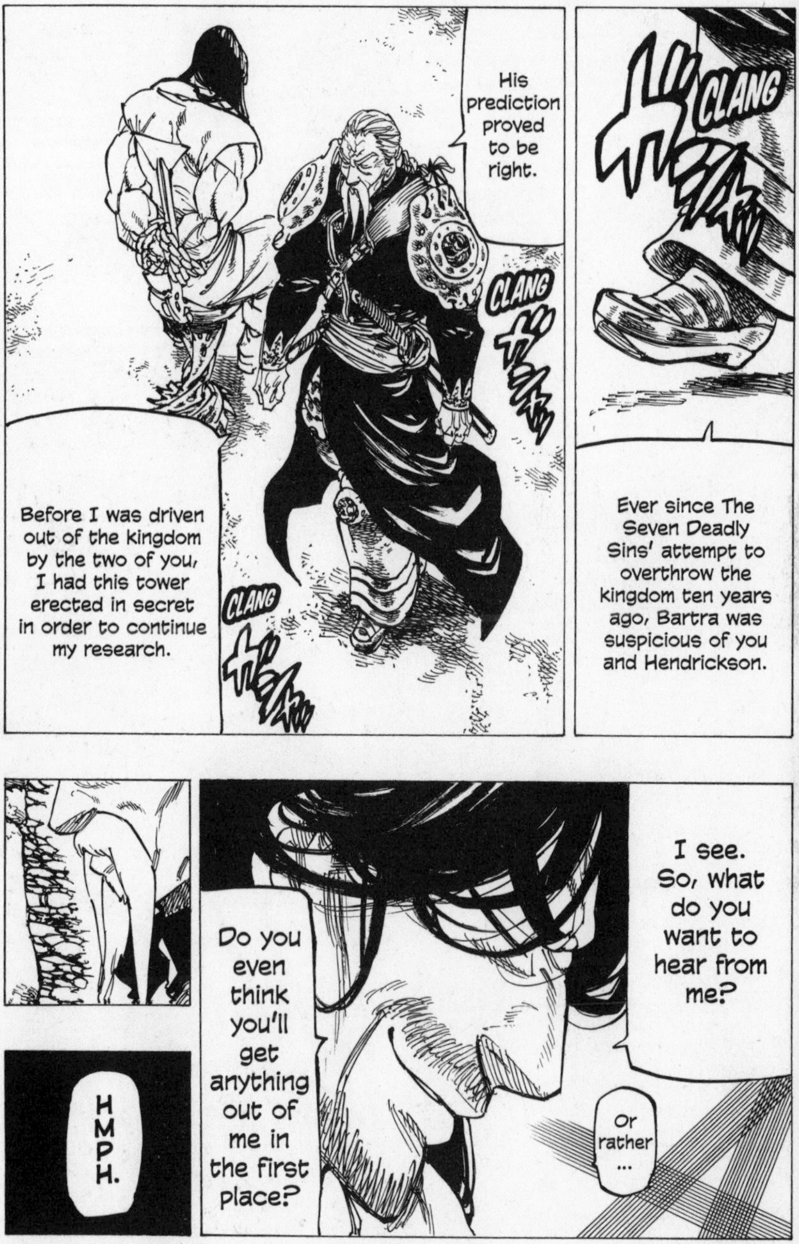
CLANG
Ever since The Seven Deadly Sins' attempt to overthrow the kingdom ten years ago, Bartra was suspicious of you and Hendrickson.
His prediction proved to be right.
CLANG
Before I was driven out of the kingdom by the two of you, I had this tower erected in secret in order to continue my research.
CLANG
I see. So, what do you want to hear from me?
Or rather ...
Do you even think you'll get anything out of me in the first place?
HMPH.

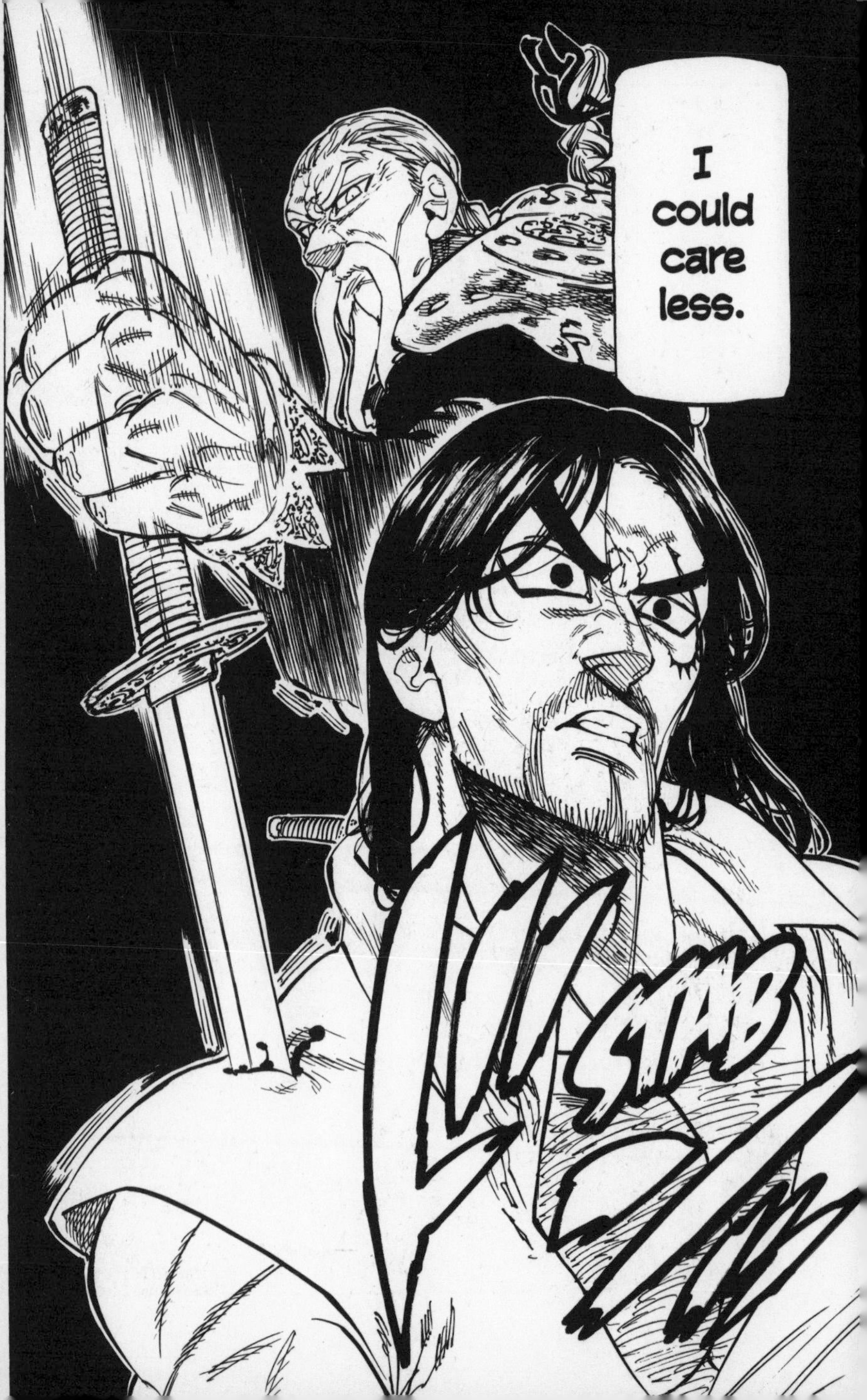
I could care less.
STAB

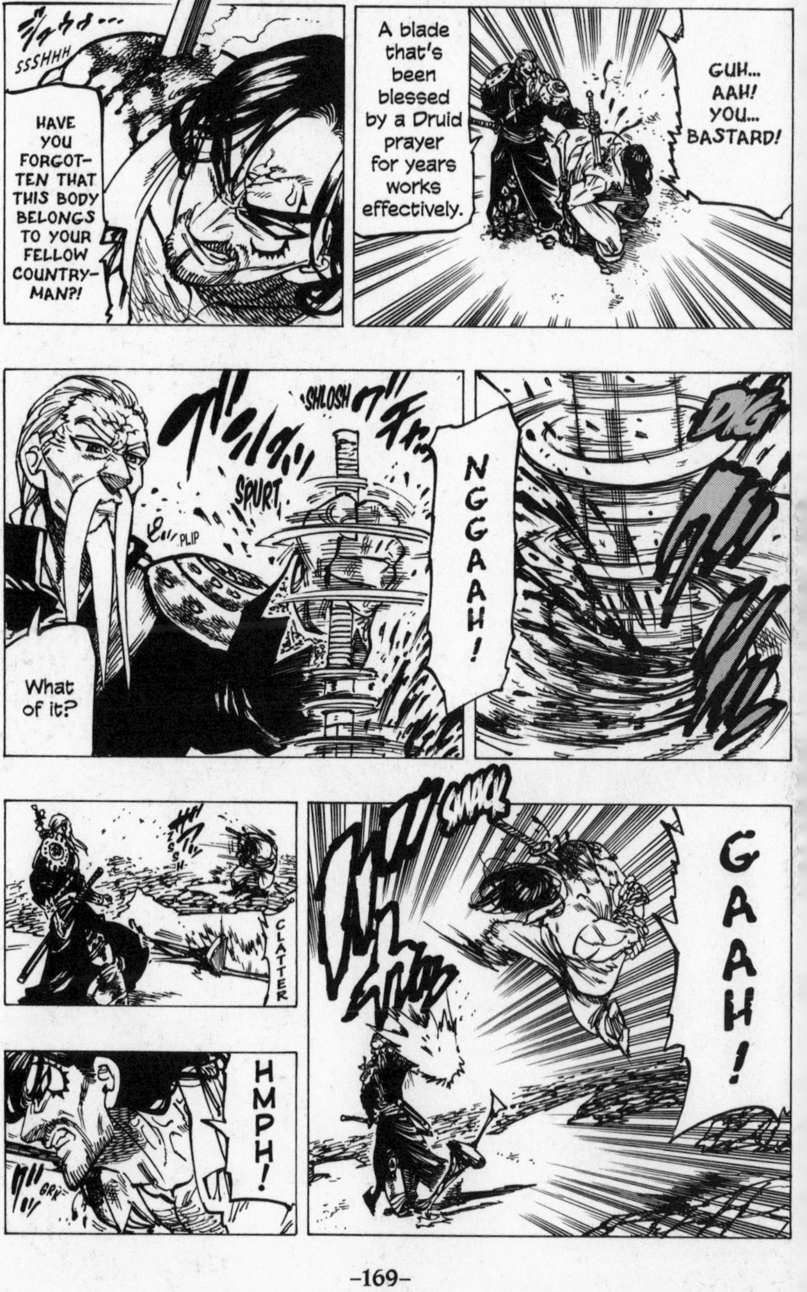
GUH... AAH! YOU... BASTARD!
A blade that's been blessed by a Druid prayer for years works effectively.
SSSHHH
HAVE YOU FORGOTTEN THAT THIS BODY BELONGS TO YOUR FELLOW COUNTRYMAN?!
DIG
NGGAAH!
SHLOSH
SPURT
PLIP
What of it?
GAAH!
SMACK
CLATTER
HMPH!
GRK

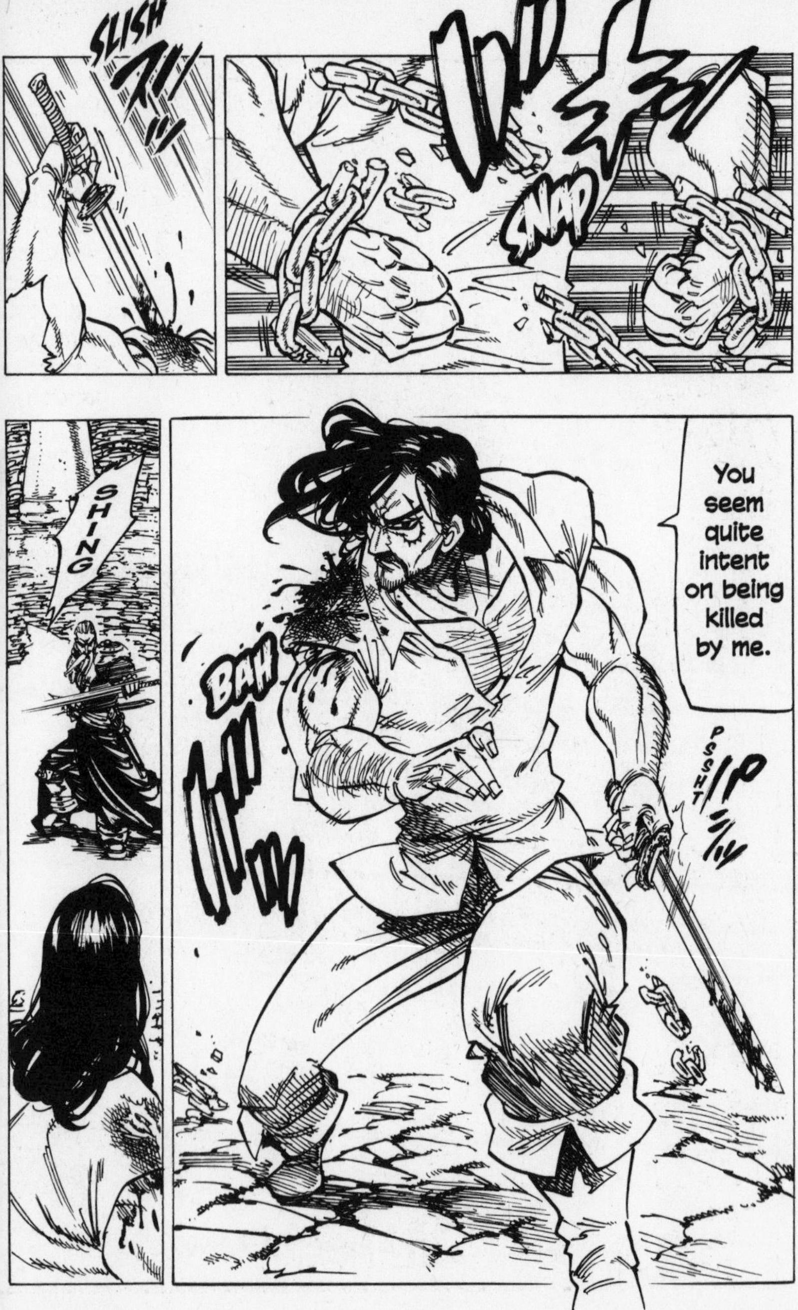
SNAP
SLISH
You seem quite intent on being killed by me.
PSSHT
BAH
SHING

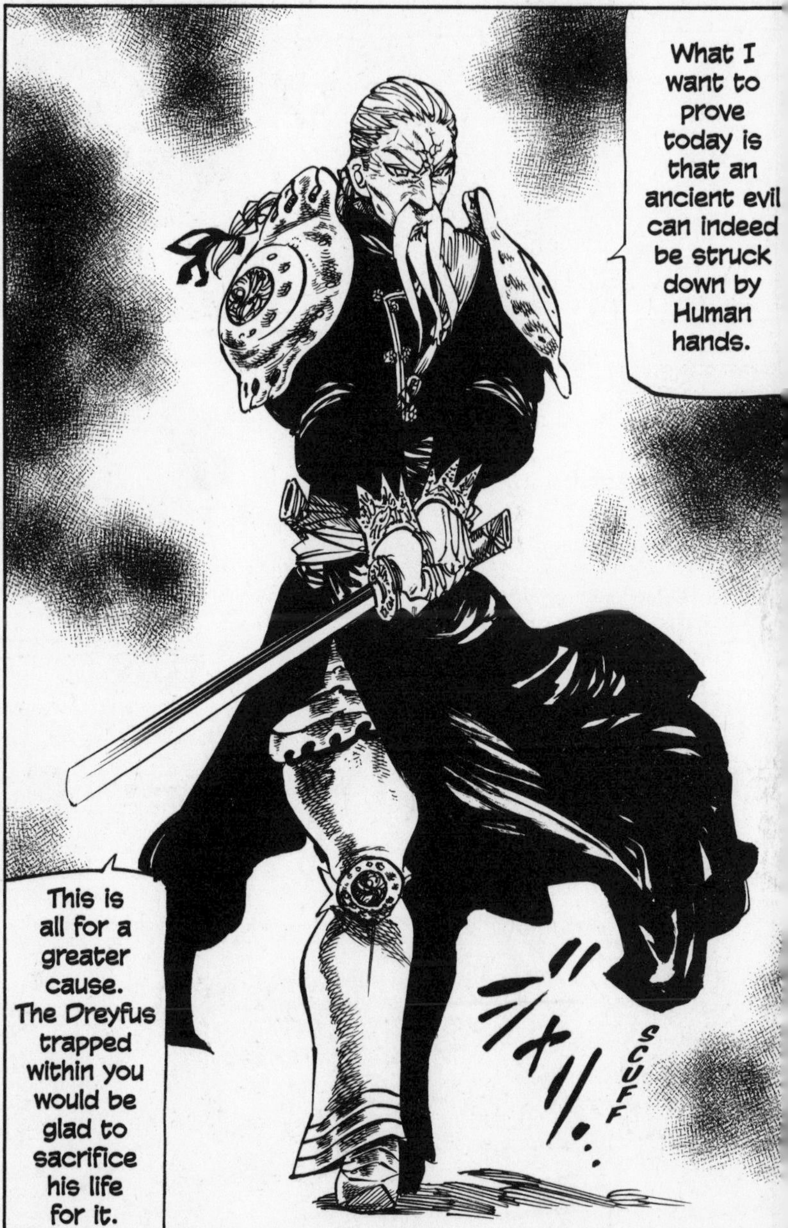
What I want to prove today is that an ancient evil can indeed be struck down by Human hands.
This is all for a greater cause. The Dreyfus trapped within you would be glad to sacrifice his life for it.
SCUFF

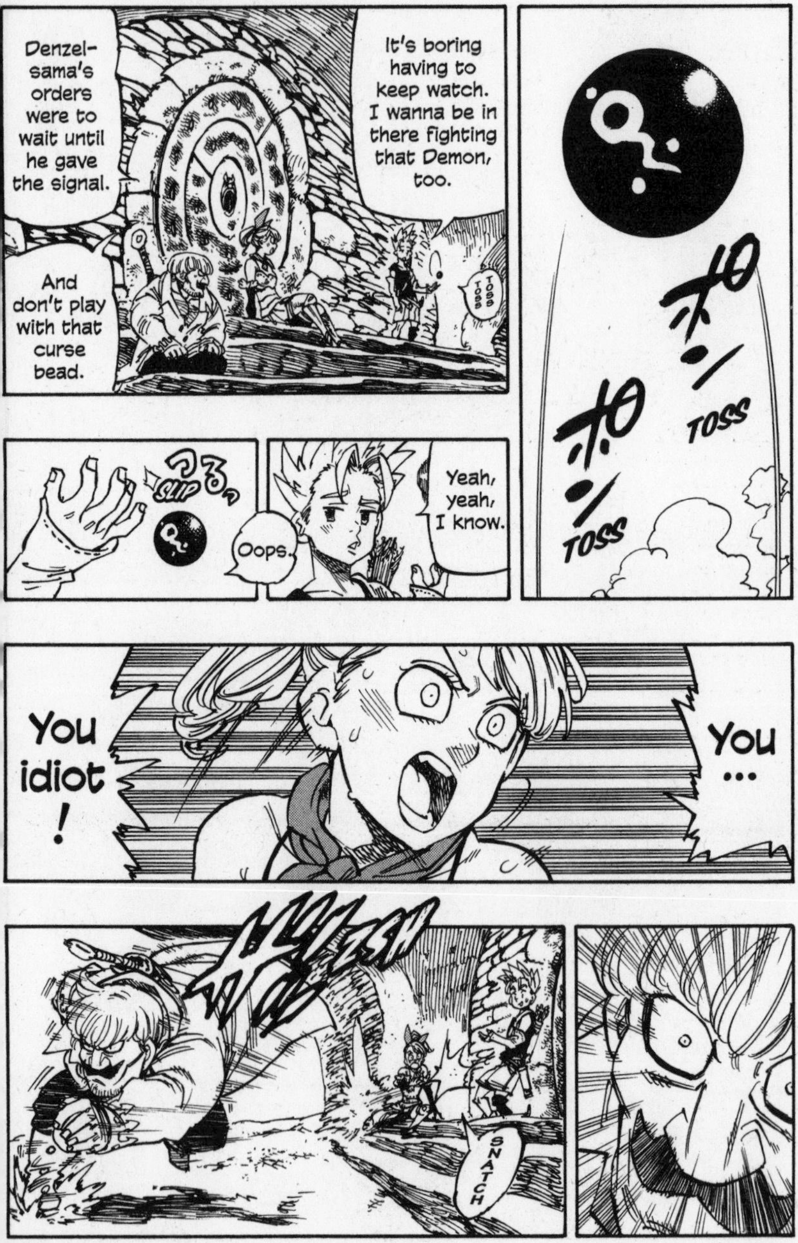
ポン
TOSS
ポン
TOSS
It's boring having to keep watch. I wanna be in there fighting that Demon, too.
Denzel-sama's orders were to wait until he gave the signal.
And don't play with that curse bead.
TOSS TOSS TOSS
Yeah, yeah, I know.
Oops.
つるっ
SLIP
You...
You idiot!
SNATCH

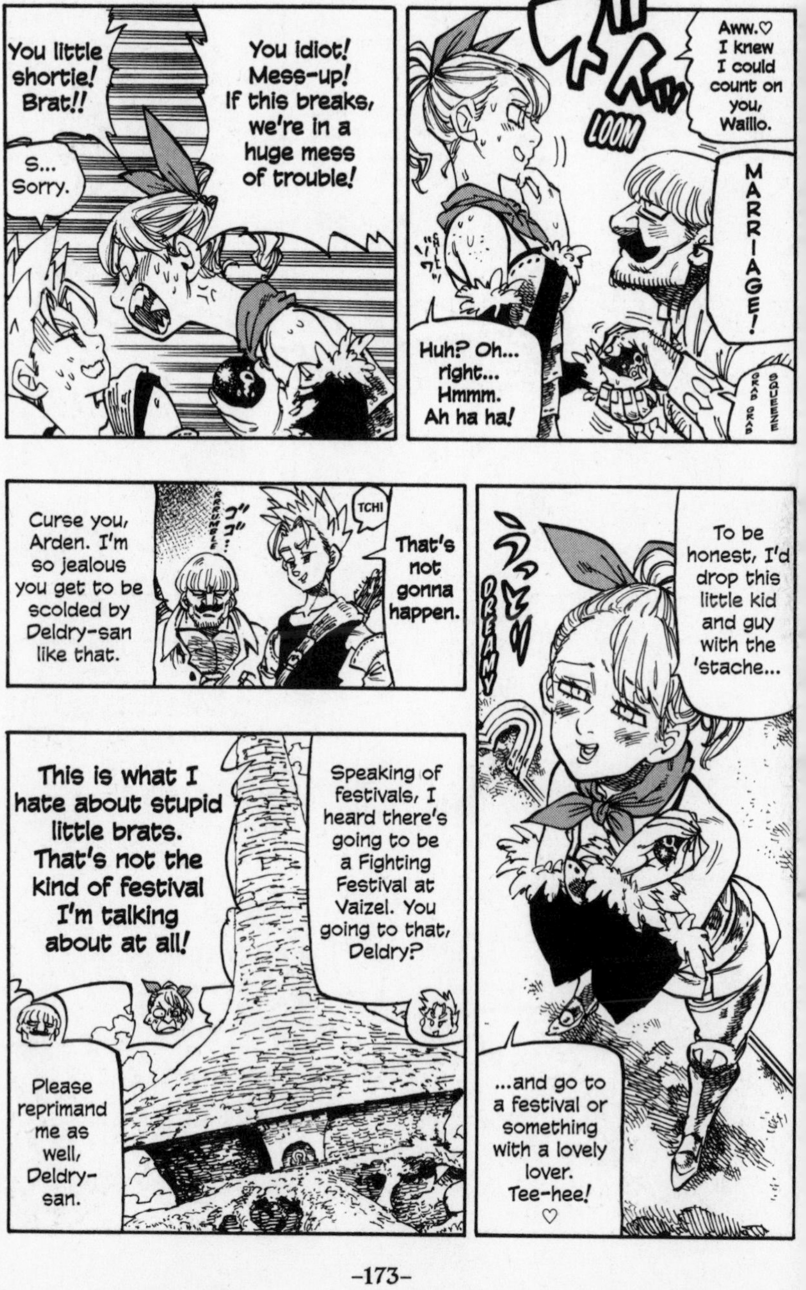
Aww.♡ I knew I could count on you, Waillo.
LOOM
MARRIAGE!
SQUEEZE
GRAB GRAB
Huh? Oh... right... Hmmm. Ah ha ha!
You idiot! Mess-up! If this breaks, we're in a huge mess of trouble!
You little shortie! Brat!!
S... Sorry.
To be honest, I'd drop this little kid and guy with the 'stache...
DREAMY
...and go to a festival or something with a lovely lover. Tee-hee! ♡
That's not gonna happen.
TCHI
RRRUMBLE
Curse you, Arden. I'm so jealous you get to be scolded by Deldry-san like that.
Speaking of festivals, I heard there's going to be a Fighting Festival at Vaizel. You going to that, Deldry?
This is what I hate about stupid little brats. That's not the kind of festival I'm talking about at all!
Please reprimand me as well, Deldry-san.

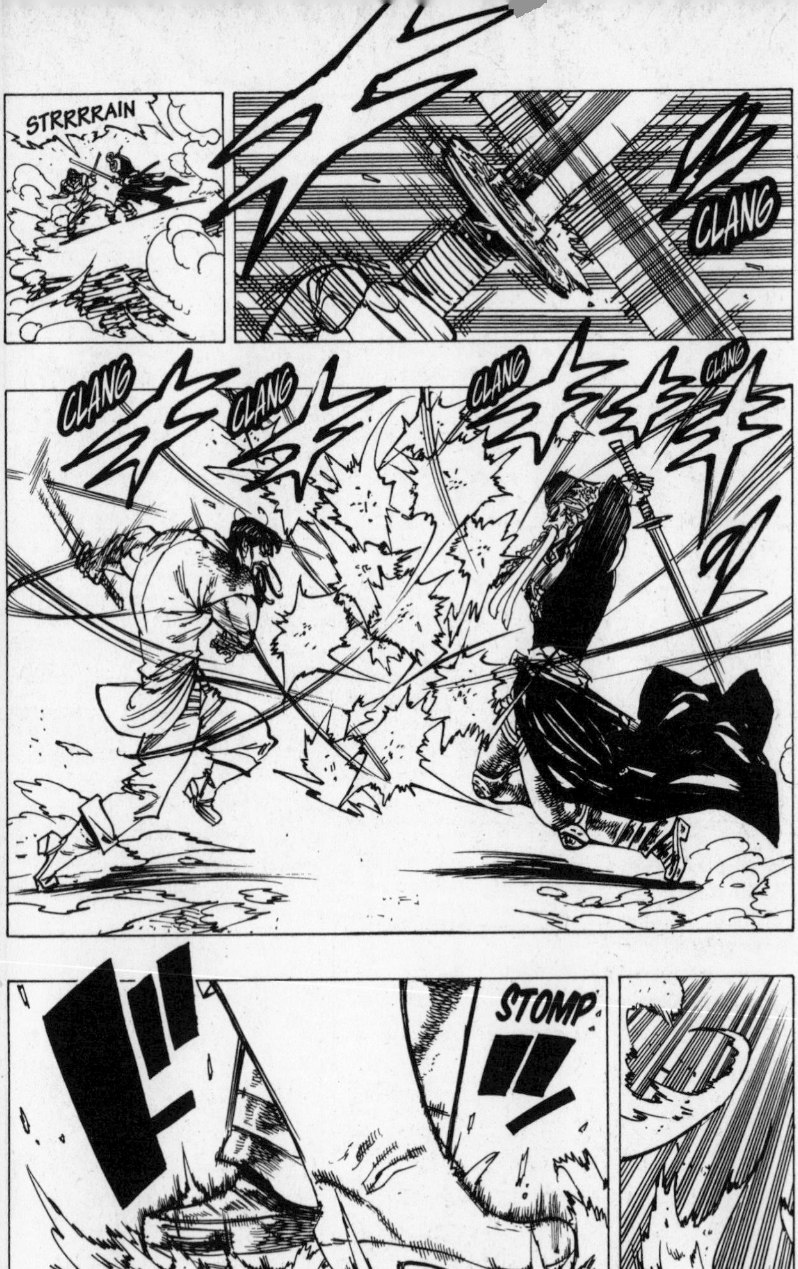
CLANG
STRRRRAIN
CLANG
CLANG
CLANG
CLANG
STOMP

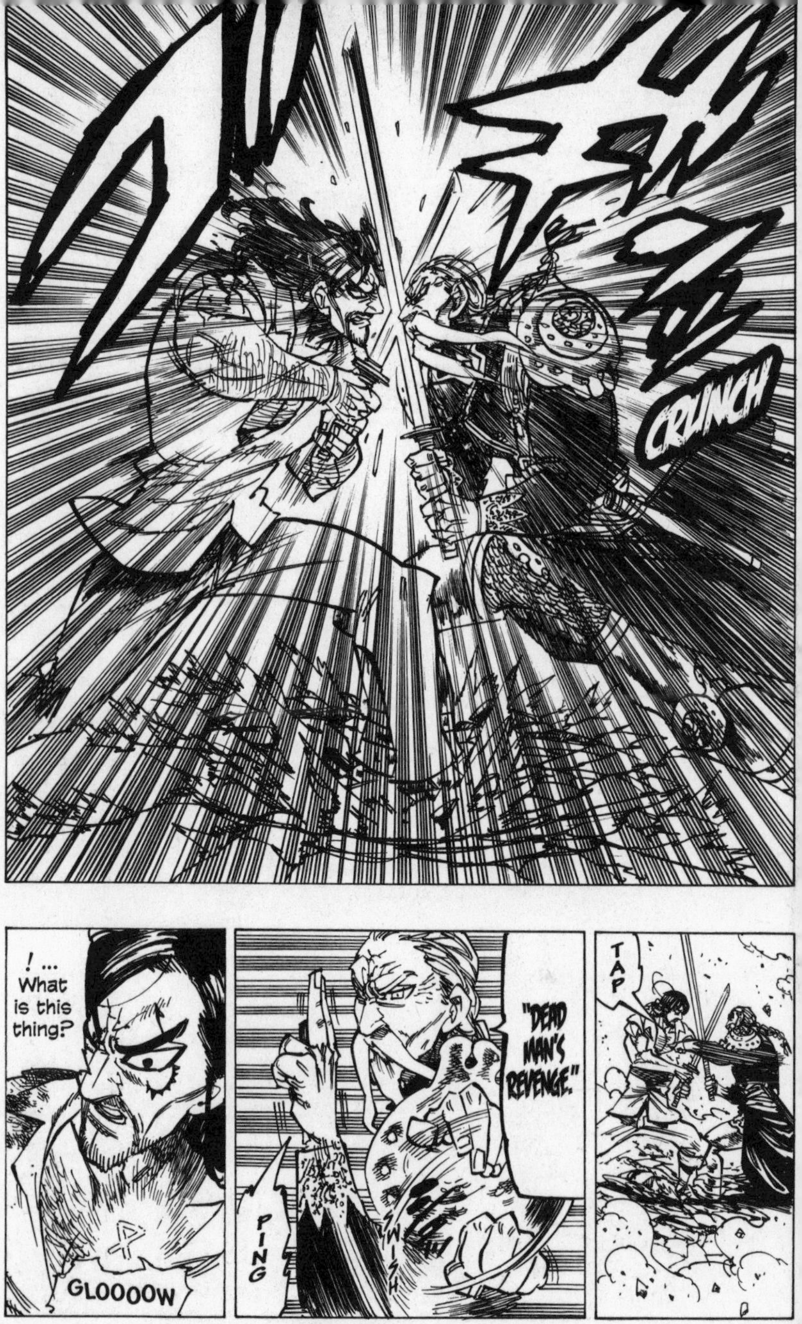
CRUNCH
TAP
"DEAD MAN'S REVENGE."
SWISH
PING
! ... What is this thing?
GLOOOOW

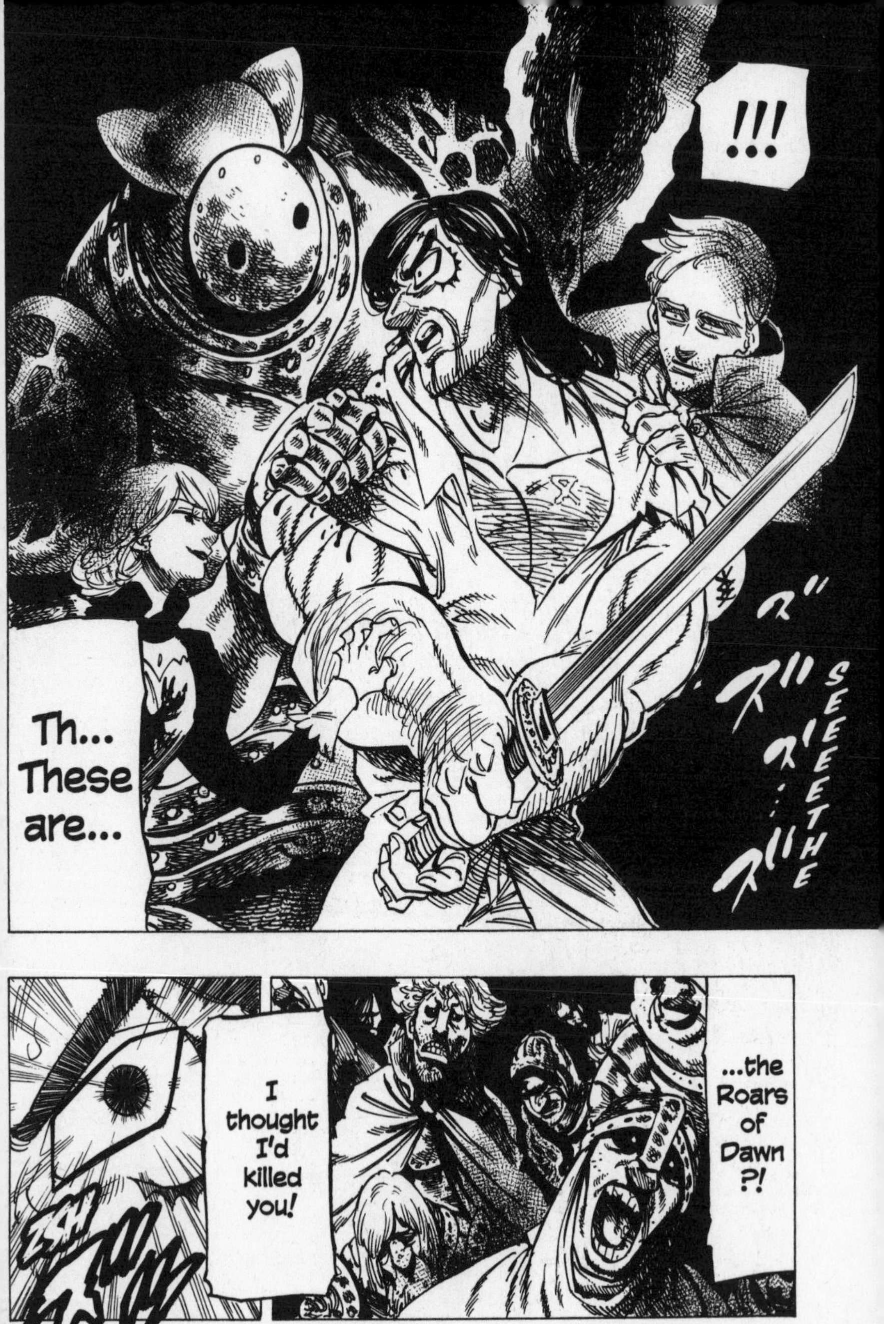
!!!
SEEEETHE
Th... These are...
...the Roars of Dawn?!
I thought I'd killed you!
ZSH

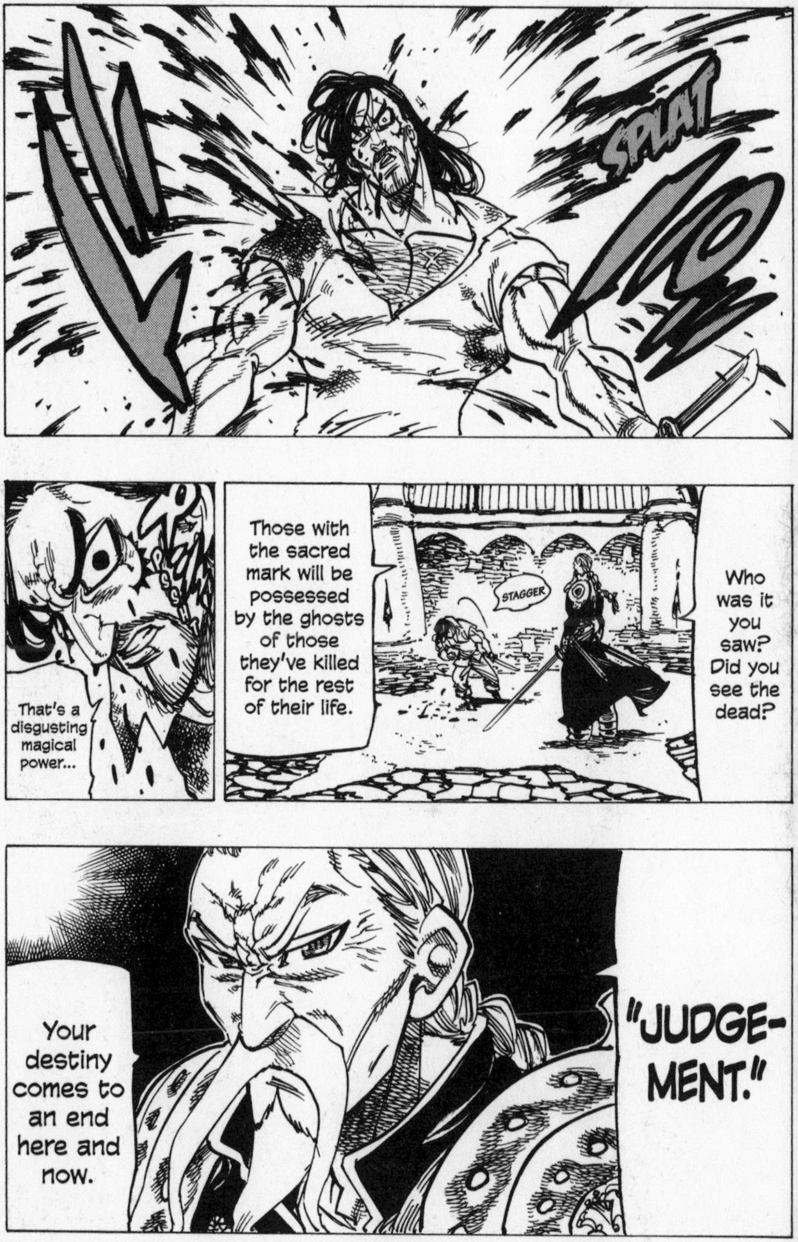
SPLAT
Who was it you saw? Did you see the dead?
STAGGER
Those with the sacred mark will be possessed by the ghosts of those they've killed for the rest of their life.
That's a disgusting magical power...
"JUDGE-MENT."
Your destiny comes to an end here and now.

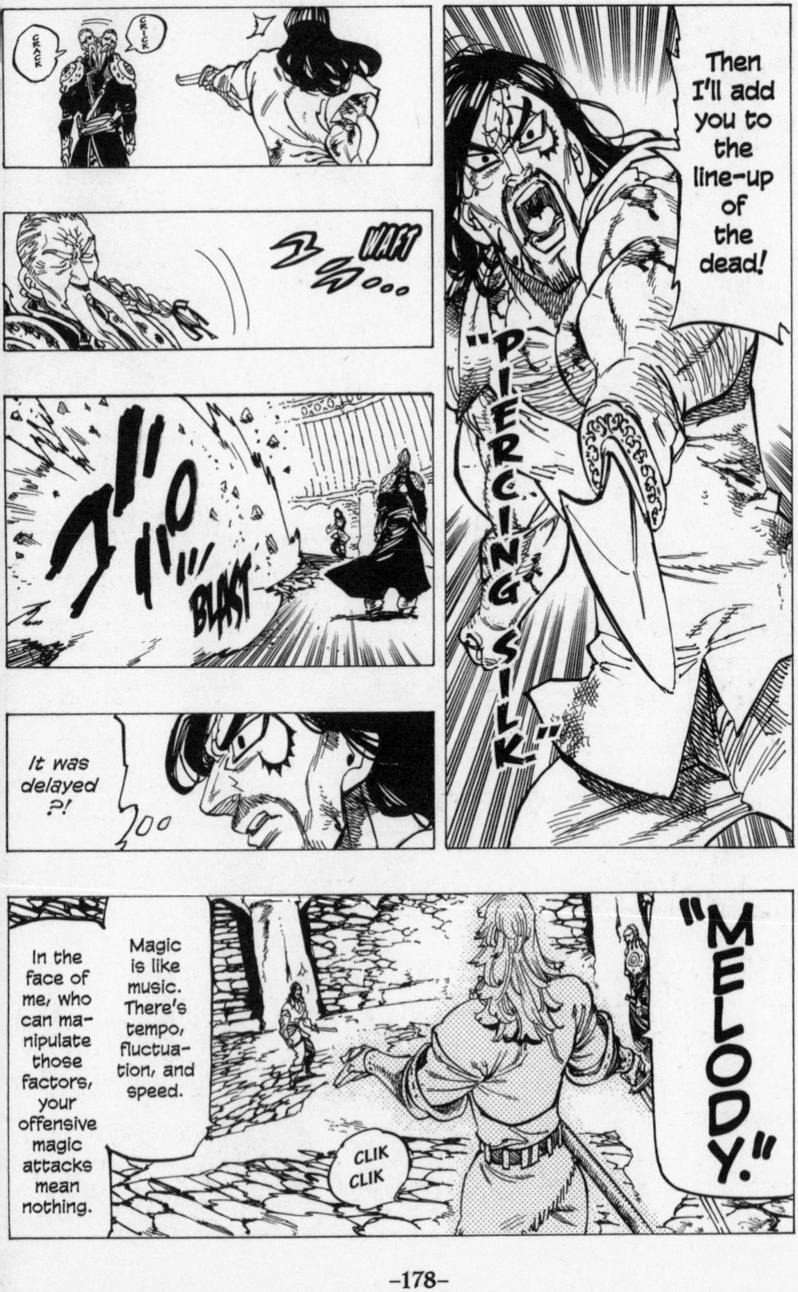
Then I'll add you to the line-up of the dead!
"PIERCING SILK."
CRICK
CRACK
WAFT
BLAST
It was delayed?!
"MELODY."
Magic is like music. There's tempo, fluctuation, and speed.
In the face of me, who can manipulate those factors, your offensive magic attacks mean nothing.
CLIK CLIK

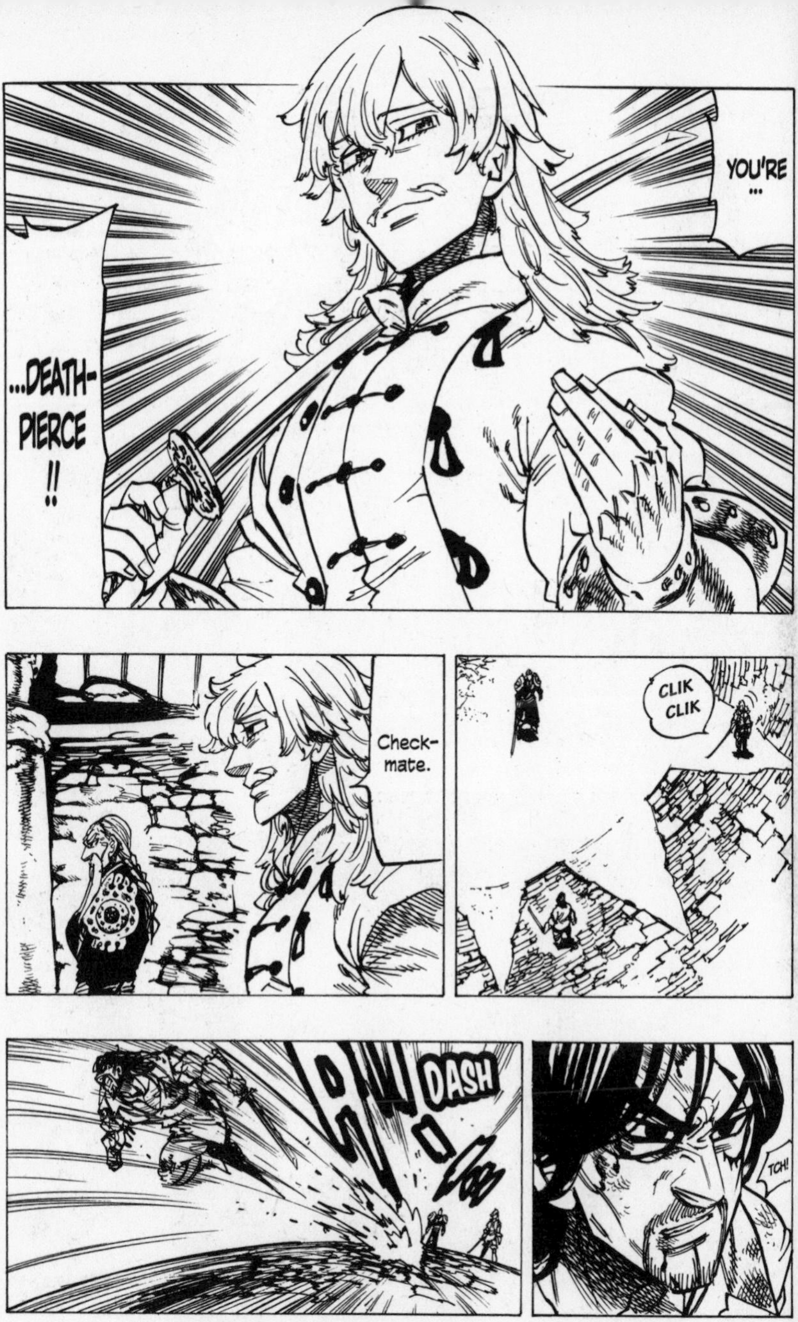
YOU'RE ...
...DEATH-PIERCE !!
CLIK CLIK
Check-mate.
TCH!
DASH

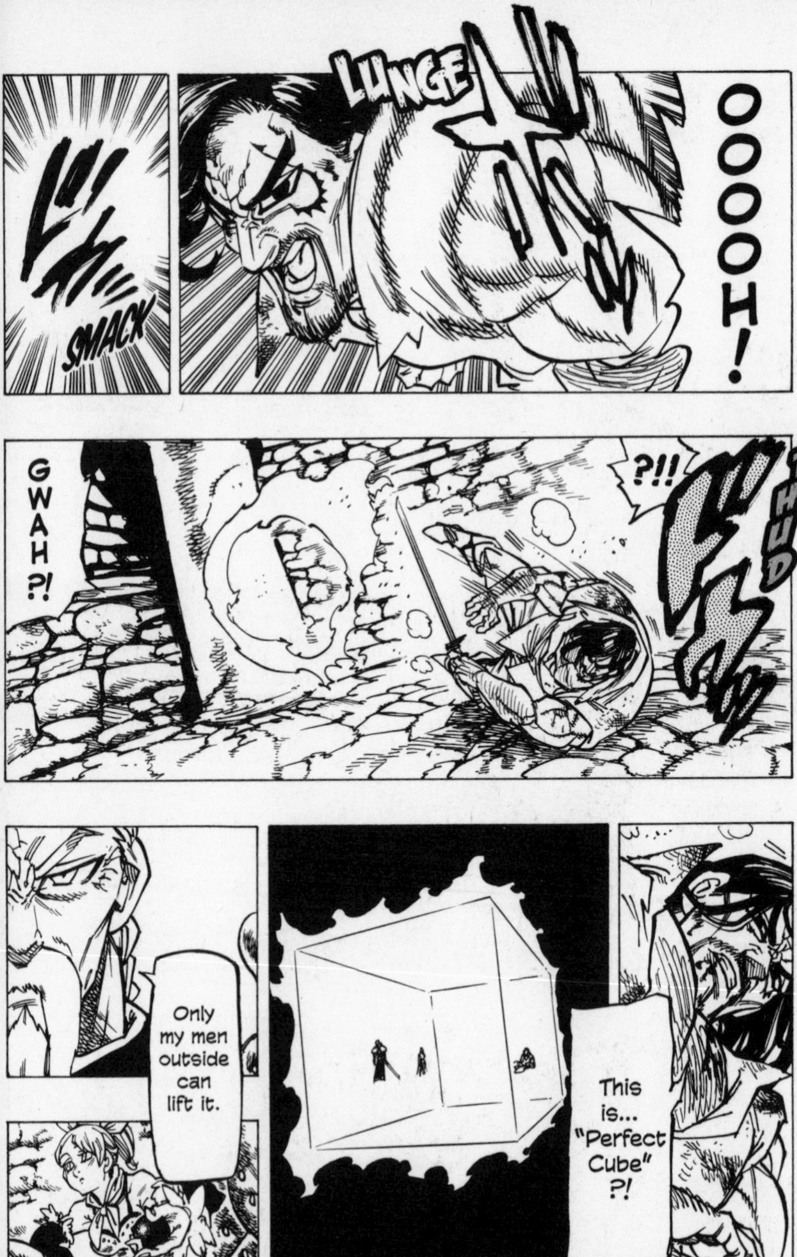
LUNGE
OOOOH!
SMACK
THUD
?!!
GWAH?!
This is... "Perfect Cube"?!
Only my men outside can lift it.

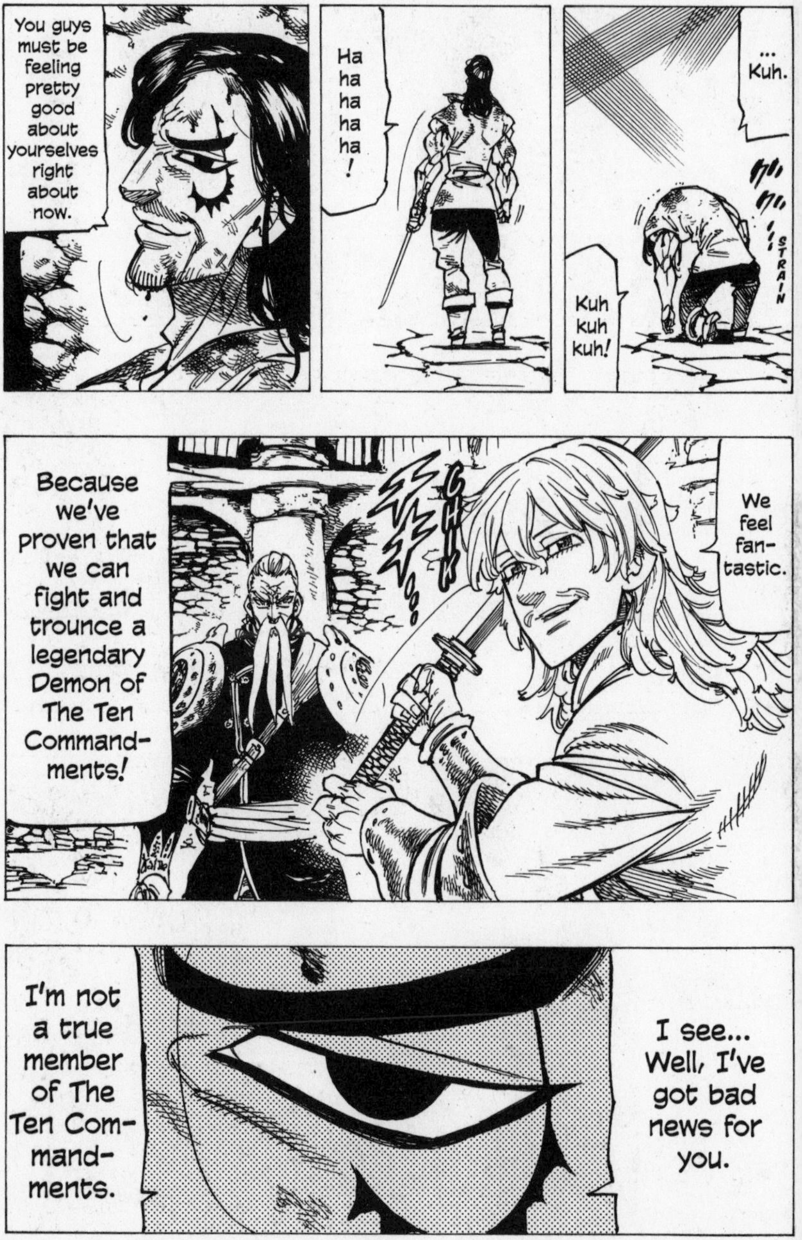

...Kuh.
STRAIN
Kuh kuh kuh!
Ha ha ha ha ha!
You guys must be feeling pretty good about yourselves right about now.
We feel fantastic.
CHIK
Because we've proven that we can fight and trounce a legendary Demon of The Ten Commandments!
I see... Well, I've got bad news for you.
I'm not a true member of The Ten Commandments.

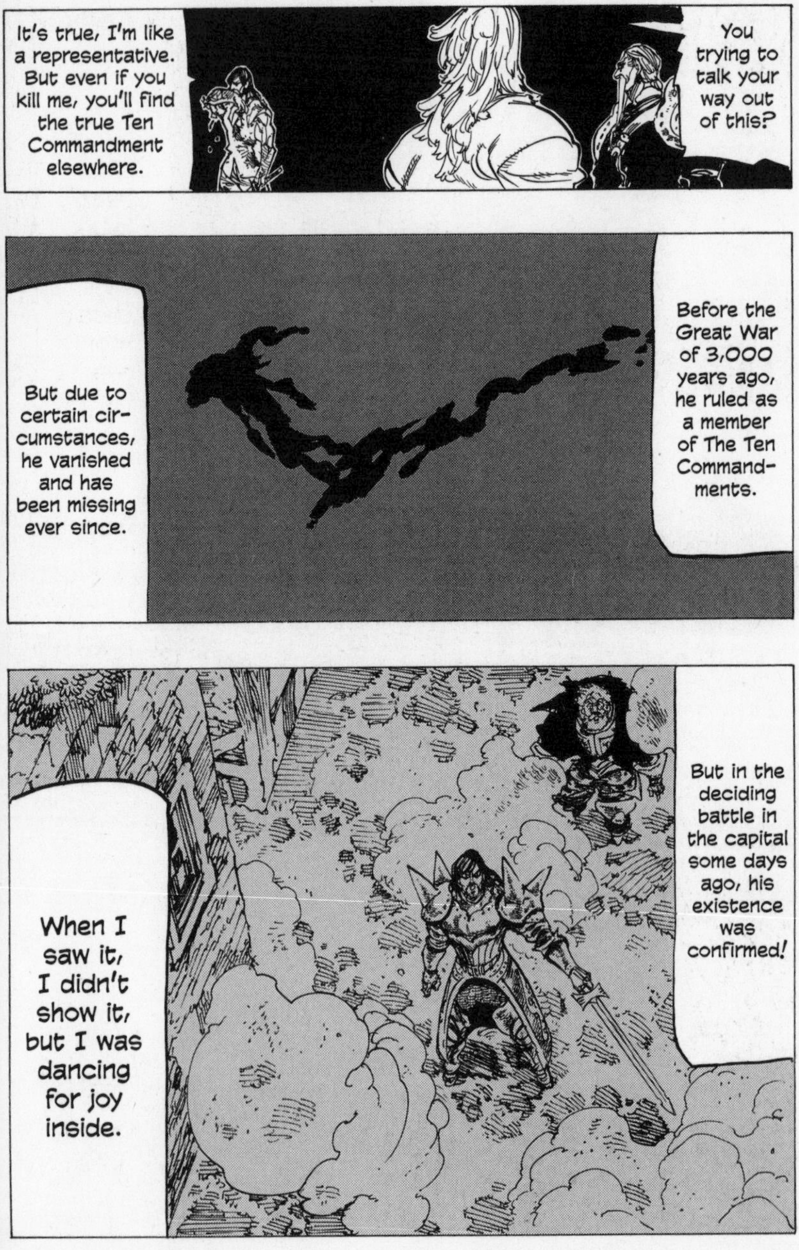
You trying to talk your way out of this?
It's true, I'm like a representative. But even if you kill me, you'll find the true Ten Commandment elsewhere.
Before the Great War of 3,000 years ago, he ruled as a member of The Ten Command-ments.
But due to certain cir-cumstances, he vanished and has been missing ever since.
But in the deciding battle in the capital some days ago, his existence was confirmed!
When I saw it, I didn't show it, but I was dancing for joy inside.

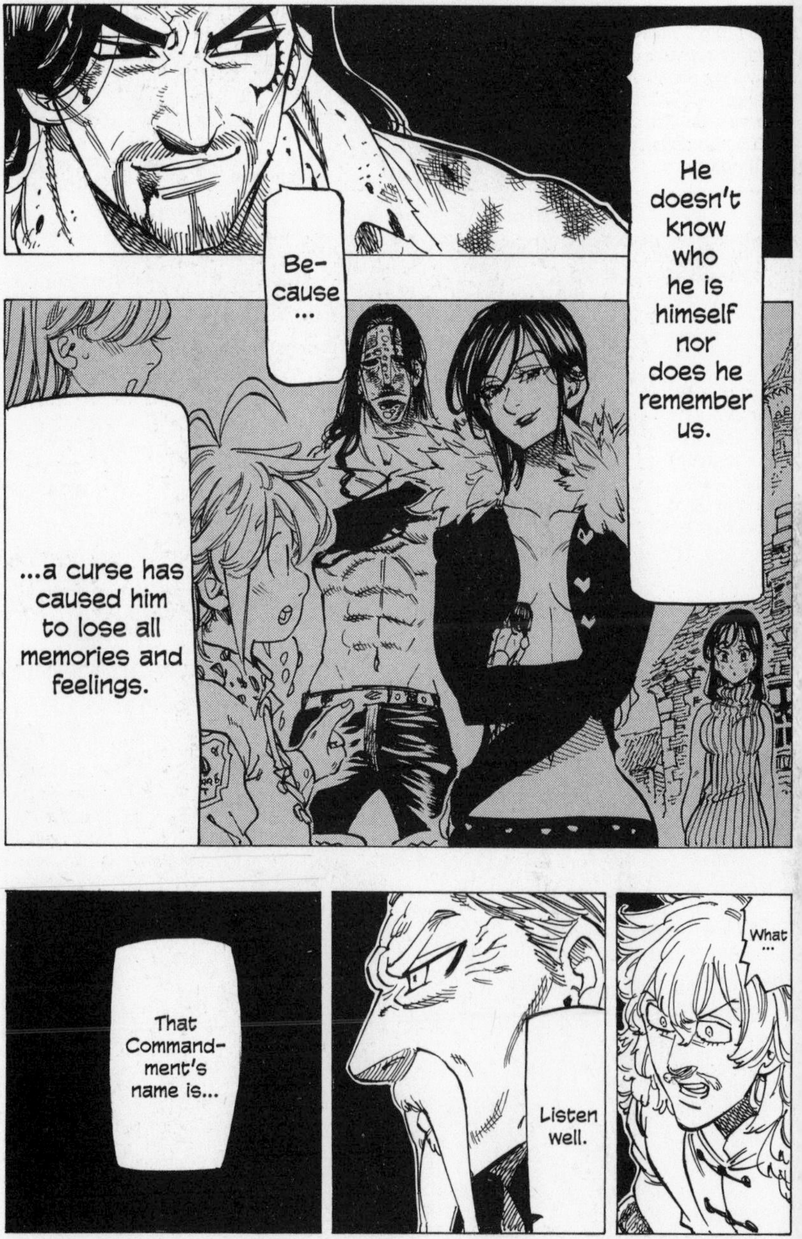
He doesn't know who he is himself nor does he remember us.
Be-cause...
...a curse has caused him to lose all memories and feelings.
What...
Listen well.
That Command-ment's name is...

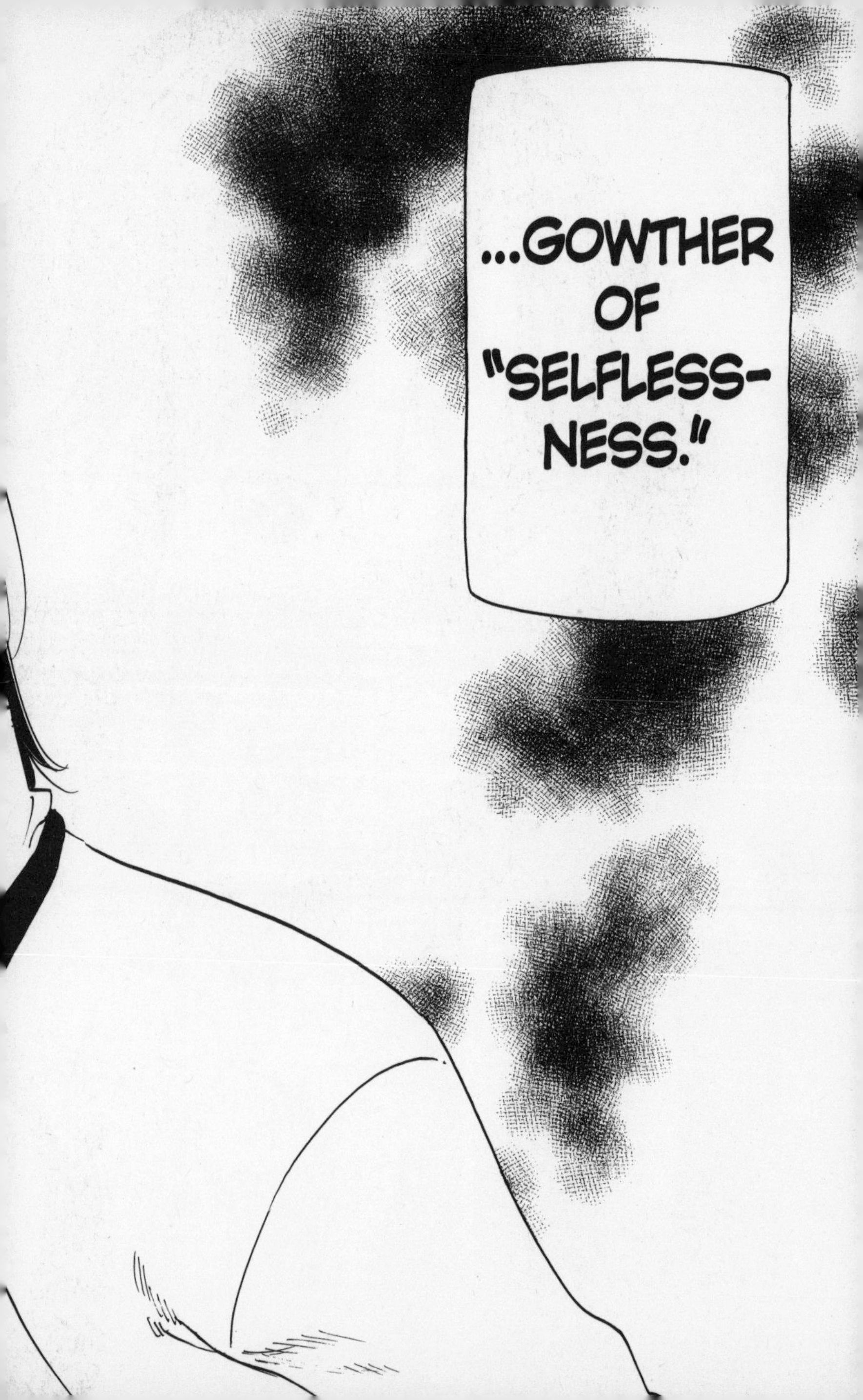
...GOWTHER OF "SELFLESS-NESS."

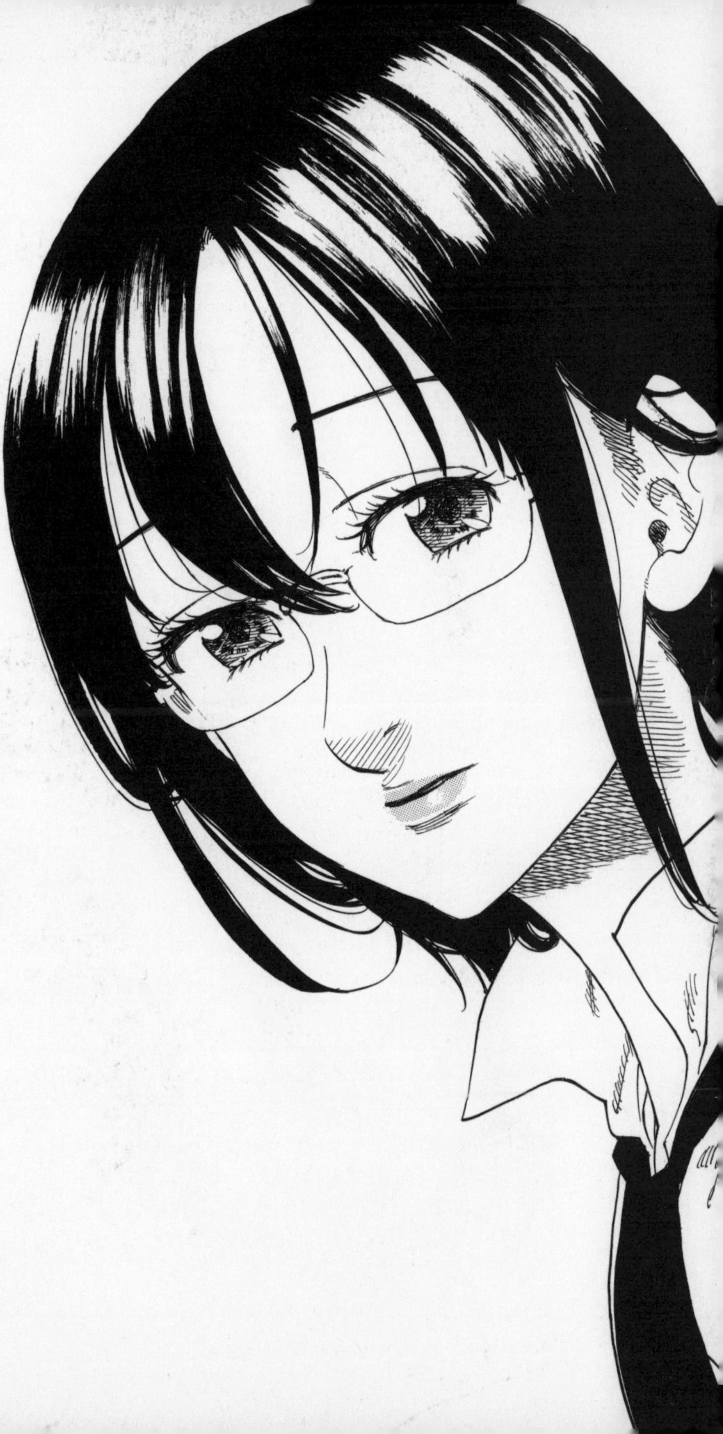

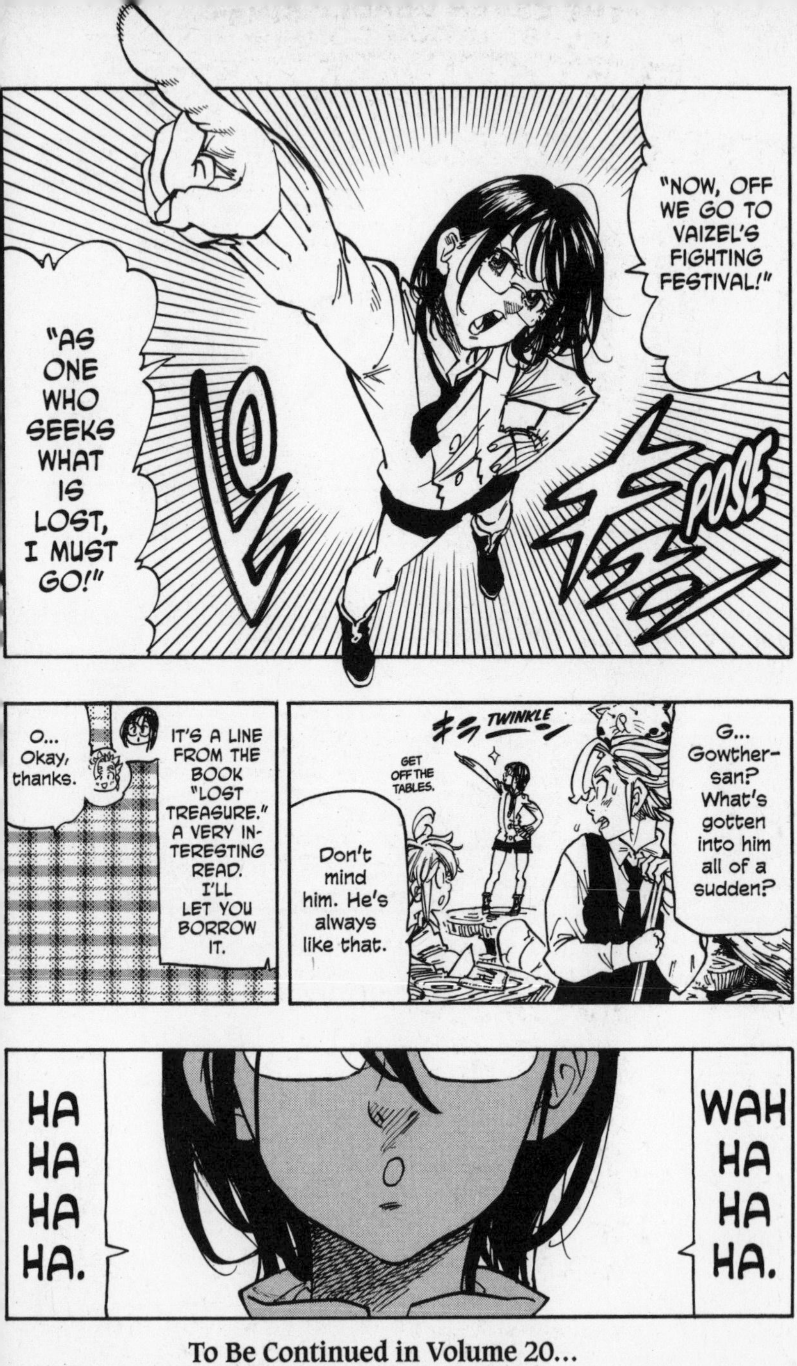
"NOW, OFF WE GO TO VAIZEL'S FIGHTING FESTIVAL!"
"AS ONE WHO SEEKS WHAT IS LOST, I MUST GO!"
POSE
G... Gowther-san? What's gotten into him all of a sudden?
TWINKLE
GET OFF THE TABLES.
Don't mind him. He's always like that.
IT'S A LINE FROM THE BOOK "LOST TREASURE." A VERY INTERESTING READ. I'LL LET YOU BORROW IT.
O... Okay, thanks.
WAH HA HA HA HA.
HA HA HA HA.

To Be Continued in Volume 20...

"THE SEVEN DEADLY SINS" ILLUSTRATION CORNER

"THE DRAWING KNIGHTHOOD" SPACE

Be sure to include your name and address on your postcard!

M = H = E = D = B = K = G = MER = Es = El = J =

SPECIAL PRIZE

七
つ
の
大
罪

KANA SATO-SAN / AOKI PREFECTURE

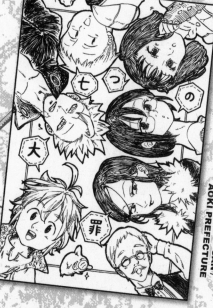

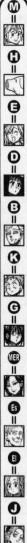

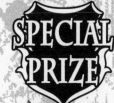

H "At long last, the seventh member has appeared!"

M "As usual, he's both super reliable and great to have on the team and, at the same time, more of a liability.

七つの大罪大好きです！
応援しています！
エリザベスちゃん
ごめんなさい

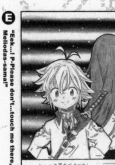

SNOWFLAKE-SAN / TOKYO

E "Eek...! P-Please don't...touch me there, Meliodas-sama!"

M "Touch you where exactly?"

H "Quit sexually harassing her!"

AYA ITO-SAN / SHIZUOKA PREFECTURE

B "It really is the good ones that die too young..."

H "At least you've got me 'n' the barkeep!"

B "Master... Thank you.♫"

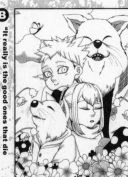

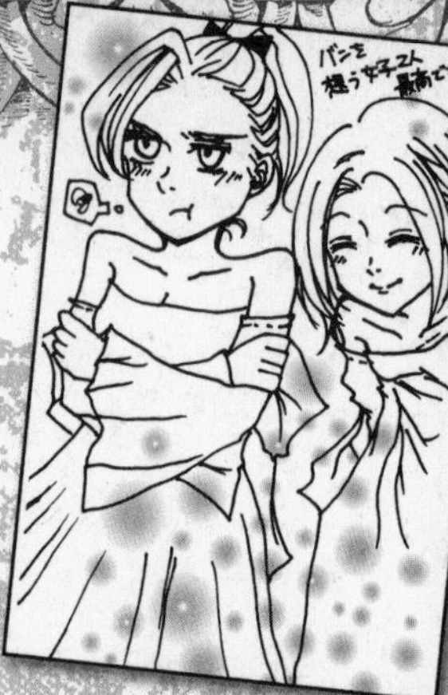
バンを想う女子2人最高です♡

HYDRANGEA-SAN / NIIGATA PREFECTURE

"I'm really glad I got to meet you, Jericho."

"D...Don't say such embarrassing things!"

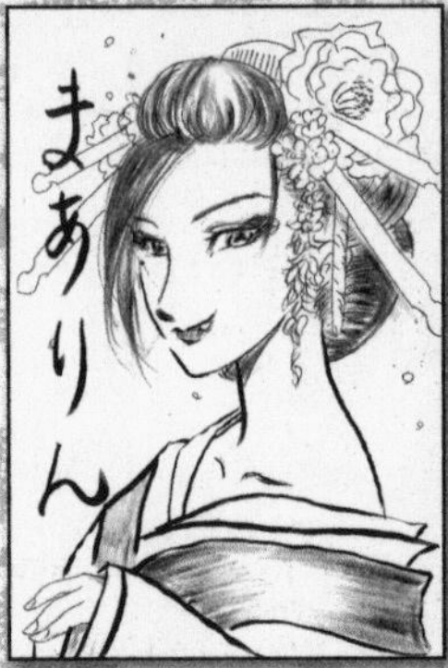
まありん

COCOA-SAN / SHIGA PREFECTURE

Es "M-Merlin-san, you look lovely in any attire. ♡"

MER "Are you saying I look the same no matter what I wear?"

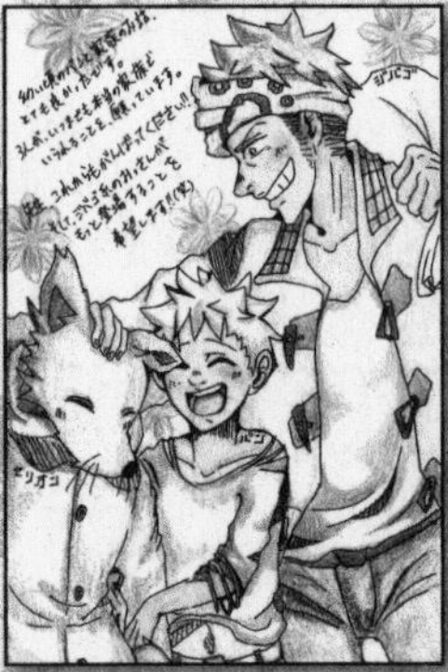

MERLIN'S WALL-SAN / HYOGO PREFECTURE

B "I'd have loved to have at least one drink with Selion and his dad."

M "Ban! Here, have an ale."

B "Oh! thanks, Cap'n! ♫"

J "So this is Ban from his youth... Heh Heh... What a cutie."

El "I'd have loved to have seen him then."

B "Cut it out, you two. ♫"

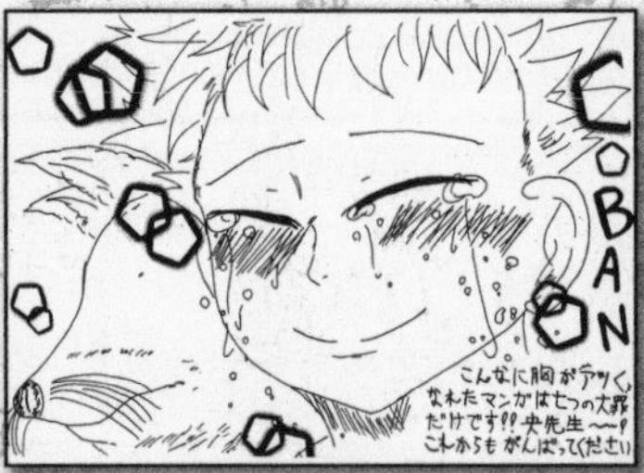
BAN

MARI-SAN / AICHI PREFECTURE

J "That reminds me that you've finally started calling me 'Jericho.'"

B "Ha ha! is that so, Joricho? ♫"

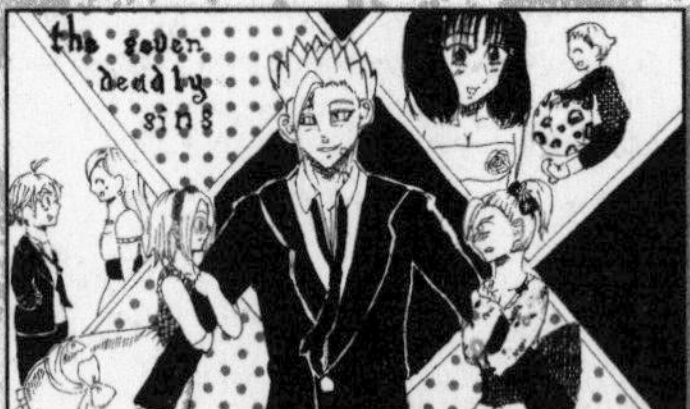

MIA MIKI-SAN / TOTTORI PREFECTURE

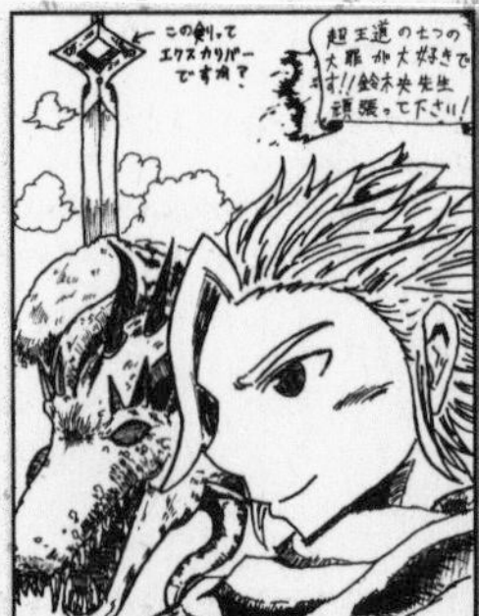
この剣ってエクスカリバーですか?
ARTHUR PENDRAGON

SHUNSUKE TANAKA-SAN / HYOGO PREFECTURE

M "Arthur's such a mysterious guy. All I know is that he's hiding amazing magical powers."

MER "I can certainly confirm that."

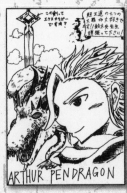

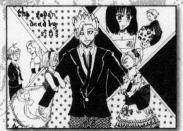

M "Elizabeth. This time...this time for sure I'll keep you safe!"

E "Huh? M-Meliodas-sama?!"

M "Urh...never mind!"

KAGAYA ATSUMI-SAN / MIE PREFECTURE

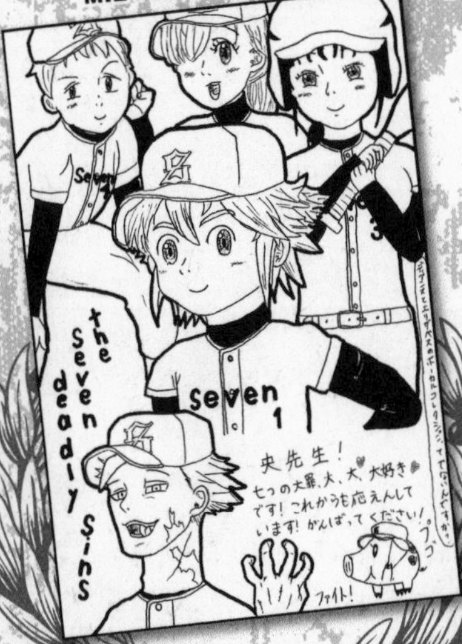
the Seven deadly Sins
Seven 1
央先生！七つの大罪、大、大、大好きです！これからも応えんしています！がんばってください！
ファイト！
ブブ

"Sweet! As of now you are all members of 'Hawks' Leftovers'!"

"You've got to change that name first!"

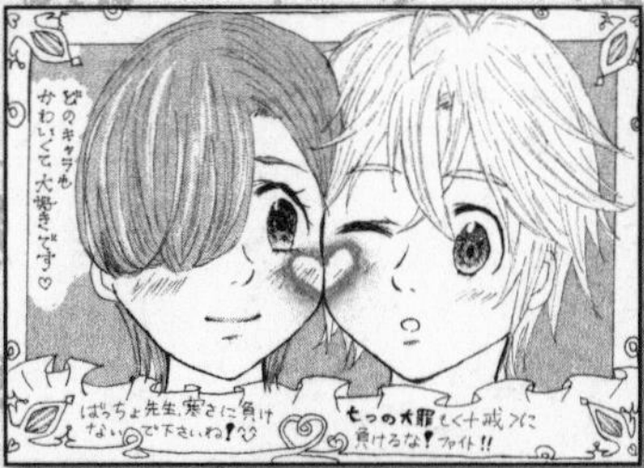
どのキャラもかわいくて大好きです♡
ばっちょ先生、寒さに負けないで下さいね！
七つの大罪も十戒に負けるな！ファイト!!

CROWN-SAN / AOKI PREFECTURE

K "Oh! Little piggy, that was pretty clever!"

B "Guys, you do realize the Cap'n's right behind you, right?"

H "Meliodas claims his creations are 'cooking,' but it's really called 'leftovers.'"

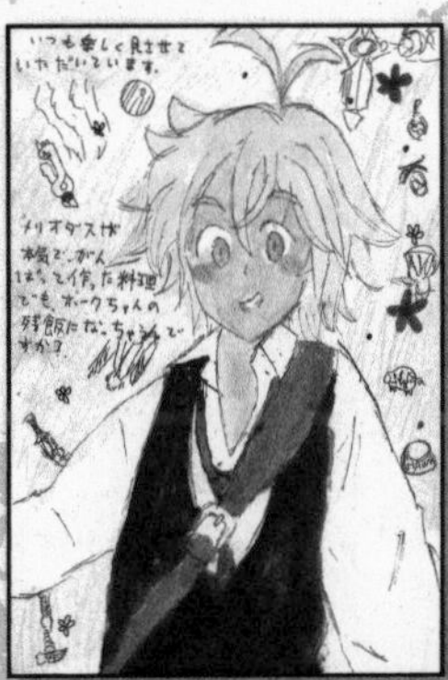
いつも楽しく見せていただいています。
メリオダスが本気で、がんばって作った料理でも、ホークちゃんの残飯になっちゃうんですか？

MOMOAN HAYASHI-SAN / KYOTO PREFECTURE

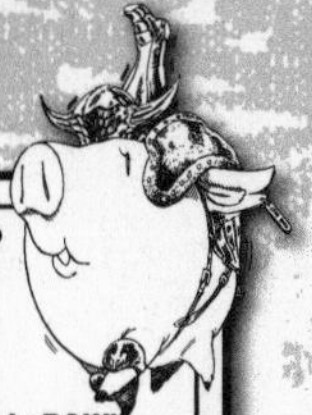

Now Accepting Applicants for the Drawing Knighthood!

- Draw your picture on a postcard, or paper no larger than a postcard, and send it in!
- Don't forget to write your name and location on the back of your picture!
- You can include comments or not. And colored illustrations will still only be displayed in B&W!
- The Drawing Knights whose pictures are particularly noteworthy and run in the print edition will be gifted with a signed specially made pencil board!
- And the best overall will be granted the special prize of a signed shikishi!!

Send to:
The Seven Deadly Sins Drawing Knighthood
c/o Kodansha Comics
451 Park Ave. South, 7th floor,
New York, NY 10016

- Submitted letters and postcards will be given to the artist. Please be aware that your name, address, and other personal information included will be given as well.

KC KODANSHA COMICS

Yamada-kun AND THE Seven Witches

"A very funny manga with a lot of heart and character."
—Adventures in Poor Taste

SWAPPED WITH A KISS?!

Class troublemaker Ryu Yamada is already having a bad day when he stumbles down a staircase along with star student Urara Shiraishi. When he wakes up, he realizes they have switched bodies—and that Ryu has the power to trade places with anyone just by kissing them! Ryu and Urara take full advantage of the situation to improve their lives, but with such an oddly amazing power, just how long will they be able to keep their secret under wraps?

Available now in print and digitally!

© Miki Yoshikawa/Kodansha Ltd. All rights reserved.

THE HEROIC LEGEND OF
ARSLAN

READ THE NEW SERIES FROM THE CREATOR OF FULLMETAL ALCHEMIST, HIROMU ARAKAWA! NOW A HIT TV SERIES!

"Arakawa proves to be more than up to the task of adapting Tanaka's fantasy novels and fans of historical or epic fantasy will be quite pleased with the resulting book."
-Anime News Network

ECBATANA IS BURNING!

Arslan is the young and curious prince of Pars who, despite his best efforts doesn't seem to have what it takes to be a proper king like his father. At the age of 14, Arslan goes to his first battle and loses everything as the blood-soaked mist of war gives way to scorching flames, bringing him to face the demise of his once glorious kingdom. However, it is Arslan's destiny to be a ruler, and despite the trials that face him, he must now embark on a journey to reclaim his fallen kingdom.

Available now in print and digitally!

© Hiromu Arakawa/Yoshiki Tanaka/Kodansha Ltd. All rights reserved.

The Seven Deadly Sins volume 19 is a work of fiction. Names, characters, places, and incidents are the products of the author's imagination or are used fictitiously. Any resemblance to actual events, locales, or persons, living or dead, is entirely coincidental.

A Kodansha Comics Trade Paperback Original.

The Seven Deadly Sins volume 19 copyright © 2016 Nakaba Suzuki
English translation copyright © 2017 Nakaba Suzuki

All rights reserved.

Published in the United States by Kodansha Comics, an imprint of Kodansha USA Publishing, LLC, New York.

Publication rights for this English edition arranged through Kodansha Ltd., Tokyo.

First published in Japan in 2016 by Kodansha Ltd., Tokyo.

ISBN 978-1-63236-349-7

Printed in the United States of America.

www.kodanshacomics.com

9 8 7 6 5 4 3 2 1

Translation: Christine Dashiell
Lettering: James Dashiell
Editing: Lauren Scanlan
Kodansha Comics edition cover design: Phil Balsman